The Effect of
Japanese Investment
on the World Economy

The Effect of
Japanese Investment
on the World Economy

A Six-Country Study, 1970–1991

EDITED BY LEON HOLLERMAN AND RAMON H. MYERS

HOOVER INSTITUTION PRESS • STANFORD UNIVERSITY STANFORD, CALIFORNIA

Hoover Press Publication No. 432

First printing, 1996

02 01 00 99 98 97 96   9 8 7 6 5 4 3 2 1

Simultaneous first paperback printing

02 01 00 99 98 97 96   9 8 7 6 5 4 3 2 1

Manufactured in the United States of America
The paper used in this publication meets the minimum requirements of
American National Standard for Information Services—Permanence of
Paper for Printed Library Materials, ANSI Z39.48-1984. ∞

Library of Congress Cataloging-in-Publication Data

The effect of Japanese investment on the world economy: a six-country
study, 1970-1991/Leon Hollerman, Ramon H. Myers, editors.
        p.   cm.
        Includes bibliographical references and index.
        ISBN 0-8179-9401-7. — ISBN 0-8179-9402-5 (pbk.)
        1. Investments, Japanese—Case studies. 2. Economic history—
1945– I. Hollerman, Leon. II. Myers, Ramon Hawley, 1929–.
HG4538.E42 1996   95-42429
332.6'7352—dc20   CIP

Contents

Tables and Figures

Chapter 4

Chapter 5

Chapter 6

Acknowledgments

The editors wish to thank the Japan–U.S. Friendship Commission for financial support of the conference and preparation of the essays in this volume. Further support from the Hoover Institution on War, Revolution and Peace also is acknowledged.

Abbreviations

AMI	Australian Motor Industries
ASEAN	Association for Southeast Asian Nations
BOI	Board of Investment
BREMA	British Radio and Electronic Equipment Manufacturers
CBI	Confederation of British Industry
CFE	Federal Electric Power Commission
CFIUS	Committee on Foreign Investment in the United States
CPI	Consumer price index (U.S.)
CSO	Central Statistical Office
DTI	Department of Trade and Industry
EC	European Community
ECLAC	United Nations Economic Commission for Latin America and the Caribbean
EEOC	Equal Employment Opportunity Commission
EETPU	Electrical, Electronic, Telecommunication and Plumbing Union
EIAJ	Electronic Industries Association of Japan
ERM	Exchange rate mechanism
EXIM	Export-Import Bank (Japan)
FDI	Foreign direct investment
GDI	Gross domestic investment
GDP	Gross domestic production
GEC	General Electric Company Ltd.
IBB	Invest in Britain Bureau
IDB	Inter-American Development Bank
IRELA	Institute for European-Latin American Relations
IRS	Internal Revenue Service (U.S.)
ISI	Import-substitution industrialization
JEBA	Japan Electronics Business Association
JESSI	Joint European Submicron Silicon Initiative
JFDI	Japanese foreign direct investment

JICA	Japanese International Cooperation Agency
JIOI	Japan Institute for Overseas Investment
LDCs	Less-developed countries
MITI	Ministry of International Trade and Industry
MNE	Multinational enterprise
NAFTA	North America Free Trade Agreement
NEDO	National Economic Development Office (U.K.)
NIE	Newly industrialized economy
NRI	Nomura Research Institute
OECD	Organization for Economic Cooperation and Development
OECF	Overseas Economic Cooperation Fund
PEMEX	Petroleos Mexicanos (Mexican Petroleum Company)
RIC	Radio Industry Council (U.K.)
SMEs	Small and medium enterprises
SMMT	Society of Motor Manufacturers and Traders
TCP	Toshiba Consumer Products
TNC	Transnational corporation
UAAI	United Australian Automotive Industries
USIMINAS	Usinas Siderurgicas de Minas Gerais

INTRODUCTION
Ramon H. Myers

A surge in foreign direct investment (FDI) from the United Kingdom and other European countries gradually transformed the nineteenth-century world economy by expanding trade and integrating foreign and domestic markets. Between 1865 and 1885, the United Kingdom's FDI alone "increased some three and a half times," far more rapidly than output, and flowed not only to its colonies, but mainly to the land-rich countries of North America and Australia.[1] For the first time, foreign multinational enterprises (MNEs) significantly increased in size and number to expand production and domestic and foreign trade. This era saw the triumph of a middle class in trade and finance.[2]

The growth of world trade and investment between 1865 and 1914 was not repeated between 1914 and 1939, when manufacturing output slowed and world trade contracted. In fact, the world economy became less integrated because each nation adopted a beggar-thy-neighbor policy to protect domestic industry and agriculture by raising protective barriers to reduce imports. Not until the "Golden Age" of the 1950s and 1960s did economic growth in the advanced capitalist countries surpass previous records.

According to Angus Maddison, the annual average growth of gross domestic production (GDP) of capitalist countries between 1950 and 1973 was 4.9 percent compared to only 2.3 percent between 1870 and 1950.[3] Three factors accounted for the growth surge after World War II: (1) Trade liberalization helped to promote industrialization and to restructure the advanced economies. (2) Economic restructuring encouraged greater exchange of manufactured goods between the advanced capitalist countries and thus accelerated world trade in those same decades.[4] (3) A surge in U.S. FDI to Europe, Australia, and Asia promoted new technology, more employment, and increased trade with the United States.[5]

A third period of world trade and FDI expansion began in the 1970s and continued until 1991, when a surge of Japanese FDI, along with MNEs, flowed to various countries of the world. This Japanese FDI generated new opportunities and benefits, as well as creating new problems for the recipient countries.

By addressing three questions, the chapters that follow examine the six countries—United States, United Kingdom, Mexico, Australia, Republic of China, and Thailand—that received nearly three-fifths of all Japanese FDI between 1980 and 1990: (1) Why did Japanese FDI increase so dramatically between 1970 and 1991? (2) What are some of the significant patterns of Japanese FDI in host countries? (3) What economic effect did Japanese FDI have on the host countries?

Japanese FDI Between 1970 and 1991

In the early 1970s Japan's gross national saving already was the highest in the world, 38.4 percent.[6] It remained over 30 percent for the next ten years. Since the 1950s Japan's government and businesses heavily invested to expand human and physical capital, along with improving technology and organizations to make capital more productive.[7] Japan's business leaders, especially those producing automobiles, realized in the 1970s and 1980s that producing cheaper, higher-quality products could be done more economically overseas than at home.[8] They also perceived that domestic investment return and profits from market shares were approaching equivalence or were lower than could be earned by investing and establishing their MNEs abroad. After many years of building networks overseas to obtain information, Japanese enterprise owners and directors began to realize that their transaction costs for overseas business were as low as at home. Rising unit costs at home and lower unit costs abroad, therefore, encouraged Japanese companies to increase FDI in the 1970s.

By the 1980s, however, new push-and-pull economic factors combined to greatly increase Japanese FDI: Rising prices of physical assets at home enabled businesses to borrow credit cheaply to finance their FDI, a booming securities market increased the value of enterprise balance sheets, and an appreciating yen strengthened enterprise purchasing power overseas.

In 1991 Japan's financial bubble burst, however, and FDI suddenly declined. Japan's securities and real estate markets turned sour. In 1992 Japan's real GDP slowed to an anemic 1.5 percent growth, with no growth registered in 1993 and growth barely recovering in 1994 and 1995. Wholesale domestic prices fell after 1990, and economic indicators between 1991 and 1995 turned downward and flattened as the economy experienced its worst economic depression since the end of World War II. In mid-1995 the Ministry of Finance said that "the nation's lending institutions are sitting on a bad debt worth 40 trillion yen, $450 billion at current exchange rates, or 9.5 percent of Japan's annual economic output."[9]

From a world economy view, Japanese FDI between 1970 and 1991 had increased nearly one-hundred-fold in nominal terms, with 44 percent of that investment going to North America, 19 percent to Western Europe, 15 percent to Asia, and 12 percent to Latin America in 1991. Japanese FDI to North America increased more rapidly, followed by that to Western Europe. Latin American and Asian shares fell. Japanese FDI to Oceania also fell, with most going to Australia. The share of Japanese FDI to the Middle East and Africa also fell. By 1991 around 65 percent of total Japanese FDI in the world economy entered the services sector, and of that amount 24 percent went to purchase real estate. Between 1970 and 1991, Japan's FDI exceeded that of any other nation (See table I.1).

Japanese Direct Investment in Six Countries: Some Patterns

Japanese FDI in the world economy has been trade-supporting, resource-seeking, low-cost-labor-seeking, trade-conflict-avoiding by transplanting assembly, surplus recycling, and strategic networking (Ozawa and Reynolds). In every country of this study some mixture of these effects flowed from Japanese FDI. Japanese MNEs located overseas in the hope of earning profit, but their expectations were not always fulfilled, particularly in the 1980s, after purchasing real estate in North America.

What is striking is that Japanese FDI began to surpass that of some longstanding foreign investors, except in Latin America. By 1987, Japanese FDI in the United States surpassed that of the Netherlands and Canada and ranked just behind the United Kingdom's (Wong and Yamamura, table 1.8). Although the volume of U.S. FDI in the United Kingdom is still ten times as great as Japan's, by 1989 Japan's share of total FDI in that nation reached 11 percent compared to the U.S. share of 36.5 percent (Hollerman, table 2.1). In Latin America between 1979 and 1990, Japanese FDI was only around $4.0 billion compared to $16.5 billion from the United States and $14.9 billion from Europe (Ozawa and Reynolds, table 3.1). Japanese FDI in Australia, however, rose rapidly in the 1980s to achieve second ranking, 17.9 percent, just behind that of the United States (19.3 percent), and slightly ahead of that of the United Kingdom (17.2 percent) (Drysdale, table 4.4). In Thailand, by 1990 Japan had become the largest foreign investor to surpass the United States, which had been the premier foreign investor in previous decades (Kaosa-ard, table 5.5). In the Republic of

China on Taiwan, Japanese FDI had ranked as the third largest between 1952 and 1970 but jumped to second rank, just after that of overseas Chinese investors in the 1980s. Similarly, Japanese FDI in South Korea eventually surpassed that of all other foreign investors (Schive, table 6.2).

In all six countries covered in this study the bulk of Japanese FDI went to purchase equity capital. In the capital-rich, urban-populated countries, however, much of that equity capital took the form of real estate purchases. In the United States, for example, only 5 percent of Japanese FDI in 1980 went to purchase real estate, but by 1991, 44.3 percent of Japanese FDI went to purchase real estate (Wong and Yamamura, table 1.10). In the United Kingdom the story was similar, with the bulk of Japanese FDI flowing into services and real estate. In Australia the rapid increase of Japanese FDI in the 1980s produced a new pattern, in which real estate and commerce absorbed $7.6 billion, or around 40 percent of the cumulative invested amount, and Japanese FDI in manufacturing, mining, and agriculture declined to 28.9 percent of total cumulated investment (Drysdale, table 4.5).

In the capital-poor, resource-abundant, or cheap-labor countries such as Mexico, Thailand, Taiwan, and South Korea, Japanese FDI flowed primarily into manufacturing and/or resource extraction. In the 1970s and 1980s Japanese trading companies increased their FDI in Mexico and other Latin American nations to produce fibers, consumer goods, motorcycles, automobiles, electronic equipment, and the like for sale in the local markets (Ozawa and Reynolds). Some Japanese companies eventually left the region, but firms such as Nissan Motor in Mexico began to assemble trucks and automobiles. In the 1970s Mexico became important because of her exports of oil and natural gas to Japan. Japanese FDI soon moved into three large Mexican government-sponsored projects to produce large steel pipe, iron and steel castings, and other steel products for the domestic market.

Labor-cheap Thailand had attracted little Japanese FDI before 1980. The Thai economy avoided inflation, heavy regulation, and budget deficit financing thanks to prudent, intelligent economic management.[10] The bulk of Japanese FDI began entering Thailand in the 1980s, flowing mainly to the manufacturing sector, rising from 58 percent of all Japanese FDI in 1986 to 86 percent in 1991 (Kaosa-ard, table 5.6). The Thai government, like other governments in this study, actively sought Japanese investors by providing financial incentives: exempting export duties for capital goods and raw materials, and allowing special deductions to reduce taxable income.

In the labor-cheap Republic of China of the 1950s and 1960s, two-thirds of all Japanese investment went to manufacturing, and that pattern continued in later decades. Even as real wages rose in that country, Taiwanese skilled labor was so productive that Japanese manufactured products remained low-cost and high-quality. The same was true in South Korea, where 85 percent of Japanese FDI went into manufacturing and only 15 percent into services (Schive, table 6.5).

The Effects of Japanese FDI

Foreign direct investment through MNEs and other organizations in host countries influences employment, income, output, trade, technology, and public opinion. The effects of FDI, however, are complex and subject to change from unexpected developments. For that reason, this volume does not attempt to assess whether the effects of Japanese FDI were either beneficial or costly to the host country. It merely tries to elucidate some of the observable short-term effects produced by Japanese FDI between 1970 and 1991, which occurred in countries where factor endowment and income and wealth levels profoundly differed.

In manufacturing and resource development, Japanese FDI created only modest new employment in host countries. The reason for this was that Japanese affiliates, whether MNEs or joint ventures, generally employed more capital and used highly productive labor and up-to-date technology than did native industries. Therefore, Japanese affiliates tended to pay higher wages to their employees than did their competitors but they employed fewer workers.

In the United States, for example, Wong and Yamamura estimated that for every $1 million of additional Japanese FDI, that investment created 16.83 man-years compared to 15.91 man-years for Japanese FDI invested in other countries. They conclude that "Japanese affiliates are not good job creators in the sense that they have relatively very high asset-employment ratios" (Wong and Yamamura, table 1.13, column 1). In 1991 Hollerman found in the United Kingdom "Japanese-owned firms provided direct employment for only around 50,000 workers, or approximately 1 percent of the labor force in manufacturing" (Hollerman). The employment multiplier effect of Japanese FDI in U.K. manufacturing probably only increased total employment by 2 or 3 percent.

We do not know the figures for total employment generated by Japanese FDI in Mexico, the Republic of China, and Thailand. In Australia, Japanese affiliates employed only 0.6 percent of total employment compared to U.S. affiliates, which employed around 5 percent of the total workforce.

Japanese affiliates increasingly purchased more goods and services from suppliers in host countries, thereby helping to generate greater output and revenue in them. In the United States, Japanese MNEs producing automobiles also purchased U.S.-made auto parts worth $9.07 billion in 1990, compared to only

TABLE I.1
JAPANESE FDI BY REGION, 1970–1991

Region	1970		1975		1985		Cumulative Through 1991	
North America	$912	25%	$3,917	25%	$26,964	32%	$155,008	44%
Western Europe	639	18	2,518	16	11,022	13	68,636	19
Latin America and offshore havens	567	16	2,881	18	15,636	19	43,821	12
Asia	751	21	4,219	26	19,463	23	53,455	15
Oceania	281	8	930	6	4,243	5	21,376	6
Middle East	334	9	976	6	2,976	4	3,522	3
Africa	92	3	501	3	3,370	4	6,574	1
TOTAL	$3,576	100	$15,943	100	$83,648	100	$352,392	100

SOURCE: For 1970 and 1975, see Sueo Sekuguchi, with the collaboration of Munemichi Inoue and Tadahisa Ooka, *Japanese Direct Foreign Investment* (Tokyo: Japan Economic Research Center, 1977), Center paper no. 32, p. 124. For 1985, see Charlie G. Turner, *Japan's Dynamic Efficiency in the Global Market: Trade, Investment, and Economic Growth* (New York: Quorum Books, 1991), p. 113. For 1991, data supplied during interview at Ministry of Finance, Japan (1993). All figures are cumulative balances in millions of then-current U.S. dollars.

$1.73 billion purchased in 1985 (Wong and Yamamura, table 1.14). The U.K. and Mexican governments encouraged Japanese investors to increase their purchase of locally produced goods and services, and they complied. In 1989, Japanese affiliates in Oceania (including Australia) purchased 87.5 percent of plant and equipment from local producers, and for Japanese MNEs engaged in manufacturing that purchase amounted to 90.0 percent of all purchased intermediate products (Drysdale, table 4.10). In the Republic of China those Japanese and other foreign affiliates conducting business there over the longest period tended to purchase more goods and services from local suppliers (Schive, figure 6.2).

Japanese MNEs and affiliates abroad also improved their host countries' economic competitiveness by transferring advanced Japanese research and development technology to local enterprises. In the United States the big three auto producers reacted to expanding Japanese market share in auto sales by redoubling their efforts and investing more to innovate and improve quality and lower the prices of their automobiles and trucks. By 1993 these developments, along with the increasing value of the yen, had reduced Japan's market share of automobiles sold in the United States. Hollerman notes that the "diffusion of Japanese management practices had indeed raised productivity and quality in British manufacturing," but "Britain still has much to learn." Japanese MNEs in Mexico and Australia also transmitted new technology and organizational methods to local enterprises. In Thailand, Japanese technology suppliers charged lower prices than did other foreign suppliers, but they also charged additional fees for components embodying new technology. In the Republic of China, Japanese FDI introduced new technology to Chinese firms. Between 1979 and 1991, Japanese MNEs also more than tripled their technical cooperative projects with Chinese firms, to exceed the same arrangements with other foreign investors.

Japanese FDI also increased the host country's foreign trade. In the United States, Japanese automakers produced a half-million automobiles in 1985 and nearly 1.5 million in 1990. As a result, U.S. automobile imports from Japan declined over the same period from 2.3 to 1.7 million, but Japanese MNEs in the United States exported more parts and automobiles in the 1987–1990 period, helped by the powerful appreciation of the yen. Japanese manufacturing MNEs in the United Kingdom, particularly of automobiles, produced for the United Kingdom and also exported to the European Commuinity. In 1991 Nissan exported 90 percent of its U.K. production. Japanese-owned consumer electronic firms in Britain currently export about one-half of their output, and for color TV and VCRs it is slightly less than one-half. Mitsubishi purchased a large saltmine complex in Baja California and exported enough Mexican salt to account for half of the total Japanese consumption, shipping the rest to the United States.

United States investors in Australia between 1950 and 1970 had hoped to

sell much of their manufacturing output to the Australian market, and they succeeded. Between 1972 and 1991, however, Japanese MNEs exported around 70
percent of their sales in the early 1970s, and 57.2 and 44.4 respectively for 1980
and 1990 (Drysdale, figures 4.6 and 4.7). While contributing to host-country
exports, Japanese MNEs initially bought less from Japan as a share of their total
purchases, and that share remained low over the next two decades. In Australia,
Japanese automakers were more export-oriented than were U.S. firms, with an
increasing share of their output being marketed to Japan. Japanese affiliates in
Thailand and the Republic of China also expanded their exports, particularly
after 1985, to outstrip U.S. enterprises in their share of total country exports.

Did Japanese FDI earn a higher rate of return abroad than at home? Wong
and Yamamura found that the rate of return on Japanese FDI was much better
than the average of the rates earned by all nations investing in the United States
between 1982 and 1986 (Wong and Yamamura, tables 1.11 and 1.12). After 1986
the rates of return for Japanese direct investment were much lower than those for
investments from other nations. The collapse of U.S. real estate prices probably
accounts for the decline in rate of return to Japanese FDI in the United States
after 1990. Japanese investors had overinvested in the late 1980s, a decision
encouraged by the real estate boom in Japan and their host countries in those
same years. Japanese FDI rates of return are unavailable for other countries.

Japanese MNEs and their FDI also created new economic difficulties in
their host countries. United States workers, especially women, employed in Japanese firms have expressed dissatisfaction about their promotions and job security. Some have taken their Japanese employers to court, and final legal settlements have yet to be reached. Another criticism is that many Japanese MNEs do
not undertake significant R & D in their host countries. In the United Kingdom, some experts complained that Japanese firms "do no real research" and
merely accumulate information for the parent company in Japan. A 1991 study
of the United Kingdom's consumer electronics industry concluded that Japanese
design and development of sophisticated key components were done mainly in
Japan (Hollerman).

Another difficulty is that Japanese firms avoid paying their fair share of
taxes because they pay higher than "justified" prices for goods and services from
their parent firms in Japan or other countries. These complaints are currently
being studied and even litigated in some countries such as the United States,
which received considerable Japanese FDI. Large Japanese purchases of real
estate caused much publicity and anxiety in the United States and Australia during the late 1980s. These purchases received high media attention, and we know
little about how such investments turned out or how they compared with real
estate purchases by foreign investors decades ago. The surge of Japanese FDI

seems to have elicited that age-old fear of foreigners cheaply acquiring national resources and controlling the economy, a fear expressed in Europe and elsewhere in the 1950s and 1960s when U.S. FDI increased. Just as those earlier fears were exaggerated, it is likely to be the same concerning Japanese FDI. Finally, it is unlikely in the near future that Japanese FDI will reach the level of the 1980s.

Conclusion

The Japanese FDI spurt in the 1970s and 1980s was rapid and similar to the United Kingdom's FDI spurt in the late nineteenth century and the United States' FDI in the 1950s and 1960s. Special push-and-pull economic factors made it possible for Japan to expand its FDI to other countries, just as had been the case for the United Kingdom and the United States in previous periods.

Japanese FDI in the advanced countries still ranks behind that of traditional large foreign investors and is a small share of total gross capital investment in those host countries. Japanese investors also did not greatly profit from their FDI in U.S. real estate. The Japanese FDI that flowed to poor, resource-rich countries such as those in Latin America developed and acquired resources and established some manufacturing. Japanese FDI flowing to the labor-abundant, resource-poor Asian countries mainly went into manufacturing, with part of that output being marketed locally and the remainder exported. We do not know the profitability of Japanese FDI in these countries, but it probably exceeded Japanese profit rates at home.

Japanese FDI promoted more host-country trade, improved their technology, and helped to integrate those countries more closely with Japan and other countries. The host countries experienced difficulties in receiving Japanese FDI, and some of those were probably connected with the world economic slowdown between 1970 and 1990, when their productivity and employment also grew more slowly than in previous decades. Under these circumstances, many critics in the United States and elsewhere perceived Japanese MNEs and FDI as causing economic dislocation and de-industrialization. It is difficult to separate the factors responsible for their economic slowdown from those caused by Japanese FDI. Critics perhaps attribute a greater dislocational role to Japanese FDI than is warranted. This is a topic awaiting more research.

In Southeast Asia and Latin America, Japanese FDI and MNEs contributed to a new division of labor based on modern manufacturing, foreign trade, and market competition. For North America and the United Kingdom, Japanese FDI and MNEs promoted new manufacturing and services. In Australia their impact was similar. In the 1970s and 1980s, global economic interdependence advanced, based on transferring new technology and high value-added production from Japan to other countries. At the same time many countries were afflicted by economic growth slowdowns as their manufacturing sectors declined and high unemployment persisted.

In the mid-1990s the world economy is at a new juncture: It can advance toward greater global economic interdependence based on FDI, technology transfer, and competition; or it can splinter into regional trading blocs characterized by that same discourse, technology transfer, and competition.

Notes

I want to express my gratitude to Leon Hollerman, Kozo Yamamura, and other conference participants for their comments.

1. Phyllis Deane and W. A. Cole, *British Economic Growth, 1688–1959: Trends and Structure* (Cambridge: Cambridge University Press, 1962), p. 273.
2. Charles Moraze, *The Triumph of the Middle Classes* (New York: Anchor Books, 1968), Chap. 11.
3. Angus Maddison, *Phases of Capitalist Development* (Oxford: Oxford University Press, 1982), Chap. 3.
4. This important interpretation of trade and industrial development for the 1950s and 1960s is presented in Alfred Maizels, *Growth and Trade: An Abridged Version of Industrial Growth and World Trade* (Cambridge: Cambridge University Press, 1970), Chap. 1.
5. Richard Caves, *Multinational Enterprise and Economic Analysis* (Cambridge: Cambridge University Press, 1982), Chaps. 7 and 9.
6. Kazu Sato, "Saving and Investment," in Kozo Yamamura and Yasukichi Yasuba, eds., *The Political Economy of Japan. The Domestic Transformation* (Stanford: Stanford University Press, 1987), Vol. 1, p. 138.
7. See Charlie G. Turner, *Japan's Dynamic Efficiency in the Global Market: Trade, Investment, and Economic Growth* (New York: Quorum Books, 1991), Chap. 1.
8. Michael A. Cusumano, *The Japanese Automobile Industry: Technology and Management at Nissan and Toyota* (Cambridge, Mass.: Council on East Asian Studies, Harvard University, 1989); see Conclusion.
9. Sheryl Wudunn, "Japan Banks Find Themselves Under the Gun," *New York Times,* July 28, 1995, pp. C1–C2.
10. For an excellent review of the successful policies Thailand used to avoid these economic dysfunctions and achieve high economic growth, see Gustav Ranis and Syed Akhtar Mahmod, *The Political Economy of Development Policy Change* (Cambridge, Mass.: Blackwell, 1992), Chap. 5.

CHAPTER 1

Japan's Direct Investment
in the United States
Causes, Patterns, and Issues

● ●

KAR-YIU WONG AND KOZO YAMAMURA

In the 1980s, Japan emerged as a major supplier of capital to the world and to the United States. Japanese foreign direct investment (JFDI) in the 1980–1985 period ($51.84 billion) easily exceeded the total JFDI made in the 1965–1979 period ($47.13 billion), and in 1986–1990 the figure rose even more sharply to $160.4 billion. In 1990, Japan accounted for 22.1 percent of the total FDI made in the world, as against 15.4 percent made by the United States, 10.3 percent by Germany, and 9.4 percent by the United Kingdom. A lion's share of the rapidly increasing JFDI in the 1980–1990 period was made in the United States (ranging from 31.6 percent in 1980 and 26.4 percent in 1981 to 48.2 percent in 1989 and 45.9 percent in 1990). Thus, by the end of 1990, the United States had received $130.53 billion or 42 percent of the total cumulative JFDI made around the globe. In the early 1990s, JFDI declined significantly, but both total JFDI and JFDI in the United States remained substantial. Japan's total FDI in 1991 and 1992 were $30.73 billion and $17.2 billion, respectively, in contrast to $44.13 billion and $48.02 billion in 1989 and 1990. However, JFDI in the United States still remained $15.21 billion in 1991 and $5.18 billion in 1992, in contrast to $21.24 billion and $25.58 billion in the preceding two years.[1]

In the 1980s, some in the United States reacted with concern or even alarm to the rapid increase in JFDI in their midst and many in Japan argued that steady and large JFDI would "hollow" their economy and exacerbate political and economic tension with the United States.[2] Today the reactions to JFDI are appreciably calmer, however, as evident in the tone and frequency of articles appearing in the mass media of both nations. Two principal reasons for this can be suggested. One is that both Americans and Japanese have "overcome," as it were, their respective initial "shock" at the novel experience of the large amount of capital flow from Japan to the United States in the 1980s, and especially in 1986–1989. The other is a combined result of the visible decline in JFDI of the past few years and an increasing realization by both Americans and Japanese that the dire effects of JFDI, predicted and feared by some both in the United States and Japan, have not occurred.

The goals of this chapter, pursued in order, are as follows: (1) To present a succinct review of the "push," i.e., the reasons for the "supply" of FDI in Japan, and the "pull," i.e., the reasons for the "demand" for it in the United States (hereafter in this chapter, unless otherwise noted, JFDI denotes JFDI in the United States); (2) to describe and discuss the patterns (growth rate and distribution by industry) and performance (returns) of JFDI; (3) to summarize and offer our views on the most significant among the political-economic and legal issues raised by JFDI (such as those on employment, bilateral trade, and technology transfer).

The Push and Pull of JFDI

We begin with a review of the push and the pull in our effort to answer such questions as: Why did Japan have so much capital to export in the 1980s and why did the magnitude rise so sharply in the second half of that decade? Why was such a large proportion of Japanese capital invested in the United States? Will Japan continue to invest abroad, and especially in the United States, through the end of the 1990s? As will be made evident in this section as well as in the following sections, the push and the pull are closely intertwined.

The Push

Let us proceed by dividing the period since 1980 into the 1980–1985 and 1986–1990 periods and the past few years, since the magnitude of JFDI differed significantly by subperiod for the reasons described below.

As seen in tables 1.1 and 1.2, the Japanese economy in the 1980–1985 period had its share of ups and downs. Because of the second oil crisis of 1979, in 1980 the current account was negative (–$10.7 billion) and the trade account showed a surplus of only $2.1 billion. Affected by the U.S. recession of 1981 and 1982 and because of the need to "adjust" for the rapid investment of the preceding few years, the rates of increase in capital investment in 1982 and 1983 were only 2.1 and 1.5 percent, respectively. Buffeted by the macroeconomic policies of both the United States and Japan, the ex-

TABLE 1.1

SELECTED TRADE-RELATED DATA, JAPAN, 1980–1991 ($US billion)

Year	Current Account (Global)	Merchandise Trade (Global)	Investment Income (Global)	Exchange Rate (¥/$1)	Exports to U.S. ÷ Total Exports
1980	–10.7	2.1	0.9	226.7	24.2
1981	4.8	20.0	–0.8	220.5	25.4
1982	6.9	18.1	1.7	249.1	26.2
1983	20.8	31.5	3.1	237.5	29.1
1984	35.0	44.3	4.2	237.5	35.2
1985	49.2	56.0	6.8	238.5	37.2
1986	85.8	·92.8	9.5	168.5	38.5
1987	87.0	96.4	16.7	144.6	36.5
1988	79.6	95.0	21.0	128.2	33.8
1989	57.2	76.9	23.4	138.0	33.9
1990	35.8	63.5	23.2	144.8	31.5
1991	72.6	103.3	26.7	134.7	29.1

SOURCES: Bank of Japan, *Balance of Payments Monthly,* April 1991 and January 1992; and Ministry of Finance, "Main Economic Indicators of Japan," August 1992.

TABLE 1.2
SELECTED MACROECONOMIC AND OTHER DATA, JAPAN, 1980–1991

Year	GNP % Change From Previous Year		Gross Private Capital Formation in Plant and Equipment		Index of Industrial Production % Change From Previous Year	Money Supply % Change From Previous Year (average outstanding) M2 + CD	Nikkei Average	CPI	WPI
	Nominal	Real	Change From % Previous Year (nominal)	% of GNP					
1980	8.2	3.5	14.2	15.7	4.7	9.2	6870.16	8.0	17.8
1981	7.2	3.4	5.7	15.4	0.9	8.9	7510.73	4.9	1.4
1982	5.1	3.4	2.1	15.0	0.4	9.2	7399.36	2.7	1.8
1983	4.2	2.8	1.5	14.6	3.0	7.4	8808.71	2.0	-2.2
1984	6.7	4.3	11.9	15.3	9.4	7.8	10560.61	2.3	-0.3
1985	6.8	5.2	12.4	16.1	3.7	8.4	12565.62	2.0	-1.1
1986	4.4	2.6	3.0	15.9	-0.2	8.7	16401.83	0.6	-9.1
1987	4.4	4.3	4.8	16.0	3.4	10.4	23248.06	0.1	-3.7
1988	6.6	6.2	14.3	17.1	9.5	11.2	27038.57	0.8	-1.0
1989	6.8	4.8	15.5	18.5	6.1	9.9	34058.81	2.9	2.5
1990	7.4	5.2	13.6	19.6	4.6	11.7	29437.17	3.3	2.0
1991	6.4	4.4	6.2	19.5	2.1	3.6	24295.57	2.8	-1.2

SOURCE: Ministry of Finance, "Main Economic Indicators of Japan," August 1992.

change rate too fluctuated more than 10 percent, recording a high of ¥220/US$ in 1981 and a low of ¥250/US$ in 1982.

Over all, however, the six-year period managed to maintain an average real GNP growth rate of 3.5 percent; the current account surplus steadily increased, led by the trade surplus, which rose rapidly from $20 billion in 1981 to $56 billion in 1985. Of course, the underlying macroeconomic reality that accounted for this steady increase in the trade surplus was "excess saving"; the gap that continued to increase between the high saving rate, around 24 percent of GNP, and the rate of investment (gross capital investment in plant and equipment), around at 21 percent of GNP.[3] The gap was made even larger because the government succeeded in its policy of reducing the deficit. The "dependency ratio"—the proportion of total expenditures and investment financed by deficit—which stood at 32.9 percent in 1979, was down to 26.6 by 1985. Along with this macroeconomic reality, we should be reminded also of the growing trade surplus, which reflected the increasing competitiveness of Japanese manufacturing industries. These facts and the rapidly increasing U.S. budget deficit of those years are the reasons why the proportion of total exports destined for the United States jumped from 24.2 percent in 1980 to 37.2 percent by 1985.[4]

This ballooning bilateral trade imbalance was an important reason for the Plaza Accord of the fall of 1985, reached by G7 under the leadership of the Reagan Administration, which abruptly shifted its international monetary policy from benign neglect to active intervention. The effect of the accord was a rapid and steady increase in the value of the yen, from around ¥250 in summer 1985 to ¥124 in spring 1986. It was this increase, *endaka*, and the monetary policy adopted to cope with its effects that determined the course of the Japanese economy and the magnitude of JFDI in the second half of the 1980s and in 1990.

Because of its magnitude and also because it came when a business cycle had just peaked (in June 1985), *endaka* quickly caused a wave of bankruptcies among export-dependent small- and medium-sized firms into 1986, and the rate of increase of investment, which had reached 12.4 percent in 1985, visibly slowed to a mere 3.0 percent in 1986. The index of industrial output, too, recorded in 1986 the first negative growth since the oil crisis of 1973. Reacting to this recession, as well as to U.S. insistence that Japan quickly stimulate its economy to enable it to increase imports from the United States, the monetary authority of Japan pursued a super-easy monetary policy. That is, beginning in January 1986, the official discount rate was reduced successively from 5.0 percent to 2.5 percent (the lowest ever in Japan's monetary history) in February 1987, and the rate remained unchanged for the following 27 months, until May 1989. The results were a very rapid increase in money supply (M2 + CD) ranging from 9.9 to 11.7 percent and the sharply lower call rates of the 1987–1990 period (see table 1.2).

The monetary policy was continued because the trade surplus in the 1986–1991 period continued to rise and remain very large (table 1.1) despite *endaka* because of the J-curve effect, "pricing to market" by Japanese firms,[5] and further increases in the competitiveness of Japanese firms, reflecting the large investments made in the preceding several years and the stability of the price level despite the monetary policy. The CPI in 1986, 1987, and 1988 rose only 0.6, 0.1, and 0.7 percent, respectively, and the WPI in those three years declined by 9.9, 1.7, and 1.0 percent, respectively.[6]

Price levels were not rising because the increasing liquidity created by the super-easy monetary policy was being diverted for transactions in assets (financial assets and land) to cause "asset inflation" (i.e., asset values were rising more rapidly than nominal GDP).[7] The asset inflation that occurred was reflected by the Nikkei index's climbing from the 12,000 to 13,000 level in 1985 to a peak of 38,915 in December 1989. The price of residential land in Tokyo and other large Japanese cities also continued to rise more than 20 percent per year in 1987, 1988, and 1989.[8]

Asset inflation raised the market value of firms' assets and the capital base of financial institutions, enabling the former to raise more capital more easily both in Japanese and foreign capital markets and the latter to make more loans and investments both in Japan and abroad. That a significant part of Japanese investment abroad included the loans, mostly short-term, obtained by Japanese firms and financial institutions in foreign capital markets is readily seen in table 1.3, showing a very rapid increase in short-term, private-sector external liabilities in the 1986–1989 period. The ease of obtaining capital at lower costs and very large capital gain (realized as well as unrealized) could not but motivate firms, financial institutions, and individuals to seek investment opportunities abroad, especially in the United States (for reasons that will be described below). The result was, as noted at the outset of this study, the very large JFDI made in these years.[9] Although we do not discuss portfolio investment, if this investment is added to JFDI, the total capital outflow from Japan in this period was even larger than JFDI, as can be seen readily in table 1.4.

However, the asset inflation that had become a "bubble"—"the portion of a movement in asset prices that cannot be explained by economic fundamentals"[10]—finally burst in December 1989. The Nikkei index tumbled in 1990 (recording a low of 20,221) and continued to decline, with some minor fluctuations, into 1992 (to reach the year's lowest level of 14,309). The in-

TABLE 1.3

EXTERNAL LIABILITIES, JAPAN, 1976–1991 ($US billion)

Year	Total	Direct Investment	Loans	Portfolio Securities	Short-term Private Sector
1976	58.4	2.2	2.1	11.1	38.3
1977	58.1	2.2	1.8	11.9	36.1
1978	82.5	2.8	1.9	18.0	48.1
1979	106.6	3.4	1.8	22.2	64.8
1980	148.0	3.3	1.6	29.7	94.5
1981	198.3	3.9	1.5	44.0	121.0
1982	203.0	4.0	1.3	47.1	118.8
1983	234.7	4.4	1.3	69.9	125.1
1984	266.9	4.5	1.3	77.1	145.9
1985	307.9	4.7	1.2	84.8	177.0
1986	547.0	6.5	1.2	143.6	341.8
1987	830.9	9.0	1.1	166.2	583.1
1988	1177.6	10.4	1.1	254.9	851.0
1989	1477.8	9.2	18.9	374.0	1004.1
1990	1529.8	9.9	58.0	334.5	1028.8
1991	1623.4	12.3	99.7	443.8	924.7

SOURCE: Bank of Japan, *Balance of Payments Monthly*.

dex of land prices, too, soon followed and began a visible descent, beginning in 1990.[11]

Although we cannot present a full discussion of many consequences of the bursting of the "bubble," let us note the following. The sharp decline in JFDI, both globally and to the United States, was accompanied by an abrupt reversal in the short-term capital account (from an inflow of $21.5 billion to an outflow of $25.8 billion, i.e., paying back short-term loans taken mostly from the Eurodollar market during the bubble years) and a rapid increase in the current account ($35.8 billion in 1990 to $72.9 in 1991). Because of the export performance and the remaining momentum of investment activities, in 1991 the economy managed to achieve a real growth rate of 3.4 percent, in contrast to 5.1 percent in 1990. With the money supply (M2 + CD) declining from 10.2 percent in 1990 to only 2.6 percent in 1991, bankruptcies rose

Table 1.4
External Assets, Japan, 1976–1991 ($US billion)

Year	Total	Direct Investment	Loans	Portfolio Securities	Short-term Private Sector	Net Assets
1976	68.0	10.3	5.4	4.2	14.5	9.5
1977	80.0	12.0	4.3	5.6	14.8	21.5
1978	118.7	14.3	8.8	12.2	55.4	36.2
1979	135.4	17.2	14.9	19.0	51.7	28.8
1980	159.6	19.6	14.8	21.4	46.0	11.5
1981	209.3	24.5	18.9	31.5	92.2	10.9
1982	227.7	29.0	23.2	40.1	88.2	24.7
1983	272.0	32.2	29.3	56.1	75.5	37.3
1984	341.2	37.9	40.6	87.6	84.8	74.3
1985	437.7	44.0	46.9	145.7	108.8	129.8
1986	727.3	58.0	69.2	257.9	207.9	180.4
1987	1071.6	77.0	97.5	339.7	343.3	240.7
1988	1469.3	110.8	123.7	427.2	538.8	291.7
1989	1171.0	154.4	137.1	533.8	666.7	293.2
1990	1857.9	201.4	130.1	563.8	682.1	328.1
1991	2006.5	231.8	141.2	632.1	685.4	383.1

SOURCE: Bank of Japan, *Balance of Payments Monthly*.

visibly (total debt involved rising from ¥3.28 trillion in 1990 to ¥8.14 trillion in 1991), and the growth rate of capital investment by all industries fell drastically (14.3 percent in 1990 to a mere 3.0 percent in 1991).[12] The post-bubble recession deepened into 1992, and as late as mid-1993, the debate continued whether or not the recession had ended. (We will offer some relevant observations of the recent past in the concluding section of this chapter.)

In understanding the push, we must also be reminded that the decreased dependence of firms on bank loans in the 1980s and the liberalization of Japanese capital markets together played important roles in determining the magnitude and manner of the push. The former enabled Japanese banks (and other financial institutions) to lend abroad (as well as to make loans to firms and individuals buying or speculating in land, contributing to the "bubble"). The latter, which proceeded during the 1970s and culminated in the 1980 change from "controlled in principle" (piecemeal liberalization) to "unrestricted in principle" (only retaining residual controls), enabled firms to raise capital (a part of which became JFDI) both at home and abroad more easily and at lower costs.[13]

The Pull

Why did the United States become the major capital importer in the 1980s, and why was the largest share of JFDI made in the United States? Since the first question has been answered by many specialists who have examined the macroeconomic effects of the Reagan policy and various long-term and structural reasons for the low saving rate and declining international competitiveness of U.S. industries, let us examine table 1.5 to summarize the following results of the policy and the structural changes.

In addition to the rapid accumulation of international liabilities that turned the United States from an international creditor into an international debtor in 1986, table 1.5 reveals several significant facts relating to the private international investment position of the United States. Both inward direct investment and inward portfolio investment grew rapidly, but the growth rate of outward direct investment was less impressive, a mere 7.6 percent annually on average. As a result, the balances of direct and portfolio investment did drop in the period from 1976 to 1991. More dramatic was the change in the balance of portfolio investment: After being positive for a long time, it has been negative from 1986 until 1991. On the direct investment side, despite the high annual growth rate of inward investment, which is more than double that of outward investment, the balance of direct investment remained

TABLE 1.5
PRIVATE DIRECT AND PORTFOLIO INVESTMENT POSITION OF
THE UNITED STATES, 1976–1991 ($US billion)

Year	Direct Investment			Portfolio Investment		
	Outward	Inward	Balance	Outward	Inward	Balance
1976	223.0	48.9	174.1	145.6	128.4	17.2
	(60.5)	(27.6)		(39.5)	(72.4)	
1977	252.8	56.7	196.1	164.3	130.9	33.4
	(60.6)	(30.2)		(39.4)	(69.8)	
1978	291.0	69.6	221.4	213.6	156.2	57.4
	(57.7)	(30.8)		(42.3)	(69.2)	
1979	343.9	88.3	255.6	248.3	201.8	46.5
	(58.1)	(30.4)		(41.9)	(69.6)	
1980	396.2	126.0	270.2	304.8	241.7	63.1
	(56.5)	(34.3)		(43.5)	(65.7)	
1981	412.4	159.9	252.5	398.4	289.5	108.9
	(50.9)	(35.6)		(49.1)	(64.4)	
1982	387.2	176.9	210.3	513.9	374.2	139.7
	(43.0)	(32.1)		(57.0)	(67.9)	
1983	371.7	184.4	187.3	594.7	452.9	141.8
	(38.5)	(28.9)		(61.5)	(71.1)	
1984	361.6	211.2	150.4	625.9	533.8	92.1
	(36.6)	(28.3)		(63.4)	(71.7)	
1985	387.2	231.3	155.9	659.7	679.8	−20.1
	(37.0)	(25.4)		(63.0)	(74.6)	
1986	421.2	265.8	155.4	759.5	884.4	−124.9
	(35.7)	(23.1)		(64.3)	(76.9)	
1987	493.3	313.5	179.8	820.2	994.8	−174.6
	(37.6)	(24.0)		(62.4)	(76.0)	
1988	515.7	374.3	141.4	908.8	1,142.0	−233.2
	(36.2)	(24.7)		(63.8)	(75.3)	
1989	522.8	433.2	119.6	988.7	1,336.5	−347.8
	(35.9)	(24.5)		(64.1)	(75.5)	
1990	623.6	466.5	157.1	1,003.7	1,341.4	−337.7
	(38.3)	(25.8)		(61.7)	(74.2)	
1991	655.3	487.0	168.3	1,067.0	1,438.2	−371.2
	(38.0)	(25.3)		(62.0)	(74.7)	
AGR	7.6	16.6		14.2	17.5	

NOTES: Direct investment is measured at current cost. Numbers in parentheses are shares in the private investment position.

SOURCE: U.S. Commerce Department, *Survey of Current Business*, various issues.

positive throughout this period, and its value in 1991 was only slightly less than that in 1976. This is because at the beginning of the period inward direct investment was much smaller than outward direct investment ($48.9 billion compared with $223 billion).

Within this broad picture, let us now ask: Why was more than 40 percent of JFDI "pulled" into the United States during the 1980–1990 period while the United States continued to be the most important host nation for JFDI in 1991 and 1992? We believe the principal answers to this question must include the following.

JFDI in the United States was large because Japanese firms wished to maintain and increase their market share in their largest market, which imported almost one-quarter of their total exports in the early 1980s and nearly one-third by the end of that decade. JFDI helped to maintain and increase their sales, as well as their long-term competitiveness, by enabling them to (1) "internalize" the gains from their technological, managerial, and other firm-specific advantages; (2) circumvent the existing or expected tariff or quota barriers; (3) gain access to U.S. technology; (4) obtain information (regarding consumer tastes and other market characteristics) more efficiently; (5) provide financial and other services needed by Japanese firms; and (6) reduce transportation costs.

As specialists of FDI have found, identifying, let alone demonstrating quantitatively, the specific motivations for FDI is extremely difficult. As results of surveys invariably reveal, most FDI, including JFDI in the United States, is made for multiple reasons. We believe, however, that the most important reasons for JFDI in the decade were the "internalization" and circumventing of trade barriers as numerous studies of JFDI in the automobile, electronics, steel, and other industries have shown. Further, as will be discussed below, there is good reason to believe that some JFDI in these industries constituted overinvestment that was made in an effort to diffuse the mounting political risks of trade restrictions that became increasingly stringent during the decade.

Neither is there little doubt that an increasing amount of JFDI was made to gain access to U.S. technology, as typified by Japanese acquisition of technological start-up firms by in Silicon Valley and elsewhere. (Since this motive for JFDI has become an important political-economic issue in bilateral relations, we will discuss the issue later in this chapter.) The JFDI that rose for those reasons required financial and other services, increasing the JFDI made by banks, security houses, and others (as will also be discussed later). Reduction in transportation costs was not likely to have been a significant reason for JFDI, since virtually all Japanese exports to the United States are high-value manufactured products for which transportation costs were only a very small fraction of the total.

In discussing the motivations for JFDI in the 1980s, we need to consider Japanese investment in real estate and the relationship between the exchange rate and JFDI. Japanese direct investment in real estate increased rapidly in the 1980s, from $264 million (or slightly less than 6 percent of total investment) to $14.95 billion in 1991 (slightly more than 17 percent). As seen in table 1.6, the average annual growth rate in this 11-year period was a remarkable 44.3 percent, which accounts for why Japanese investment in real estate provoked a heated debate in the United States.

To gain a perspective on this investment, we obtained the following data contained in an extensive survey done by the Department of Commerce on foreign investment in the United States in 1987. The area of land in the United States owned by other countries was 13.65 million acres. The four nations whose citizens collectively owned the largest amounts of land in the United States were the United Kingdom (24.6 percent), Canada (15.0 percent), France (9.2 percent), and Switzerland (5.5 percent). That is to say, despite the many negative observations made in the mass media regarding the Japanese "buy-

TABLE 1.6
JAPANESE DIRECT INVESTMENT BY INDUSTRIES IN SELECTED YEARS
($US million)

Year	1980	1984	1987	1991	AGR, %
All industries	4,723	16,044	34,421	86,658	30.3
Petroleum	−232	−88	−56	113	—
Manufacturing	1,033	2,460	4,970	18,657	30.1
Wholesale trade	3,177	9,689	15,927	26,935	21.4
Retail trade	78	252	373	1,102	27.2
Banking	645	1,853	3,655	6,797	23.9
Finance (exc. banking)	D	513	2,994	9,120	50.9
Insurance	D	138	188	572	22.5
Real estate	264	744	4,386	14,948	44.3
Others	274	482	1,984	8,413	34.2

NOTES: D = Suppressed to avoid disclosure of data of individual companies.
AGR = annual growth rate, 1980–1991 (1984–1991 for finance [excluding banking] and insurance). The growth rate of petroleum is not shown because of its negative investment position.

SOURCE: U.S. Department of Commerce, *Survey of Current Business*, various issues.

ing of America," the area of land owned by Japanese investors was much smaller than that owned by the Swiss and was only 0.8 percent of the foreign-held land in the United States.

The reasons for the strong negative reaction to Japanese acquisitions, we believe, were that Japanese acquired several well- known properties; their investment rose very rapidly in the 1986–1989 period; and Japanese acquisitions were concentrated heavily in California, Hawaii, and a few other states. (The percentages of investment in California and Hawaii were, respectively, 18.8 and 14.3 percent; Washington and Minnesota were next with 5.4 percent each.) We should, however, note that, for two reasons, the number of acres may not truly reflect the importance of Japanese investment in real estate. In many instances, Japanese firms purchased high-rise buildings, for which the number of acres does not reflect the amount of investment. On the other hand, Japanese have purchased many golf courses, for which the number of acres may exaggerate the investment.

Despite such estimation difficulties, one thing is clear. Japanese investors were and are eager to acquire land in the United States for an obvious reason: Land is scarcer and much more costly in Japan than in the land-abundant United States, and during the "bubble" years this price differential became even larger.[14]

Another analytically important point relates to the frequently asserted view that FDI in the United States is substantially affected by exchange rates. Ever since the collapse of the Bretton Woods system in the early 1970s, the price of the dollar against the Japanese yen has been moving lower and fluctuating widely. In 1973, the year the Bretton Woods system collapsed, the average price of the dollar was ¥271.70, but in 1990 the average price dropped to ¥144.79, representing a devaluation of the dollar of 47 percent. This made U.S. products and assets more attractive to Japanese buyers. The change in the exchange rate has been used to argue that the prices of assets in the United States have become too low and that Japanese investors have been spending their more valuable yen on buying out America.[15]

Despite its intuitive appeal, this "fire sale" argument must be examined critically.[16] Whether or not an asset in another country is cheaper depends on many factors, including but not limited to the exchange rate. For example, an investor must evaluate the price of an asset in the local currency, and also that price as compared with the price of a comparable asset in the currency of the investor's own country. During the period from 1973 to 1990, although the price of the dollar dropped, local prices in the United States and Japan changed, too. For example, the consumer price index (CPI) in the United States rose 194 percent (from 41.28 to 121.43, with 1985 = 100), while in

Japan it increased 133 percent (from 45.99 to 106.94). Surprisingly, the growth rate of the U.S. CPI minus that of the price of the dollar approximates that of Japan's CPI. This is consistent with the relative version of the purchasing power parity.[17] This means that in a relative sense, consumer goods in the United States have not become cheap despite the devaluation of the dollar.[18]

Moreover, whether or not a Japanese firm chooses to invest in the United States depends not only on the present exchange rate but also on the costs of production in the two countries, and also on the expected exchange rate in the near future when the Japanese firm repatriates the profit back to Japan. After all, the major motive of a foreign firm for investing in the United States is to earn profit, and it is the profit expressed in the firm's own currency that counts. If the recent devaluation of the dollar is an indication that the dollar will continue to slide, then, other things being equal, a Japanese firm will be deterred from investing in the United States.

Another factor that may affect JFDI in the United States is the variation of exchange rates and prices. For example, from 1974 to 1989, the coefficient of variation of the end-of-month price of the dollar in terms of the yen was 24 percent.[19] The coefficients of variation of the U.S. consumer price index (CPI) and the wholesale price index (WPI) for this period were 28 and 17 percent, respectively, while the corresponding numbers for Japan were 22 and 11 percent.[20] These numbers do not suggest that the exchange rate fluctuated widely as compared with commodity prices, although wholesale price indices on the whole were more stable.[21] The preceding is to argue that no convincing or conclusive evidence has been found to enable one to conclude that exchange-rate variations encourage or discourage foreign investment.[22]

Finally, we should also note that JFDI in the United States was larger than elsewhere because the United States is politically more attractive—a safe haven—compared to the EC, Eastern Europe, many Asian nations, and developing economies around the globe, and because the United States is the largest market for Japanese firms. We must, of course, be careful to note that, as many economists have argued, the size of a market in itself is neither a necessary nor a sufficient reason for FDI.[23]

Patterns and Performance

Having examined the push and pull of JFDI, we now turn to a brief discussion of its patterns and performance in the 1980–1991 period.

Patterns

Table 1.7 compares the direct investment position of all nations and that of Japan measured at historical cost.[24] The investment position of all nations grew from $13,270 million in 1970 to $407,577 million in 1991, with an annual growth rate of 17.7 percent. The investment position of Japan at the same time increased at a much faster rate, 32.7 percent annually. As a result, the share of the investment position of Japan swelled from a mere 1.7 percent in 1970 to a sizable 21.3 percent in 1991.

Another way to illustrate the influx of Japanese investment is to compare its position in the United States with the positions of other major investing countries. Table 1.8 presents the shares of the investment positions in the 1980–1991 period of four major investing countries from 1980 to 1991: Japan, United Kingdom, Netherlands, and Canada. In 1980, the Japanese investment position was only about 6 percent of the total foreign investment position, far behind those of the other three investing countries. In the first half of the 1980s, the shares of Japan and the United Kingdom rose gradually while those of the Netherlands and Canada declined. The result was that around 1982 the United Kingdom became the largest investor, and around 1984 Japan emerged as the third largest investor. As the share of Japanese investment continued to grow in the second half of the decade, Japan surpassed the Netherlands in 1987 to become the second largest investor.

As noted earlier, an important source of JFDI was capital inflow consisting of equity capital inflow, reinvested earnings, and intercompany debt. Indeed, Japanese capital inflow in 1986 was as high as 97 percent of the change in Japanese investment position, and the number for 1990 reached 107 percent (with negative valuation adjustment).

Table 1.9 shows the Japanese capital inflow and its composition from 1980 to 1991. Note how capital flow changed during the 1980–1991 period. Column 2 of table 1.9 shows that capital inflow, which grew from $948 million in 1980 to $17,336 million in 1990, declined sharply to $5,183 million in 1991. The growth of capital inflow in the 1980–1991 period, however,

TABLE 1.7
FOREIGN DIRECT INVESTMENT POSITION AT HISTORICAL COST, 1970–1991

Year	All Nations $, Million	Japan $, Million	Share, %
1970	13,270	229	1.7
1971	13,914	227	1.6
1972	14,868	154	1.0
1973	20,556	152	0.7
1974	25,144	345	1.4
1975	27,662	591	2.1
1976	30,770	1,178	3.8
1977	34,595	1,755	5.1
1978	42,471	2,749	6.5
1979	54,462	3,493	6.4
1980	83,046	4,723	5.7
1981	108,714	7,697	7.1
1982	125,677	9,677	7.8
1983	137,061	11,336	8.3
1984	164,583	16,044	9.7
1985	184,615	19,313	10.5
1986	220,414	26,824	12.2
1987	263,394	34,421	13.1
1988	314,754	51,126	16.2
1989	368,924	67,268	18.2
1990	396,702	81,775	20.6
1991	407,577	86,658	21.3
AGR, %	17.7	32.7	

NOTE: AGR = annual growth rate, 1970–1991, %.

SOURCE: U.S. Department of Commerce, *Survey of Current Business*, various issues.

was quite uneven. After an increase of about 213 percent in 1981, capital inflow dropped in the next two years, before it grew again at an impressive rate of 164 percent in 1984. It also increased by more than 100 percent in 1986 and 1988. In the next three years, 1988 to 1990, capital inflow remained fairly constant around $17.3 to 17.4 billion. As noted above, in 1991, capital inflow dropped abruptly to $5.2 billion.

TABLE **1.8**

SHARES OF INVESTMENT FROM MAJOR INVESTING COUNTRIES, 1980–1991 (%)

Year	Japan	United Kingdom	Netherlands	Canada
1980	6	17	23	15
1981	7	17	25	11
1982	8	23	21	9
1983	8	23	21	8
1984	10	23	20	9
1985	10	24	20	9
1986	12	25	18	9
1987	13	26	12	12
1988	16	26	11	11
1989	18	28	15	8
1990	21	26	16	8
1991	21	26	17	8

SOURCE: U.S. Department of Commerce, computer disks.

The last three columns of table 1.9 show the sources of investment funds: equity capital inflow, reinvestment earnings, and intercompany debt inflow. In almost every year, the major component of capital inflow was equity capital inflow. Except in three of the years (1981, 1984, and 1985), more than half of the capital inflow was due to equity capital inflow; in fact, in 1988 to 1990, the shares of equity capital inflow reached nearly 80 percent. On the other hand, the importance of reinvestment earnings was declining over time. In 1987, its share fell so much that it was negative. Its share was barely positive in 1988, and was negative again in 1989 and 1991. Negative reinvestment earnings represent a net withdrawal of the funds originally invested.[25] The major reason for the declining importance of reinvested earnings was the low or negative earnings of Japanese investment in those years, as will be discussed below. The shares of intercompany debt inflow, on the other hand, were fairly constant, ranging from 20 percent to 40 percent of the total capital inflow of 9 out of 11 years during the 1980–1990 period.

Table 1.6 showed the growth rate and distribution of JFDI across various industries in 1980, 1984, 1987, and 1991. Aggregate Japanese investment rose at a remarkable compounded annual growth rate of 30.3 percent from 1980 to 1991, and the rates differed significantly by industry, ranging from 21.3 percent for wholesale trade to 50.9 for nonbanking finance.[26] The

TABLE 1.9
JAPANESE CAPITAL INFLOW, 1980–1991

Year	Capital Inflow, $, million	Shares, %		
		Equity	Reinvest.	Int. Debt
1980	948	53	61	−14
1981	2,970	35	22	44
1982	1,977	54	6	40
1983	1,653	55	35	10
1984	4,374	41	30	29
1985	3,394	36	25	39
1986	7,268	53	2	46
1987	8,791	62	−2	40
1988	17,287	77	1	22
1989	17,425	79	−3	24
1990	17,335	89	−18	30
1991	5,183	191	−71	−20

NOTES: Equity = Equity Capital Inflow.
Reinv. = Reinvested Earning.
Int. Debt = Intercompany Debt Inflow.

SOURCE: U.S. Department of Commerce, *Survey of Current Business,* various issues.

rapid growth of nonbanking financial investment from Japan in those years can be attributed to three reasons: (1) Such investment had a much smaller initial value, $513 million in 1984; (2) the interdependence among many Japanese firms created increasing demand for Japanese financial services as JFDI rose;[27] and (3) such investment was needed because of the growth of Japanese portfolio investment in the United States, which required the services of Japanese financial institutions.

Another sector that saw significant Japanese investment was real estate, as discussed earlier. Here let us add only that the magnitude of investment in real estate differed significantly within the period, reflecting a steady rise in the trade surplus during the 1980–1985 period, *endaka* of 1985 and 1986, and the "bubble" and its bursting in the 1987–1990 period. That is, while the annual growth rate rose gradually from 15.5 percent in 1981 to 44.5 percent in 1984, it jumped to a record high of 100.6 percent in 1985 and stayed at 91.5 percent in 1986. Although the rate fell to 48.1 percent in 1987, it climbed back to 86.7 percent in 1988 and then slowed to below 40 percent in 1989 and 1990.

TABLE 1.10
DISTRIBUTION OF JAPANESE DIRECT INVESTMENT
BY INDUSTRIES IN SELECTED YEARS (%)

	1980		1986		1991	
	All Nations	Japan	All Nations	Japan	All Nations	Japan
All industries	100.0	100.0	100.0	100.0	100.0	100.0
Mining	1.6	0.1	2.3	D	0.0	0.0
Petroleum	14.7	− 4.9*	13.2	−0.1*	9.8	0.1
Manufacturing	39.8	21.9	32.6	13.3	40.0	21.5
Wholesale trade	13.9	67.3	15.4	51.0	13.0	31.1
Retail trade	4.4	1.7	4.0	1.1	1.7	1.3
Banking	5.6	13.7	5.6	10.1	5.1	7.8
Finance (exc. banking)	1.6	D	3.3	7.8	2.3	10.5
Insurance	7.3	D	7.0	D	8.2	0.7
Real estate	7.4	5.6	10.2	11.0	8.3	17.2
Others	5.4	5.8	8.6	4.9	11.8	9.7

NOTES: D = Suppressed to avoid disclosure of data of individual companies.
*Negative JFDI in the petroleum sector in 1980 and 1986 means a divestment. Direct investment can be disaggregated into capital inflow and valuation adjustment, both of which can be either positive or negative. For example, negative capital inflow means withdrawal of some existing facilities, and negative valuation adjustment can be due to a drop in value of existing facilities.

SOURCE: U.S. Department of Commerce, *Survey of Current Business,* various issues.

Other than wholesale trade, which had the lowest annual growth rate, several other industries also had relatively low growth rates: Insurance, retail trade, and banking all had annual growth rates of 25 percent or less, and the rate for manufacturing was only 30 percent. In noting these facts, we must of course be aware that both wholesale and manufacturing had larger shares of JFDI than others, as seen in table 1.10. Wholesale received the largest share of JFDI, i.e., 67.3 percent in 1980 and, although this figure declined gradually over time, the figure still stood at 33.1 percent in 1991. However, it is important to be aware that these numbers overstate the growth of investment in wholesale trade because several Japanese automobile makers invested heavily in the United States during the 1980s and some among them classified (and still classify) themselves as wholesale traders. (Unfortunately, no data are available to enable us to discriminate between investments made by automobile makers and those made by others.) The second largest amount of JFDI went to the manufacturing industry. In 1980, this industry accounted for 22 percent of JFDI and, although the proportion fell to 13.3 percent in 1986, it climbed back up to 21.5 percent in 1991.

Because of the significantly different growth rates of investment by sector, as seen in table 1.6, the distribution of JFDI changed dramatically over time. In 1980, manufacturing and banking respectively received the second and third largest shares of JFDI (21.9 and 13.7 percent). In 1991, although wholesale trade still had the largest share of JFDI, its share had dropped to 31.3 percent while the share of real estate had risen to the second largest with 17.2 percent. The share of manufacturing industries in 1991 remained at a level slightly lower than in 1980, while that of banking fell to 7.8 percent. The rapid rise in investment in nonbanking finance pushed its share in 1991 to 10.5 percent.

Table 1.10 also shows the distribution of investment from all countries. The average share by industry of FDI made by all nations investing in the United States was highest for the manufacturing industry. The petroleum industry and wholesale trade were second and third, with 14.7 and 13.9 percent, respectively,[28] and all other industries had less than 10 percent of all investment. Table 1.10 also shows that there were three noteworthy differences between the distribution of Japanese investment and that from all nations. First, although the distribution of investment from Japan changed visibly between 1980 and 1991, those of all nations remained fairly constant in that decade. Second, the average share invested by all nations was highest for the manufacturing sector whereas Japanese investors' favorite target for investment was wholesale trade (with the above-noted caveat that some automobile makers still classify themselves as wholesale traders). Third, Japan in 1991 had high proportions of investment in nonbanking finance and real estate.

Confirming what is widely believed, the growth of JFDI in the 1980s was rapid indeed—rapid enough to make Japan the second largest investor in the United States by the end of the decade. Unlike the FDI of other nations in the United States, a substantial amount of JFDI was made, especially in the "bubble" years, in the nonbanking finance and real estate sectors.

Performance

One way of examining the performance of an investment is by its rates of return. Because returns can be measured in various ways, we chose to examine the rates earned by JFDI in the United States comparatively vis-a-vis

TABLE 1.11

A COMPARISON OF RATES OF RETURN OF FOREIGN AND JAPANESE INVESTMENT IN THE UNITED STATES, U.S. DIRECT INVESTMENT, AND ALL U.S. BUSINESSES, 1982–1991 (%)

Year	Returns Based on Market Value			Returns Based on Current Value		Returns Based on Historical Cost		
	FDIUS	USDIA	All US	FDIUS	USDIA	FDIUS	USDIA	Japanese
1982	n.a.	n.a.	11.0	1.2	6.0	2.7	11.4	4.6
1983	4.0	11.4	9.9	2.3	7.0	3.9	12.9	9.6
1984	5.7	11.6	11.1	4.4	8.3	6.3	14.4	13.8
1985	3.2	9.1	8.7	3.3	7.9	4.3	12.6	8.8
1986	2.2	7.2	7.2	2.8	7.6	3.7	12.2	4.4
1987	2.5	7.7	8.1	2.6	8.3	3.6	13.4	1.9
1988	3.9	8.4	9.0	3.4	10.0	4.4	15.5	3.4
1989	2.2	7.9	7.6	1.6	10.2	2.2	15.2	1.1
1990	-0.3	7.6	7.7	0.2	9.4	0.4	13.8	-1.7
1991	-0.2	6.9	6.0	-0.8	7.7	-0.7	11.2	-1.8

NOTES: n.a. = Not available.
FDIUS = Foreign direct investment in the United States.
USDIA = U.S. direct investment abroad.
All US = All U.S. businesses.

SOURCE: U.S. Department of Commerce, *Survey of Current Business*, various issues.

those earned by (1) U.S. direct investment abroad (USDIA), (2) FDI in the United States (FDIUS), and (3) all U.S. businesses calculating the value of assets at market value,[29] and at current cost,[30] as shown in table 1.11. Because of data limitations, the rates for return on JFDI (the ratio of investment income to the mean of the investment at the beginning and end of the year) are for all industries during the 1982–1991 period, calculated using historical cost. We find in the table that Japanese investment performed much better than the average of the rates earned by all nations investing in the United States between 1982 and 1986. After 1986 the picture changed, however. The post-1986 rates of return (i.e., 1987–1991) for Japanese direct investment were much lower than those for investment from all nations.

The interesting questions are why in the above-mentioned period foreign capital invested in the United States was consistently not performing as well as U.S. capital both at home and abroad, and why there was a difference in profitability between investment from Japan and that from all nations (i.e., why did the returns to Japanese investment that were above those of FDI of other nations until 1986 decline visibly beginning in 1987?).

One possible reason for lower rates of return for FDI (including JFDI) in the United States is that it is newer or the average age is younger because FDI in the United States has risen rapidly in the past decade in contrast to older U.S. investment abroad, which took place mainly in the 1960s and 1970s. However, for this explanation to be valid, the rate of return must increase substantially with the age of an investment during its early years and the aging of an investment must not seriously affect its profitability. In other words, the rate of return must rise during the early years of an investment, and then stay fairly constant. We do not believe that the observed pattern of changes in the rates and the significant difference seen between the returns of foreign investment and those of U.S. investment abroad and at home support this explanation.

Another possible explanation for the differing performances of FDI in the United States (including JFDI) and foreign and U.S. investment abroad is that foreign investors have overinvested in the sense that they invested beyond the amount that would have earned a rate of return equal to the rate realized by U.S. investment. We believe this is a strong hypothesis. However, to be able to conclude that FDI in the United States earned less than did U.S. investment abroad in the 1980–1991 period mainly because of overinvestment, we need to carry out much more extensive research. (Conversely, a no-less-interesting question to examine is why U.S. firms did not make or did less overinvestment abroad as evidenced in the higher returns their investment abroad earned.[31])

Table 1.12
Rates of Return by Industries in Selected Years, Japan and All Nations (%)

	1982		1984		1986		1988		1991	
	All Nations	Japan	All Nations	Japan	All Nations	Japan	All Nations	Japan	All Nations	Japan
All industries	2.7	4.6	6.1	13.8	2.7	4.4	4.7	3.4	-0.7	-1.8
Manufacturing	0.1	-4.6	4.9	-1.6	0.1	-6.8	6.9	-2.8	0.6	-9.1
Wholesale trade	0.1	3.8	11.6	17.3	4.7	4.8	6.0	6.4	-1.0	0.3
Retail trade	7.3	-6.4	13.6	-2.5	10.4	-5.9	2.2	3.1	-18.4	-9.2
Banking	8.3	19.0	7.9	24.5	12.2	25.3	9.5	13.0	-1.5	10.6
Finance (exc. banking)	-4.3	D	1.7	D	1.3	-5.1	-2.3	2.2	-4.2	1.6
Insurance	4.5	D	-7.0	-3.8	12.5	D	0.8	13.2	1.3	6.9
Real estate	-1.6	*	4.6	2.1	0.4	*	0.5	1.9	-5.3	-0.5
Others	-0.3	4.4	-3.1	5.8	-3.9	6.4	-2.1	-5.6	-1.9	-7.2

NOTES: D = Suppressed to avoid disclosure of private information.
* = less than 0.05% in magnitude.

SOURCE: U.S. Department of Commerce, *Survey of Current Business*, various issues.

Let us focus our attention more specifically on the performance of JFDI vis-a-vis that of FDI made by other nations in the United States and on the visibly lower return earned by JFDI after 1987 (relative to both the return JFDI earned before 1987 and to the return earned by FDI of other nations).

Table 1.12 presents the rates of returns by industries for investment from these countries in 1982, 1984, 1986, 1988, and 1991. (The rate of return of an investment in a particular year is defined as the ratio of income in that year to the average of the year-end investment position and the previous year-end investment position.) In general, the rates of return for all nations and those of Japanese investment fluctuated considerably both in signs and magnitudes. It is difficult to identify an industry that was profitable in those years. Roughly speaking, investment from all nations in the banking and retail trade industries appeared to perform better than the average in those years, and investment in the nonbanking finance and real estate industries did poorly.[32]

There are some similarities and differences between the performance of investment from all nations and that of JFDI in the United States. For example, the banking industry seemed to be quite profitable for all investors in general. However, the similarities nearly stop here. Japanese investment in the banking industry convincingly outperformed investment from other nations in all these years. Even in 1991, when the returns to all investment as a whole were negative, the loss the Japanese banks experienced in that year was significantly less than that experienced by other banks. This interesting phenomenon deserves closer examination. Another interesting feature in the table is that Japanese investment in the United States did better than the investment from all other nations until 1987, but JFDI in the manufacturing sector in the United States performed poorly in the 1980–1991 period (i.e., its returns were consistently negative).

Why did JFDI in manufacturing industries, accounting for a lion's share of JFDI (recall that some JFDI made in wholesale trade, too, was JFDI made in the automobile industry) fail to earn positive returns? Although we need to consider the fact that in some years during the 1980–1991 period many U.S. manufacturing firms (e.g., U.S. automakers) also recorded losses, we believe the principal reason for the consistently negative returns earned by JFDI in manufacturing industries was the overinvestment made by Japanese firms (especially automakers) in attempting to jump the quota restrictions and to diffuse the American protectionist threat. The latter is what Bhagwati called "quid pro quo" investment: FDI made when the possibility of trade restriction in the near future is sufficiently high.[33]

The main reason for the distinctively lower post-1987 performance of

TABLE 1.13
PERFORMANCE OF AFFILIATES OF MAJOR INVESTORS, 1989

Country	A/E	C/E	I/A	IT/A
Japan	651	39	2.4	5.0
Canada	266	30	18.1	5.6
United Kingdom	259	29	12.1	11.9
Netherlands	275	30	11.6	9.6
Germany	201	33	9.7	12.7
All nations	316	32	8.4	7.2

NOTES: A/E = Asset/Employment, $1,000/worker.
C/E = Compensation/Employment, 1,000/worker.
I/A = Income/Asset, $/$1,000.
IT/A = Income Tax/Asset, $/$1,000.

SOURCE: U.S. Department of Commerce, computer disks.

JFDI in comparison to FDI made by other nations in the United States, we believe, is the "bubble." That is, the "bubble" substantially increased the value of collateral (stocks and land) necessary to raise lower-cost capital at home and abroad,[34] causing Japanese investors to become less risk-averse (or even prompting them to make erroneous risk assessments). Put simply, many Japanese firms and individuals invested too much between 1987 and 1990 to be able to maintain positive reasonable rates of return on their investments in the United States. Indeed, as numerous mass media reports attest, much of the "bubble"-induced JFDI, especially that made in real estate, proved to be unwise.[35]

Let us now turn to the following additional observations on JFDI as summarized in table 1.13, which compares the asset-employment ratio (A/E), compensation per employment (C/E), income-asset ratio (I/A), and income tax-asset ratio (IT/A) in 1989 of affiliates of firms in Japan, Canada, United Kingdom, Netherlands, Germany, and all nations. The asset-employment ratios given in column 2 of the table can be regarded as the degree of capital intensiveness. By this measure, Japanese affiliates in 1989 had a capital-labor ratio much higher than those of other countries' affiliates. In fact, the affiliates of all other countries had capital-labor ratios lower than the average. From the viewpoint of the United States as a host country, is a higher capital-labor ratio better? It depends. Since a higher capital-labor ratio means a lower labor-capital ratio, the job-creating power of Japanese investment is very small compared with that of other major investors' investment. However, the higher capital-labor ratio in the Japanese affiliates means a higher productivity of labor and thus, as shown in column 3 of the table, a higher rate of compensation. Affiliates of all other major investing countries (except Germany) pay rates of compensation lower than the average.

The fourth column in table 1.13 confirms one thing we saw in tables 1.10 and 1.12: Japanese affiliates have low profit rates. Affiliates of all other major investors did better than the average of $8.4 per $1,000 of asset. The income-asset ratio for Japanese affiliates was a very disappointing $2.4 per $1,000. Because of their lowest income-asset ratio, Japanese affiliates paid the lowest income taxes per asset.

How JFDI affects the employment level in the United States is one of the most important questions concerning JFDI made in recent years. The asset-employment ratio explained above is one way to measure such employment effects. However, the ratio is an average: the ratio of the total assets in Japanese subsidiaries to the total employment level of these firms. In measuring the job-creating ability of these firms it is useful to consider employment effects of additional FDI, i.e., how many jobs additional amounts of FDI create.

Let us begin with an estimation of the job-creating abilities of foreign investment and Japanese investment made by Wong in 1989.[36] The estimation was made first by disaggregating the U.S. economy into ten main industries. These ten industries and the number for each industry of the increase in employment resulting from an additional investment of $1 million in the industry in 1986 (under the assumption that wage rates do not change) were as follows (numbers are man-years):

Agriculture, forestry, and fisheries 8.9
Mining 2.6
Construction 1.0
Durable goods 25.7
Nondurable goods 22.3
Transportation and public utilities 5.0
Wholesale trade 24.1
Retail trade 65.1
Finance, insurance, and real estate 5.8
Services 29.6

These results show that an investment in the retail trade sector creates the most employment, but the same amount of investment funds spent in the construction industry would create the least employment.

This estimation was made for each of these industries and did not distinguish between local investment and foreign investment, or between Japanese investment and investment from other countries. (Ideally, this estimation should be made for the investments from major investing nations; however, these procedures require information that is not given in government publications and is difficult to obtain.) Thus, we adopt in the following an alternative method to estimate the employment effects of JFDI and investment from other nations. This method is based on several assumptions: First, we start with the investment patterns of JFDI and direct investment from all nations as given in table 1.10. We assume that as more investment comes from Japan and other nations, it will be distributed among the industries according to the investment patterns given in table 1.13. For example, if extra investment funds of $1 million come from Japan to the United States, $215,000 will be invested in the manufacturing sector, $311,000 in the wholesale trade sector, $172,000 in real estate, and so on. Similarly, for the same amount of investment funds from the rest of the world, $400,000 will go to the manufacturing sector, $130,000 to the wholesale trade sector, and so on. Next, we assume that every dollar invested in a particular industry in the United States, no matter where that dollar comes from, will create employment opportunity as shown above. For example, $1 million invested in the wholesale trade sector will create 24.1 jobs per year. Third, using the above assumptions, we can then estimate the employment created by a new investment from Japan.[37] Of course, to make use of the employment figures so derived, we must assume that the wage rate remains fairly constant. This is a reasonable assumption if significant unemployment exists in the local economy. We then perform the same exercise to determine the employment effects of investment from the rest of the world.

The results we obtained are as follows: For additional JFDI of $1 million, new employment of 16.83 man-years is created. For the same amount of investment from the rest of the world, new employment of 15.91 man-years is created. These results suggest that the job-creation ability of JFDI is larger than what table 1.13 implies. Some explanation can be offered. First, a significant percentage of JFDI goes to the wholesale trade sector, which is a big job creator. Second, 40 percent of the investment from the rest of the world goes to the manufacturing sector, and the employment effect of this sector is not as significant as that of some other sectors, such as services and retail trade. Third, about 10 percent of the investment from the rest of the world is in mining, which has the lowest employment effect.

Let us summarize how JFDI performed in the past decade. JFDI has performed quite poorly in the "bubble" years even in comparison to FDI made in the United States by other nations. Overinvestment—made to jump trade restrictions, "quid pro quo" investment, and "bubble"-induced—are the primary reasons for this low performance of JFDI. Japanese affiliates are not good job creators in the sense that they have relatively very high asset-employment ratios. However, it is these high asset-employment ratios that allow those Japanese firms in the automobile, steel, electronics, and other industries to pay higher wage rates to their workers. Thus, when one tries to evaluate the benefits of JFDI to the U.S. economy, one has to make clear whether one is more concerned about employment per se or the wage rates of the employed workers.

Political-Economic Issues

JFDI in the United States raises numerous political-economic issues not only because of its magnitudes and patterns but also because some of the Japanese economic policies, institutions, and practices are subjects of intense debate within the United States itself as well as between the United States and Japan. The debate continues with seemingly little likelihood of resolution for the following reasons: There are conflicting interest groups in the United States and Japan as well as interest groups within each nation; neoclassical economic theory is ill-equipped to offer unambiguous answers (except by making strong—unrealistic—assumptions); the data necessary to resolve the debate are either unavailable or are obtained only by making assumptions that are themselves debatable. With this caveat, the next section summarizes the conflicting views about several political-economic (and legal) issues raised by JFDI that are most significant, and offers our judgments of them.

The Keiretsu *Issue*

One of the most intensely debated questions relating to JFDI has been: Does JFDI contribute less than the FDI in the United States made by other nations to increase American employment and to improve the American trade balance because of the enterprise groups (*keiretsu*) maintained by Japanese firms?[38] Put differently, the question is whether or not *keiretsu* ties cause or motivate Japanese firms in the United States to employ fewer Americans than do the firms of other nations because Japanese firms import more from *keiretsu* firms in Japan and/or buy more from *keiretsu* firms in the United

States (which also employ more Japanese and import more from Japan).

Analytically, this is a subset of questions regarding the substitutability of FDI and trade[39] (i.e., does FDI increase or decrease trade and with what effects on allocation and prices of resources in the investing and host nations in the short and/or long runs?) which continued to be debated among economists.[40] Since it is beyond the scope of this study to engage in an analytic discussion, we shall summarize two sharply contrasting answers offered to date to the question and attempt to show that the reality lies somewhere between them.

Many Japanese and some American economists argue that Japanese affiliates (Japanese-owned or -controlled firms) in the United States behave no differently from firms in the United States that are owned or controlled by firms of other industrial nations, i.e., the former employ Americans as would the latter and do not buy from other Japanese affiliates in the United States or import from firms in Japan except when price and quality considerations make doing so more profitable. Those holding this view argue that any observed differences in employment and trade practices between Japanese and non-Japanese affiliates in the United States can be explained by Japan's comparative advantage in production, the relative youth and capital and/or technology intensity of JFDI. This is because, they argue, the *keiretsu* ties that might have affected the behavior of Japanese firms in the rapid growth period (until the late 1960s or the early 1970s depending on industry) no longer determine the behavior of Japanese firms, or that what is often referred to as *keiretsu* relations differ little today from the interfirm relations maintained in the West to minimize transaction costs or otherwise maximize gains that result from maintaining continuing trading relations.[41]

Some Japanese and U.S. economists and other social scientists challenge the above view strongly and argue that *keiretsu* relations maintained both in Japan and by Japanese affiliates in the United States cause them to behave substantively differently from the affiliates of other nations in the United States and the former's behaviors have significant effects on both their employment in the United States and their patterns of trading. That is, they employ fewer Americans because they import more from Japan and/or buy more from *keiretsu* firms in the United States than do firms that are non-Japanese affiliates in the United States. The proponents of this view argue that the *keiretsu* relations maintained among Japanese firms (and the policies and institutions in Japan that enable Japanese firms to maintain distinctive *keiretsu* relations) differ substantively from interfirm relations existing in other industrial economies.[42] An examination of analyses and evidence presented in recent years by those who hold both views reveals that neither view is compelling. As an extended examination of the literature cannot be attempted in this study, here let us present only the following to justify this observation.

Even though Saxonhouse's works[43] are often referred to as an important effort providing support to these who argue that the patterns of Japan's intra-industry trade (thus employment patterns in the host nations of JFDI) can be fully explained by Japan's comparative advantages (in capital and human resources), his analysis is far from persuasive. Among several who criticized his analysis, Lawrence and Lincoln offer the most effective criticisms. For Lawrence, "these empirical tests" as conducted by Saxonhouse "do not settle the issue" because:

> The problem with all these tests is that they do not explicitly test for the presence of trade barriers. They are tests for determining if Japanese imports are unusually low. But even if Japanese imports are unusually low, other facts that do not appear in the model, such as unusual preferences or technology, rather than trade barriers, might be the reason. To provide a flawless test, it appears that barriers must be explicitly modeled. But this is rather difficult when, by their very nature, they are "intangible" or even invisible.[44]

Lincoln is no less critical. After criticizing Saxonhouse's use of data and assumptions in detail,[45] Lincoln concludes that "as interesting as the Saxonhouse approach is, it does not seem fully convincing."

Representing the Japanese economists arguing that *keiretsu* play little role in affecting Japan's trade pattern, Komiya and Irie offered a tour de force neoclassical argument in two parts: (1) Japan could not have achieved high economic performance had *keiretsu* been restricting competition in Japan and distorting Japan's trade patterns (i.e., limiting imports that would have occurred had exporters to Japan had comparative advantage). (2) The long-term and intensive relationships maintained among Japanese firms differ little from those maintained among Western firms for the sake of increasing productive, marketing, and other efficiencies.[46] We believe, as do a very large number of U.S. and Japanese scholars, that such a view is unsustainable in the face of substantial evidence demonstrating that the character and behavior of *keiretsu* differ from interfirm relations maintained among Western firms and do continue to affect Japan's trading patterns and the behavior of Japanese affiliates in the United States.[47]

In contrast, the views of those who argue that *keiretsu* virtually dictate or play a dominant role in determining Japan's trade patterns and the behavior of Japanese affiliates in the United States commit two serious errors: (1)

exaggerating the roles of *keiretsu* based on limited (anecdotal) evidence[48] and (2) failing to note that the character and behavior of *keiretsu* have been changing significantly during the past two decades because of changing international and domestic economic conditions. One among numerous examples of those who exaggerate the roles of *keiretsu* and ignore recent changes in their behavior is the following:

> One of Japan's major contributions to modern industrial organization is the "industrial group." . . . Examples include the cooperation among different firms, banks, and trading companies in the Mitsubishi or Sumitomo groups and the integration of heavy electrical machinery with advanced electronics and telecommunications in the Hitachi, NEC, and Toshiba *keiretsu* . . . . There is no such thing as pure competition in any high technology industry. . . . Managed trade exists in such sectors as fuels, food, automotive products, steel, textiles, clothing, and consumer electronics.[49]

We believe that the reality lies somewhere in between these two contrasting views and that the behaviors of *keiretsu* and Japanese affiliates (many of which are *keiretsu*-related firms) are changing in significant ways, as Lawrence noted in concluding his important empirical study of the roles of *keiretsu* in Japan's trade pattern:

> But there are also signs that, since 1985, the Japanese economy has made major adjustments . . . in the first quarter of 1989, Japan imported twice the volume of manufactured goods it imported in 1985. . . . Japanese manufacturing firms are playing an increasing role in "reverse imports" . . . the intrafirm shipments of Japanese trading companies has [*sic*] declined conspicuously.[50]

In support of our view and to stress that the behavior of the *keiretsu* and *keiretsu*-related affiliates in the United States are changing, let us present the following observations and facts relating to Japanese automakers in Japan and in the United States. The following are also useful, we believe, in better understanding the roles JFDI plays in the industry in which most JFDI has been made affecting trade and employment patterns of the U.S. economy.

1. Despite the oft-made criticism that Japanese automakers in the United States buy little from U.S. auto-parts suppliers (i.e., they buy from Japanese affiliates in the United States or import from Japan), there is little doubt that purchases made in the United States (local content) are steadily increasing, as shown in table 1.14. The total procurement of U.S.-made auto parts by the Japanese automakers in the United States has risen from $1.73 billion in 1985 to $9.07 billion in 1990.[51] Some argue that the pace of increase is still

TABLE 1.14
PROPORTION OF LOCAL CONTENT (RAW MATERIALS AND PARTS)
OF JAPANESE-OWNED FIRMS IN THE UNITED STATES, 1987 AND 1990

	Local Content				
	100%	*70–99%*	*50–69%*	*10–49%*	*Below 10%*
1987					
Total firms					
348	57	100	51	96	54
	(15.9)	(27.9)	(14.2)	(26.8)	(15.1)
Electric/electronics					
91	1	21	18	27	24
	(1.0)	(23.1)	(19.9)	(29.7)	(26.4)
Transportation (equipment, automobiles, etc.)					
27	0	0	13	12	2
			(48.1)	(44.4)	(7.4)
1990					
Total firms					
743	158	257	124	151	35
	(21.3)	(37.0)	(16.7)	(20.3)	(4.7)
Electric/electronics					
135	10	34	40	41	10
	(7.4)	(25.2)	(29.6)	(30.4)	(7.4)
Transporation (equipment, automobiles, etc.)					
55	4	15	15	12	9
	(7.3)	(27.3)	(27.3)	(21.8)	(16.3)

NOTE: Numbers in parentheses are percentages.

SOURCE: JETRO, *Sekai to Nihon no kaigai chokusetsu toshi* (FDI of the world and Japan) (Tokyo: JETRO, 1992), p. 79.

slow but the fact remains that as American auto-parts producers acquire requisite capabilities to supply auto parts to Japanese automakers and in reaction to the rising value of the yen, local contents have been rising.

2. Few knowledgeable observers question the fact that the Japanese automakers' competitive ability to gain an increasing market share in the Unites States was one of the most important reasons for the recent effort made by the U.S. Big Three to increase their productive efficiency and quality. Had it not been for this stimulus, the U.S. automakers could not have begun to regain their collective market share beginning in 1992, when the share of Japa-

nese automobiles (exports from Japan and those produced by Japanese automakers in the United States) peaked at 32.9 percent.[52] To be sure, the share of Japanese automobiles in the United States began to decline in 1993 in part because of the increasing value of the yen, but there is little doubt that the desire of U.S. automakers to compete against the Japanese producers is the principal reason for this development.

3. As the total output of Japanese automakers in the United States rose steadily (from less than half a million automobiles in 1985 to almost 1.5 million by 1990), imports from Japan declined by about 0.6 million automobiles during the same period (2.3 million to 1.7 million).[53] Exports of autos produced by Japanese transplants back to Japan began in 1987 and rose to 158,000 in 1992.[54] Again, a significant reason for these developments is the increased value of the yen. However, these developments are continuing despite the fact that they force Japanese automakers in Japan to scale down their production and cause them to experience sharply declined profits.[55]

4. As numerous studies both in English and Japanese show, despite various recent developments, an important reason for the difficulties of the American automakers to export their cars to Japan (numbering less than 40,000 in 1992) and the lopsided auto-parts trade imbalance (ranging from 4 to 1 to 5 to 1 in favor of Japanese exports) in the 1990–1992 period continues to be the *keiretsu* ties maintained between the Japanese automakers and their subsidiaries (including distributors). Although the trade-inhibiting roles of *keiretsu* should not be exaggerated, we should be reminded that they do continue to be significant in affecting the U.S.-Japan trade balance.[56]

Employment Practices of JFDI

Worthy of our attention are the Japanese affiliates' employment practices, which have received frequent negative mass media and congressional attention during the past two decades. As JFDI increased rapidly during the 1980s, it appears that Americans' unfavorable perceptions of Japanese employment practices also rose visibly. For example, a 1989 survey made on behalf of several Japanese firms found that a majority of those sampled indicated they found employment by Japanese firms less attractive than that offered by Canadian, British, and West German firms in the United States because they believed Japanese firms discriminate against women and are reluctant to promote and provide job security to Americans.[57] Behind such a perception lies a complex issue involving the character of Japanese management-labor relations, what constitutes legally permissible discrimination, difficulties of obtaining unbiased information and data, and even cultural differences and racism (on the part of both Americans and Japanese).

Both the essential validity of the American perception and the complexity of the issues involved become evident in a score of legal cases that have attracted national attention (and many more cases settled out of court or adjudicated at lower court levels around the United States). Let us cite only a few examples. In a precedent-setting case generating a Supreme Court decision that civil rights laws apply to U.S. subsidiaries of foreign firms,[58] Sumitomo Corporation of America paid $2.6 million in 1987 to settle a 12-year-old federal lawsuit brought against it for systematic and persistent discrimination against female employees. In 1988, Honda of America Manufacturing, Inc., in Marysville, Ohio, agreed to pay damages of $6 million to resolve charges made by the Equal Employment Opportunity Commission (EEOC) that the firm had deliberately excluded a large pool of the minority population in Columbus, Ohio, only 40 miles from Marysville.[59] In 1991, Recruit, USA, Inc., lost a circuit court case brought against it by EEOC for the firm's practice of destroying, altering, or removing business records pertaining to the alleged discriminatory practice of coding comments to limit the pool of job applicants by gender, race, and ethnic origin.[60]

In addition to examples involving discrimination by gender, race, and ethnicity, others involved denial of promotion, lower compensation, and dismissal on the grounds that the U.S. employees involved were not effective in maintaining communication with their superiors or failed or were unable to perform assigned duties. In these cases, the decisions of courts were divided between the plaintiffs and defendant Japanese firms, because what constitutes legally defensive discrimination by the management of foreign firms in the United States is not as yet firmly established, circumstances vary significantly from case to case, and evidence is invariably disputed.

Typifying these difficulties is the 1991 case Fortino v. Quasar Co.,[61] in which the court permitted the subsidiary of a Japanese firm in the United States to assert the rights of its parent in Japan to dismiss the U.S. plaintiffs under Article VIII(1) of the Treaty of Friendship, Commerce, and Nation (signed between the United States and Japan to foster bilateral commercial relations), which enables "companies of either Party to engage . . . executive personnel . . . of their choice."

The effect of this ruling (which was standing as of summer 1993) was to create an exemption from the above-noted Supreme Court ruling made against Sumitomo Corporation of America and to validate the dismissal of the American plaintiffs—Fortino and two other American managers—by the Japanese subsidiary by denying their claim that they were dismissed because of their national origin (as shown, they alleged, by the fact that their positions, which were terminated because of the claimed need by the subsidiary to reduce employees, were restored immediately after their dismissal to employ Japanese nationals). The opinion of the court is worthy of quotation here:

> In the case of a homogeneous country like Japan, citizenship and national origin are highly correlated; almost all citizens of Japan were born there. But to use this correlation to infer national origin discrimination from a treaty-sanctioned preference for Japanese citizens who happen to also be of Japanese national origin would nullify the treaty. . . . The exercise of a treaty right may not be made the basis for inferring a violation of Title VII.[62]

The ruling will most likely be challenged and reversed by the Supreme Court sometime in the near future. What is significant is not the legal developments that are likely to unfold, however, but the employment issues of this type that occurred and will continue to occur in many other forms because of Japan's distinct management practices and the homogeneity of Japanese society and all it implies. As economists, we only invite attention to this complex social and legal issue that must be dealt with by all concerned as JFDI continues to increase.

Technology Transfer Issues

JFDI has also raised several important questions relating to technology transfer. Two that are most important are: Does JFDI constitute a means by which Japanese firms acquire U.S. technology to the detriment of the competitiveness of U.S. firms? And do Japanese firms threaten the national security of the United States by acquiring or controlling U.S. firms possessing technology crucial to national defense?

Two conflicting answers for the first question are found in the literature. One is that an important reason for JFDI is to increase Japanese technological ability at the expense of future U.S. competitiveness, as seen in the fact that Japanese firms acquire a disproportionately large number of smaller U.S. technology start-up firms as well as many established firms possessing significant technology. This is why Krause noted that "the Japanese more systematically transfer technology they buy back to Japan. Furthermore, the Japanese firms may well be following a strategic plan whereby they scan U.S. technology and purchase small firms not only to enhance their own position, but also to deny U.S. competitors access to this technology."[63] Spencer was able to demonstrate that Japanese firms, especially the largest firms in various *keiretsu*, acquired between 1988 and March 1993 a disproportionately large number of U.S. firms with high-technology capabilities.[64]

Diametrically opposed to the preceding view is the argument that Japanese firms are behaving no differently from all other firms in that they are engaging in market transactions of technology between U.S. sellers of technology and themselves to the advantages of both parties, and that such transactions benefit all consumers of both nations as well as those of all other nations. The fundamental belief of those who hold this view is that the nationality of technology matters little because gains realized from it are shared by all, since no technology remains proprietary for long. This position, supported by many economists, is well summarized, for example, by McCulloch who observed in seeing Japan's rapid acquisition of U.S. technology:

> Although catch-up abroad entails painful adjustments for the U.S. economy, it also means a potential increase in the U.S. gains from technological imports. Although the specter of other nations closing the technology gap is evidently distasteful to some nationalistic Americans, over the long term it offers the opportunity for mutual gains through expanded two-way trade in new knowledge.[65]

The second question—whether or not Japanese firms can threaten the national security of the United States by acquisition or control of U.S. technology via JFDI—also elicits two sharply conflicting responses. One is that, because of the real danger of this threat, all acquisitions of sensitive technology, broadly defined, by any foreign firm should be prevented and that the Exon-Florio amendment to the Defense Production Act (finally passed in August 1988 after narrowing the definition of "harm to national security" to overcome the objection of the White House) is still unsatisfactory.

Those expressing this view have vociferously argued that the Committee on Foreign Investment in the United States (CFIUS), appointed by President Bush under the terms of the Exon-Florio amendment, failed to perform its roles adequately. The evidence they cite includes the following. Of 540 instances of foreign investment involving possible violation of the amendment, CFIUS formally investigated only twelve cases and found it necessary to prevent acquisition by a foreign (Chinese) firm in only one case. Three cases in which CFIUS chose not to take action involved Japanese acquisition of technologies that it believed were militarily significant. Strongly opposing such a view is that expressed by the Reagan and Bush administrations and many others, i.e., we should not hinder in any way the free inflow of FDI, and national security should not be interpreted too broadly.[66]

This complex issue involves genuine concerns regarding the desirability of retaining under U.S. control technology important for national security (and arriving at an agreement as to what constitutes such technology) vis-a-vis the need to safeguard against the likelihood of invoking national security concerns as a pretext for restricting the international flow of technology and capital.[67]

The Transfer Price Issue

Yet another issue attracting increasing attention because of increased FDI, and especially JFDI, and because of the magnitude of the U.S. budget deficit, is the taxation issue: whether or not foreign-controlled firms in the United States are paying their fair share, i.e., not avoiding corporate tax in violation in particular of Section 482 of the Internal Revenue Code (prohibiting transfer of income from one corporate entity to another for the purpose of avoiding U.S. corporate tax). At the heart of the issue are cases in which foreign subsidiaries transfer income to their parents abroad by paying prices higher than would firms maintaining "arms-length" relations for products and/or services provided by the parents. Estimates of the loss of revenue due to violation of Section 482 range from $10 to 13 billion to as much as $40 billion.[68] Congressional investigations and hearings and mass media reports on the issue frequently cite Japanese-controlled firms as the major violators of Section 482 (as typified in a 1990 Senate hearing on the issue during which Senator Jesse Helms singled out Sony and other Japanese and Japanese-controlled firms).[69]

On this issue, those who identify Japanese-controlled firms as major violators cite the examples of several settlements reached between the Internal Revenue Service (IRS) and large Japanese subsidiaries in the United States of major Japanese automakers and electronic firms and others during the past few years and suggest that *keiretsu* relations maintained among Japanese firms are conducive to such violations. Others argue that such examples and anecdotal evidence frequently enlisted to show that Japanese-controlled firms are more likely to violate Section 482 fail not only to present sufficient credible data but also ignore facts such as that many Japanese-controlled firms are still young (still amortizing high initial costs of entry), that the corporate tax rate in Japan is higher than in the United States (offering no incentive to transfer income), that Japanese firms maintaining *keiretsu* relations are legally independent profit-maximizing entities with stockholders who would not permit transfer of income to another firm even if it might belong to the same *keiretsu*, and so forth.[70]

We offer two observations on this issue. One is that we do not believe we have sufficient reliable data to prove or disprove either of these conflicting views. Even the data presented by the IRS and those who made studies on behalf of congressional committees and individual congressmen or senators are very limited samples gathered and analyzed making use of disputable assumptions. The problem here is the lack of reliable and sufficient data. This is why the Investment Data Improvement Act of 1990 was enacted, enabling the Census Bureau and the Bureau of Economic Analysis of the Commerce Department to share certain data, allowing Commerce to exchange specified data with the Labor Department, and requiring the Government Accounting Office to make annual recommendations to Congress as to how data collection and data sharing can be improved. The act is seen as "too weak" by some because the authority of Commerce to collect certain data is limited to firms that are at least 50 percent controlled by foreigners. However, we believe we will be able to obtain more reliable data because of the act and be better able to evaluate the magnitude of violation of Section 482 by foreign firms controlled by Japanese and other foreign hands. If the issue is not resolved by the increased data obtained under the act, it may become necessary to strengthen the act.

Another observation we make is that *keiretsu* and generally long-term and closer relations maintained among Japanese firms will continue to be a knotty problem of considerable importance for the IRS. In lieu of the long discussion necessary to justify this observation, let us present the following examples of the reasons for this observation:

1. A Japanese subsidiary in the United States (S) is owned by two firms in Japan (A and B) maintaining long-standing cross-shareholding relations with interlocked management (i.e., *keiretsu*). A is a majority shareholder and B is a minority shareholder in S (and both have directors in S in numbers proportionate to their respective shareholding). B supplies product X to S at a price the IRS believes exceeds the market price that would have been charged by an "arms-length" (unrelated) supplier. S claims that the price is the market price because, had it not been so, A, holding a majority share, would not have tolerated such a transfer of S's income to B. Given the frequent difficulty faced in conclusively establishing S is paying to B for X a price below the "market price of comparable products" (due to numerous quality, performance, warranty, service, and other differences existing among manufactured products such as X), the IRS needs to demonstrate the existence of the close relationship existing between A and B in Japan, i.e., to show that B has opportunities and incentives to compensate A for the income transferred from S to B, thus enabling A and B to share, in effect, the

transferred income at the expense of the IRS. However, the IRS lacks the power to obtain information and data necessary to demonstrate the relevant aspects of the relations maintained by A and B in Japan.

2. Although the Japanese nominal corporate tax rate may be marginally higher than that in the United States, it is far from warranted to conclude that Japanese subsidiaries in the United States have no incentive to transfer their incomes to their parents in Japan. This is because of complex differences in the ways many similar deductions and exemptions are calculated under Japanese and U.S. laws and because Japanese tax laws are more generous in allowing deductions for investment made to increase productivity over time and substantially less stringent in limiting the transfer of income, in numerous forms, among firms in a *keiretsu* and between parents and subsidiaries. The effective tax rate may be appreciably lower in Japan than in the United States in many instances. The IRS has neither sufficient manpower nor expertise necessary to establish the effective tax rate paid by the parents in Japan.

3. As in the case of many multinational enterprises (MNEs), Japan's MNEs engage in business globally. However, Japanese MNEs' networks around the globe are significantly denser (longer term, multifaceted, and extensive, involving a large number of *keiretsu* firms and their subsidiaries). This fact limits the ability of the IRS to identify fully all possible and complex ways the income of a Japanese subsidiary may be transferred abroad, i.e., to related firms (parents, *keiretsu* firms, and their subsidiaries) in Japan and elsewhere. For example, a Japanese subsidiary of A in the United States is transferring income to B_Y, a subsidiary of B in country Y (both A and B are in Japan). In such a case, even if A is believed to be compensating B via trading and other relationships they maintain in Japan and elsewhere, the IRS is not able to show successfully that the Japanese subsidiary of A is evading U.S. taxes for the same reasons noted in case 2 above.

We conclude this section by noting that there are other issues raised by the large JFDI such as the reasons for, and the trade consequences of, extremely small U.S. investment in Japan and the behavior of Japanese banks and other financial institutions in the United States. However, not to further lengthen this study, we refer interested readers to the sources cited in the notes.[71]

Conclusion

Foreign direct investment is a difficult subject to analyze for many reasons, including the complexities of motivations, patterns, performance, and short- and long-term effects (thus, the inadequacies of various theories advanced to date) and unavailability in many instances of necessary data. Japanese FDI in the United States is especially difficult to study because of the unique bilateral economic relation characterized by rapidly increasing interdependence and seemingly perpetual trade conflict. This study, within the allotted space, was able to (1) examine only some of the reasons for JFDI and for the significant changes in its magnitude since 1980, (2) analyze the patterns and performance of JFDI in a limited fashion, and (3) discuss selected political-economic issues raised by JFDI.

When we reflect on all the findings and observations presented in the preceding sections, we realize that the 1980–1991 period was an unusual one. It was the dozen years during which Japan emerged as a major supplier of capital in the world and made nearly 40 percent of its very large FDI in the United States. In addition to the contrasting trends of competitiveness of several major manufacturing industries of both nations, much of this growth was a combined outcome of the macroeconomic forces generated by Reaganomics and the sustained super-easy monetary policy of Japan that caused the "bubble." Such an outcome is not likely to recur in the near future.

These years were unusual also because a significant part of the very large JFDI was undoubtedly motivated by politics of trade, that is, the desire on the part of Japanese automakers and other manufacturing firms to diffuse the trade tension and to "jump" the existing or threatened trade restrictions. This is why the returns on JFDI made in manufacturing industries ranged from very meager to negative. It is not likely that we will again soon observe another instance of a nation making tens of billions of dollars of FDI as strongly affected by politics as in this case.

Yet another factor making these years unusual was that, in contrast to FDI made by an advanced nation in developing nations or even to most instances of FDI made by one advanced nation in another in which a broad consensus as to the net welfare effects of such FDI is reached, no consensus has yet emerged among U.S. scholars as to the net welfare effects of JFDI made in their country during the past decade. Many can compile a long list of gains, including infusion of capital, jobs created, technology and managerial skills transferred, competition by Japanese affliates stimulating the efforts of many American firms to increase productive efficiency, and many other short- and long-term gains. Others, however, can compile an equally long list of losses that include a trade deficit increased due to increased intra-firm and intra-*keiretsu* trade by Japanese affliates in the United States, market shares (thus profits and jobs) lost to Japanese affiliates, technology acquired by Japanese affiliates to the detriment of U.S. competitiveness over time, and many other observed or claimed losses.

The debate, both political-economic and economic-analytic, on the net welfare effects of JFDI continues for many reasons (e.g., conflicts of ideology and interest and the absence of a theory capable of offering unambiguous answers). Few would deny, however, that a very important reason for the lack of consensus on the net welfare effects of JFDI is that it is made by Japan—in which economic policies, institutions, and practices differ in many significant ways from those found in the United States.

Put differently, the level of Japanese investment in the United States from 1980 to 1991 is not likely to be repeated because an increasingly larger proportion of Japanese FDI will be made in Asia, Europe, and elsewhere rather than the United States compared to the late 1980s.[72]

Notes

1. All data are on a calendar-year basis, reported in IMF format settlement basis. Ministry of Finance, *Zaisei kinyū tōkei geppō* (The Financial and Monetary Monthly Report).

2. For such reactions in the late 1980s, see, for example, Kozo Yamamura, ed., *Japanese Investment in the United States: Should We Be Concerned?* (Seattle: Society for Japanese Studies, 1989).

3. For example, as defined in the text, investment and saving as proportions of GNP were 20.0 percent and 22.5 percent in 1981 and 22.1 percent and 25.5 percent in 1985. Calculated from Supplements to Ministry of Finance, *Financial Statistics of Japan 1992*.

4. See, for example, Robert Z. Aliber, "The Evolution of the Japanese Trade Surplus," in Yamamura, ed., *Japanese Investment in the United States*, pp. 227–51.

5. See, for example, Richard C. Marston, "Price Behavior in Japanese and U.S. Manufacturing," in Paul Krugman, ed., *Trade with Japan* (Chicago: University of Chicago Press, 1992), pp. 121–48.

6. Ministry of Finance, "Main Economic Indicators of Japan," 1992.

7. Between 1981 and 1989, the prices of stocks (listed in the first section of the Tokyo Stock Exchange) and residential land in Tokyo rose 650.6 percent and

497.0 percent, respectively, while the nominal GDP rose 154.4 percent. Yukio Noguchi, *Baburu no keizaigaku* (Economics of the bubble) (Tokyo: Nihon Keizai Shinbunsha, 1992), p. 23.

8. For these and other data relating to the asset inflation and the reason why this inflation occurred, see Noguchi, *Baburu no keizaigaku*, pp. 117–42, and Institute of Fiscal and Monetary Policy, Japanese Ministry of Finance, *The Mechanism and Economic Effects of Asset Fluctuations* (Tokyo: Ministry of Finance, 1993).

9. Behind this, of course, were the continuing high saving rate, large trade surplus, and the declining "dependency ratios," i.e., the proportion of government expenditure financed by deficit continued to decline, from 23.2 percent in 1987 to 11.6 percent in 1990. See Institute of Fiscal and Monetary Policy, *The Mechanism*, pp. 6–31.

10. Ibid., p. 3. The authors then say that "in reality, though, as it is now used in Japan, however, the term 'bubble' refers to more than the existence of a deviation between actual and theoretical asset prices. In effect, it has gained wide currency as a key word symbolizing the immense impact an eventual collapse in inflated asset prices can have on the economy."

11. See Kozo Yamamura, ed., *Land Issues in Japan: A Policy Failure?* (Seattle: Society for Japanese Studies, 1992).

12. Institute of Fiscal and Monetary Policy, *The Mechanism*, pp. 86–95.

13. Ibid., pp. 66–72, and Noguchi, *Baburu no keizaigaku*, pp. 118-25, for a full discussion.

14. Undoubtedly, some acquisitions were due to entrepreneurial errors made in the "bubble" years, but such acquisitions, we believe, were only a small part of the total acquisitions made in the 1980s.

15. These figures, and the figures for consumer and wholesale price indices, are taken from International Monetary Fund, International Financial Statistics (1991).

16. For another criticism of the "fire sale" argument, see Edward M. Graham and Paul R. Krugman, *Foreign Direct Investment in the United States* (Washington: Institute for International Economics, 1991), pp. 44–47 and 79–81.

17. The relative version of the purchasing power parity states that the rate of growth of the price level in one country is equal to the sum of the rate of depreciation of its exchange rate (expressed as the price of the foreign currency in terms of the domestic currency) and the rate of growth of the foreign price level.

18. The purchasing power parity did not hold too well in that period in terms of the wholesale producer price index. The U.S. index grew by 158 percent (from 43.63 to 112.69) while the Japanese index increased by 61 percent (from 56.30 to 90.64).

19. The coefficient of variation is the ratio of the standard deviation to the mean. This variable is unit-free and is suitable for comparing different prices or other variables.

20. All these numbers were calculated from the exchange rates and price indices taken from the Citibank database available at the University of Washington.

21. It is true that the exchange rate fluctuated much more widely relative to commodity prices in the 1980s. From 1980 to 1989, the coefficient of variation of the end-of-month exchange rate was 24 percent. The coefficients of variation of the

U.S. CPI and WPI were 12 and 5 percent, respectively, while the corresponding numbers for Japan were 6 and 7 percent.

22. The study by Bailey and Tavlas did not find any conclusive evidence to show that exchange-rate variability has hurt direct investment. Martin J. Bailey and George S. Tavlas, "Exchange Rate Variability and Direct Investment," in Michael Ulan, ed., *Annals of the American Academy of Political and Social Science*, No. 516 (Newbury Park, Calif.: Sage Publications, 1991), pp. 106–16.

23. The size of a market is not a sufficient, and possibly not a necessary, condition for FDI. Many countries are important exporters of goods to the United States, but they have insignificant direct investment in this country. Examples are textile and clothing manufacturers in some Asian countries. Although these firms depend heavily on the U.S. market, their investment in this country, if any, is negligible. On the other hand, some relatively much smaller countries are host to many big foreign investors. Thus the size of the U.S. market alone does not explain why this country experienced the influx of foreign investment.

24. As explained in the previous section, a country's international investment position in the United States can be measured by the position at current cost, the position at market value, and the historical-cost position. The first two series better reflect the true investment position of foreign countries. Unfortunately, these two series are shorter and less disaggregated. To get more details about Japanese investment in the United States, we thus have to rely on the historical-cost series. A comparison of column 2 of table 1.7 and column 3 of table 1.3 illustrates the gap between the estimated historical-cost and the current-cost series of foreign investment positions.

25. The significant divestment in 1991 was due also to the negative intercompany debt.

26. The growth rates for nonbanking finance and insurance were for the period from 1984 to 1991 because the corresponding figures for 1980 were not disclosed.

27. Note that because investment in the financial sector is a stock, the demand for financial services generated by direct investment in other industries could lead to multiplier effects—in other words, a dollar's worth of direct investment could lead to more than a dollar's worth of investment in the financial sector.

28. Investment in petroleum comes mainly from the United Kingdom and the Netherlands.

29. This measure is a weighted average of the after-tax earnings per dollar of stock for Standard and Poor's Composite 500 companies and the average yield on corporate bond holdings rated AAA by Moody's Investors Services.

30. This measure is the ratio of after-tax profits from the national income and product accounts plus net interest paid to the average of beginning- and end-of-year total assets for all U.S. nonfinancial corporations.

31. An argument is sometimes made that some countries, such as Japan, make overinvestment because the cost of capital is lower in than in the United States (thus, Japanese have a low rate of discount, i.e., longer time horizon). However, that some countries have lower costs of capital is not sufficient for the observed lower rates of return for foreign investment in the United States. Even if the costs of capital for some investors are lower, it does not mean that they have to invest in the United States. As table 1.11 shows, U.S. direct investment abroad

received high returns in the past decade.

32. Investment in the "other" industries, which include mining and services, also did poorly.

33. For more discussion of quid pro quo investment, see Jagdish N. Bhagwati, "Investing Abroad," Esmee Fairbain Lecture, University of Lancaster, United Kingdom, November 1985; reprinted in Douglas Irwin, ed., *J.N. Bhagwati: Political Economy and International Trade* (Cambridge, Mass.: MIT Press, 1991), pp. 309–39; Bhagwati, Elias Dinopoulos, and Kar-yiu Wong, "Quid Pro Quo Foreign Investment," *American Economic Review* 82 (May 1992), pp. 186–90; Dinopoulos, "Quid Pro Quo Foreign Investment," *Economics and Politics* 1 (1989), pp. 145–60; Dinopoulos and Wong, "Quid Pro Quo Foreign Investment and Policy Intervention," in K. A. Koekkoek and C.B.M. Mennes, eds., *International Trade and Global Development: Essays in Honour of Jagdish Bhagwati* (London: Routledge, 1991), pp. 162–90; and Wong, "Optimal Threat of Trade Restriction and Quid Pro Quo Foreign Investment," *Economics and Politics* 1 (1989), pp. 227–300.

34. See, for examples, K. A. Froot, "Japanese Foreign Direct Investment," NBER Working Paper, No. 3737, 1991; and R. E. Lipsey, "Foreign Direct Investment in the U.S.: Changes over Three Decades," NBER Working Paper, No. 4124, 1992.

35. Among the factories of the Japanese affiliates that began production in 1987 and 1988, 60 percent (593 factories) were not profitable in 1991. *Asahi*, March 23, 1991.

36. Wong, "The Japanese Challenge: Japanese Direct Investment in the United States," in Yamamura, ed., *Japanese Investment in the United States*, pp. 63–98.

37. We group construction, durable goods, and nondurable goods together to form the manufacturing industry. The investments from Japan and other nations in agriculture, forestry, fisheries, mining, transportation, and public utilities are assumed to be negligible.

38. *Keiretsu* (plural) refer to subcontracting relations maintained between parent firms and their subcontractors or distributors (wholesalers and retailers) and among the largest firms in different industries that hold each other's shares, engage in numerous types of joint activities (e.g., R&D, marketing and investment both at home and abroad). Many observers and analysts believe that *keiretsu* relationships differ from interfirm relations seen in Western economies because the former are significantly more intensive, multifaceted, and longer-term than the latter. An excellent description of *keiretsu* is found in Michael L. Gerlach, *Alliance Capitalism* (Berkeley: University of California Press, 1992).

39. Different concepts of substitutability and complementarity between foreign trade and international factor movements are discussed in Wong, "Are International Trade and Factor Mobility Substitutes?" *Journal of International Economics* 21 (1991), pp. 25–43.

40. The analytic answers to the substitutability and the effects on resources differ depending on whether one uses a partial or a general equilibrium analysis. In both analytic approaches and especially in the general equilibrium analysis, analytic outcomes are highly sensitive to the assumptions made. See, for examples of these analyses and analytic discussion of each analytic method: Lipsey, "Foreign Direct Investment in the United States and U.S. Trade," in

Ulan, ed., *Annals of the American Academy of Political and Social Science*, No. 516, pp. 76–90; Krugman and Graham, *Foreign Direct Investment in the United States*, pp. 35–38 and 57–84; and Wong, "International Factor Mobility and the Volume of Trade: An Empirical Study," in Robert Feenstra, ed., *Empirical Methods for International Trade* (Cambridge, Mass.: MIT Press, 1988).

41. See, for example, Ryutaro Komiya and Kazutomo Irie, "The U.S-Japan Trade Problem: An Economic Analysis from a Japanese Point of View," in Yamamura, ed., *Japan's Economic Structure: Should It Change?* (Seattle: Society for Japanese Studies, 1990), pp. 80–98, and Ken-ichi Imai, "The Corporate Network in Japan," *Japanese Economic Studies* 16 (1987–88), pp. 3–37.

42. See, for example, Robert Z. Lawrence, "Imports in Japan: Closed Markets or Minds?" Brookings Paper on Economic Activity, No. 2 (1987), pp. 517–48; Michael Gerlach, "Keiretsu Organization in the Japanese Economy: Analysis and Trade Implications," in Chalmers Johnson, Laura D'Andrea Tyson, and John Zysman, eds., *Politics and Productivity: How Japan's Development Strategy Works* (Cambridge, Mass.: Ballinger, 1989), pp. 141–76, and Edward J. Lincoln, *Japan's Unequal Trade* (Washington: Brookings Institution, 1990), p. 694.

43. Among several of his recent articles, the most representative are: Gary R. Saxonhouse, "Evolving Comparative Advantage and Japan's Imports of Manufactures," in Yamamura, ed., *Policy and Trade Issues of the Japanese Economy: American and Japanese Perspectives* (Seattle: University of Washington Press, 1982), pp. 239–70, and "Comparative Advantage, Structural Adaptation, and Japanese Performance," in Takashi Inoguchi and Daniel I. Okimoto, eds., *The Political Economy of Japan, Vol. 2: The Changing International Context* (Stanford: Stanford University Press, 1988), pp. 225–48.

44. Robert Z. Lawrence, "How Open Is Japan?" in Krugman, ed., *Trade with Japan*, p. 25.

45. Lincoln, *Japan's Unequal Trade*, pp. 23–25.

46. Komiya and Irie, "The U.S-Japan Trade Problem," pp. 90–98.

47. For example, see Yamamura, "The Significance of Japanese Investment in the United States: How Should We React?" and Wassmann and Yamamura, "Do Japanese Firms Behave Differently? The Effects of *Keiretsu* in the United States," both in Yamamura, ed., *Japanese Investment in the United States*.

48. See, for example, Drysdale's chapter in this volume which offers serious shortcomings—analytic weaknesses, smallness of sample size, etc.—of Mordechai Kreinin's "How Closed Is the Japanese Market? Additional Evidence," *The World Economy* 11 (1989), pp. 529–42, which has been frequently cited as evidence of the closedness of the Japanese market because of *keiretsu* trading.

49. Chalmers Johnson, "Trade, Revisionism, and the Future of Japanese-American Relations," in Yamamura, ed., *Japan's Economic Structure*, pp. 120–21.

50. Lawrence, "How Open Is Japan?" pp. 35–36.

51. MITI data as quoted in Japan Automobile Manufacturers Association, *Forum*, Vol. 10, No. 1 (March 1992), p. 4.

52. *Asahi*, May 13, 1993.

53. Ibid.

54. Japan Automobile Manufacturers Association, *Forum*, Vol. 11, No. 3 (May

1993), p. 4.

55. *Asahi*, May 19, 1993.
56. The definition of auto parts used here includes engines, tires, and tubes. For the data, see Bureau of Economic Analysis, U.S. Department of Commerce, *The U.S. Export-Import by the End-Use Category*, annual. For literature on the U.S.-Japan automobile and auto-parts trade, see Wassmann and Yamamura, "Do Japanese Firms Behave Differently?" pp. 119–40.
57. "Cultures Clash as Japanese Firms Set up Shops in the United States," *Journal of Commerce*, March 1, 1989.
58. 457 U.S. 176, 1982.
59. Japan Economic Institute, *JEI Report*, May 4, 1990, p. 9.
60. 939 F.2d 746 (9th Cir. 1991).
61. 950 F.2d 389 (7th Cir. 1991).
62. Fortino, 950 F.2d at 393.
63. Lawrence Krause, "Japanese Investment in the United States," in Yamamura, ed., *Japanese Investment in the United States*, p. 114.
64. Linda M. Spencer, "High Technology Acquisitions," *Summary Charts* (Washington: Economic Strategy Institute, 1993), unpaginated. This source also shows that total Japanese acquisitions in the period noted in the text were 193 out of 363 majority acquisitions and 184 out of 228 minority acquisitions made by all foreign firms.
65. Rachel McCulloch, "The Challenge to U.S. Leadership in High Technology Industries: Can the United States Maintain Its Lead? Should It Try?" in Gunter Heiduk and Yamamura, eds., *Technological Competition and Interdependence: The Search for Policy in the United States, West Germany, and Japan* (Seattle: University of Washington Press, 1990), pp. 197–98.
66. Linda Spencer, *Foreign Investment in the United States: Unencumbered Access* (Washington: Economic Strategy Institute, 1993), pp. 1–20.
67. Graham and Krugman offer a thoughtful policy suggestion on what they call the "FDI and National Security" issue (i.e., compulsory licensing with safeguards). Graham and Krugman, *Foreign Direct Investment in the United States*, pp. 149–58.
68. Japan Economic Institute, *Report*, July 20, 1990, p. 3.
69. Ibid.
70. The observations made in this and the following paragraphs (describing specific examples) are based on Yamamura's discussions of this issue with IRS officers during 1991. The three examples described are adapted from the generic problems the IRS encountered in recent years in dealing with the 482 issues involving Japanese-affiliate taxpayers.
71. For the data, the main issues, and useful sources relating to these issues, see, for example, The House Wednesday Club of the Congress of the United States, *Beyond Revisionism: Toward a New U.S.-Japan Policy for the Post Cold-War Era* (Washington: House Wednesday Club, 1993), and Japan Economic Institute, *JEI Report*, August 31, 1990.
72. This observation is not likely to be contested by most analysts of Japanese FDI (including the contributors to this volume) or by the executives of Japanese firms contemplating future FDI.

CHAPTER 2

Japan's Direct Investment in Britain
A Case Study of Industrial Policy on the International Plane

• • • • • • • • • • •

LEON HOLLERMAN

"Supposing it was possible to set up factories which simply use the best practice, best technology, best management, best quality control. Supposing the government set them up and brought up teams of businessmen and trade unions to look at it and say, 'This is what you should do.'"

". . . It would be very expensive. Actually, we are getting the Japanese to do this for us." —Walter Eltis, Director-General of Britain's National Economic Development Office (NEDO), quoted in *Japan Times, International Edition*, October 26–November 1, 1992, p. 17.

Following World War II, Japan created institutional arrangements, policies and instruments of policy that gave rise to its economic "miracle" of 1955–1970. Industrial policy, Japanese-style, was one of its central underpinnings. That policy provided for a high degree of government-business collaboration, initially with government in the driver's seat. As the economy matured, big business—especially *keiretsu* (conglomerate industrial groups)—assumed a larger role in the policy process. Industrial policy has been consistently dedicated to the national interest, however. In a phrase attributed to the late Prime Minister Masayoshi Ohira, Japan's principal national interest is the achievement of "comprehensive economic security." From a Japanese point of view, economic security implies a high if not comprehensive degree of influence over foreign markets and foreign sources of supply. To achieve it, the principles and some of the instruments of Japan's domestic industrial policy have been applied on the international plane, especially by means of foreign direct investment (FDI). The case of Japan's FDI in Britain is an interesting example of how this has been done and with what results. Britain accepted Japan's FDI and the strategy that went with it because it seemed to be in Britain's national interest, yet each party thought it was coopting the other.

The Place of Britain in Japan's Global Strategy

As the Japanese economy emerged from its dormant state under the Occupation, it became known as the "workshop of Asia." This development was astonishing because the same tools of economic control that had stultified and paralyzed the economy during the Occupation turned out to be compatible with dynamic growth when they were bequeathed to the peacetime government that followed. The tools included comprehensive government control of foreign trade and foreign exchange, rationing of scarce materials, rationing of credit, price and interest rate controls, licensing and approval regulations, "administrative guidance," and subsidies in the form of tax and other incentives. With these instruments and their modifications, the economy was rehabilitated and a virtuous circle of exports and domestic investment was set in motion. The 10 percent average annual growth rate Japan achieved under this regime was associated with the corresponding growth of major *keiretsu* and their chief members, including international banks, insurance companies, securities companies, and general trading companies (*sogo shosha*), as well as major manufacturing firms.[1] In the 1980s it was the *keiretsu* with their interlocking networks of production, distribution, finance, and information that performed the task of transposing Japan's domestic industrial policy to the international plane.

In this process, the key industry concept, which is at the core of Japan's industrial policy, was also placed in a global context. As the postwar economy evolved, its center of gravity shifted first from traditional labor-intensive, low-tech industries to heavy and chemical industries, then to high-tech, sophisticated industries on the knowledge frontier. By 1980, some of the key industries in the middle range, such as consumer electronics and motor vehicles, were approaching maturity in Japan's domestic market. First-time demand was being superseded by replacement demand. These industries, accordingly, became candidates for expatriation by FDI. Expatriation was further prompted by push and pull factors (described below). Geographically, Japan advanced from Asia to North America in the transplantation of its maturing industries. Its ties with each of these were close and dense; its European ties were weak. However, as the European Community (EC) progressed toward organizing the world's largest single market (EC 92), it could no longer be neglected. Britain was Japan's choice as a launching pad for FDI in Europe. Capital for performing the launch was accumulated by revaluation of the yen (following the Plaza Accord of September 1985), by huge surpluses generated in commerce with Japan's major trading partners, and by capital produced "out of thin air" in the rise of securities and land prices during the speculative "bubble" of the 1980s. (How much of this was planned and how much unforeseen would be an interesting subject for debate.)

The Milieu: Push and Pull Factors

Given its strategic decision to enter European markets, what prompted Japan to do so via the United Kingdom? Push factors refer to domestic forces inducing direct investment outside Japan; pull factors refer to forces attracting it to a specific destination. With much overlapping, the factors are economic, political, and cultural.

For the most part, factors tending to push direct investment out of Japan are not destination-oriented. They include such well-known problems as the high price and limited availability of land, urban congestion, and the high cost of labor. The strong yen has been (theoretically) discouraging to exports and facilitates the purchase of assets abroad; thus it pushes trade-replacing FDI. Banks have lost business due to the aggressive expansion of securities companies in Japan; they have tried to compensate by expanding their international activities through establishing subsidiaries abroad. (They have been *pulled* toward Britain, which has a comparative advantage in finance arising from the expertise of the City of London.)

A significant institutional push factor is the policy on the part of the government and major banks, *sogo shosha*, and insurance companies, among others, to establish FDI information departments for the guidance of their clients and business associates. The Mitsubishi Corporation, for example, inaugurated its Overseas Operations Support System, which provides FDI assistance. Government collaborates with industry by providing informal coordination of the FDI departments in private-sector firms. This service is performed by the Industrial Policy Department of the Ministry of International Trade and Industry (MITI). In addition, an FDI Advisory Service was established in 1987 by a government bank, the Export-Import Bank of Japan (EXIM), which is controlled by the Ministry of Finance. Prospective investors are advised concerning the volume, composition, and geographical distribution of their FDI. (In pushing and guiding direct investment abroad, the government seeks to avoid creating Japanese "overpresence" in any particular host region.)

A noteworthy feature of the Japanese system is the way collaborative planning in behalf of the national interest, the interests of the bureaucracy, and the interests of big business has been institutionalized. One such arrangement provides for auxiliary organs of government (*gaikaku dantai*), which are accorded quasi-official status. Under ministerial auspices, they number in the hundreds. They are staffed chiefly by former government officials (whose retirement is in effect a form of secondment) and are supported partly by government and partly by private funds. A new member of this group, the Japan Institute for Overseas Investment (JOI), was authorized by the Ministry of Finance in December 1991. The institute takes account of the fact that FDI is one of the chief instruments of Japan's industrial policy on the international plane. Its purpose is to coordinate government and business planning for the implementation of that policy. As an auxiliary organ of government, the JOI takes instruction from the EXIM Bank, by which it is administered. It provides information on FDI acquired by JOI itself as well as by EXIM through its lending activities. It serves as a forum for exchange of views among Japanese investors, host governments, and financial institutions. As of March 1992, its membership comprised 166 major Japanese companies that are heavily involved in overseas business. Through their *keiretsu* affiliations, these major firms substantially determine the international strategy of Japan's entire industrial sector. They dominate the flow of Japan's FDI with regard to its composition, volume, geographical distribution, and timing.

Concerning pull factors, Britain appeals to the Japanese for cultural and political as well as economic reasons. Culturally, the British are congenial to the Japanese because of their concern for "face," their indirect manner of negotiating, and the belief—as I was told—that (in contrast to Americans) "they do not shout." The convenience of using English (Japan's second language) is greatly appreciated, as is the benefit of being able to apply in Britain many of the lessons from Japan's experience in America. In the United States, Japanese learned how to manage Anglo types, how to deal with local conditions, and what to avoid. For example, in America they learned to soft-pedal the visibility of their *sogo shosha* and *keiretsu*. (At present, the Japanese party line is that the importance of *keiretsu* has been exaggerated.) Japanese firms, moreover, have been able to transfer some of their U.S.-trained personnel to Britain and thus gain an additional return on their investment. In Britain they may also earn a further return on the success of brand names they nurtured in America. This is one of the fundamental push factors for international expansion.

The political attraction of Britain for Japan lies largely in the warm welcome it has received, both at the national and local levels. The national government has helped local governments to attract Japanese companies. Moreover, the highly centralized nature of the British government and its engrossment of political power enhances Japan's appreciation of its pro-Japanese policy. Britain's political stability, a prime desideratum of all Japanese FDI, is likewise important. The Japanese also respect the fact that British authorities have always delivered what they promised. Within the EC it is of special importance to Japan that the British government stands up for the interests of Japanese subsidiaries (as well as Britain's own interests) in disputes concerning the national origin of products made by those subsidiaries in Britain.

Concerning economic attraction, the opportunity for Japan's FDI in British manufacturing was to produce both for export and for the domestic market. In manufacturing, a strategic attraction was gaps in the product chain for motor vehicles and consumer electronics. (In vehicles, however, there were survivors in the components industry, which later helped Japan to cope with the local content problem.) Logistically, economic attractions included good infrastructure for transportation and communication. In finance and commerce, including retail distribution, Japan has been attracted by Britain's strength and comparative advantage. (Whereas the U.K.'s weakness in manufacturing was the chief reason for its welcome to Japan's FDI, its strength in finance and commerce was an opposite reason for its failure to resist the entry of competing Japanese firms in those sectors.) The prior establishment of Japanese subsidiaries in finance and distribution, moreover, was in itself an attraction for Japanese manufacturers to then seek entry into Britain.

Economically, the U.K. tax system is highly favorable to inward investment. The maximum U.K. national corporate tax rate on profits was reduced to 33 percent in 1991, the lowest in the industrialized world. There is no local tax on profits.[2] The tax system also provides for capital expenditure allowances. Furthermore, a variety of subsidies and incentives is available in the Assisted Areas, in enterprise zones, new towns, and other local jurisdictions. (At Sunderland, in an Assisted Area, Nissan received a £125 million subsidy to construct its £850 million manufacturing plant.) Antitrust laws in Britain are permissive as compared with those in America; this may help explain why firms in Britain are more collaborative than those in the United States.

Concerning labor-management relations, employment laws in Britain are less prescriptive than elsewhere in EC. In Strasbourg in December 1989, all EC member states with the exception of the United Kingdom signed the Community Charter of the Fundamental Social Rights of Workers. In June 1992, EC employment and social affairs ministers agreed in principle to limit the working week to 48 hours, but again the proposed legislation contained a provision allowing Britain to remain exempt. Post-Maastricht, the IBB (Invest in Britain Bureau of the Department of Trade and Industry) has been promoting inward investment partly on the ground of avoiding the social costs of FDI elsewhere in Europe. Accordingly, social security, retirement, and other welfare costs to British employers are relatively low. Britain has national health insurance for all workers, funded by national insurance payments made by all. In the past (but no longer) wage inflation has been outstripped by price inflation, tending to make real wages low. These advantages have been substantially offset by the low absolute level of productivity of British labor, which, however, is extremely variable by sector. On the whole, so-called "cheap labor" in Britain has been of little advantage to Japan.[3]

The British Welcome to Japan

In the 1970s the British economy was uncompetitive and demoralized. Measured by its share of world exports in manufactures, Britain had been in decline for a century. In 1983, for the first time since the Industrial Revolution, Britain's balance of payments in manufactured goods fell into deficit. Increasingly, it has remained in deficit ever since. As variously defined, Britain was described as having been "deindustrialized." Its declining industries included steel, textiles, metal manufacturing, and coal. In terms of the trade accounts, Britain's areas of comparative advantage were mainly confectionery, alcoholic drinks, and cosmetics. Virtually no sector of the economy was free of government intervention or control.

When Margaret Thatcher became prime minister in 1979, "Britain was assumed to be a land of mediocre management, adversarial industrial relations, old-fashioned industries, second-rate schooling, poor marketing, insufficient research and development, a disdain for business and a liking for tea breaks."[4] Upon assuming office, therefore, Mrs. Thatcher undertook a program to "reindustrialize" Britain and to cultivate an "enterprise culture." The program included reduction of corporate income taxes, a monetarist approach to squeezing out inflation, reduction of subsidies, financial deregulation (including abolition of exchange controls in October 1979), reform of labor union restrictive practices, and privatization of national enterprises. However, throughout her term of office (ending 21 November 1990), manufacturing remained in low esteem in Britain. A structural shift in favor of services and away from manufacturing continued during the 1980s.[5] The shift away from manufacturing was significant because of its disproportionate role in Britain's foreign trade. Although it produces only about 20 percent of the national output, in 1992 manufacturing earned about 60 percent of Britain's foreign exchange.[6]

One of Mrs. Thatcher's first acts as prime minister was to visit Japan with an appeal to the Japanese government. She vigorously invited Japanese direct investment in Britain in support of her reindustrialization program. She sought help from Japan to fill the empty spaces in Britain's industrial structure, to smash labor-union power, to provide employment, and to improve the trade balance. In each of these respects, Mrs. Thatcher's program was wholly in accord with Japan's national interests and global strategy.[7] Mrs. Thatcher hoped that Japan's FDI would raise the technological level of British industry and revive the Assisted Areas, a.k.a. "the regions," where traditional industries had crumbled. The government provides subsidies (with matching EC finance) to investors—domestic or foreign—who bring projects to the Assisted Areas. Elsewhere in Britain, in accordance with EC rules, no direct investment subsidies are officially granted.[8]

In their original form as "screwdriver" plants, Japanese FDI has been a subject of controversy in Britain as elsewhere. It is understood, however, that if Japan places its FDI in France or Germany, it would create products competitive with British exports; these could even be imported into Britain; so why not induce the Japanese to perform assembly operations in Britain? In the course of time, it could be anticipated that in Japan's interest, as well as Britain's, screwdriver plants would mature into integrated manufacturing operations. Furthermore, the net externalities of Japan's FDI in Britain would be favorable. If transplants were to help relax the balance of payments constraint, British macroeconomic policy could therefore be more flexible. There would also be multiplier effects from the employment provided by the Japanese. As the purchasing power of workers increased, it would revolve through-out the economy.

Abroad, moreover, Japanese firms are dedicated to maintaining a free market—in Britain more so than either British or American firms. This is because they have their eye on the EC as a whole, whereas some British firms and even American firms in Britain are primarily interested in the domestic British market and thus are protectionist-minded.

In encouraging Japanese entry, the British government has allowed Japan to set up wholly owned subsidiaries, which is far from universal practice in Europe. In June 1991, the DTI (Department of Trade and Industry) organized a trade association, the Japan Electronics Business Association (JEBA), which it finances and for which it acts as a secretariat. The Invest in Britain Bureau (IBB) of the DTI was established in 1977 under a Socialist government. Upon taking office, Prime Minister Thatcher supported and strengthened it. Annually, IBB holds a major seminar in Tokyo, as well as regional seminars elsewhere in Japan. In April 1991, Peter Lilley, Secretary of State for Trade and Industry, inaugurated the Priority Japan Campaign (successor to the Opportunity Japan Campaign, which had been launched in 1988) in an effort to put government support behind the efforts of British business in dealing with Japan. The Priority Japan Campaign has three objectives:

1. Selling to the Japanese: sales in Japan, to Japanese companies in third countries and in the U.K., and sales to Japanese visitors[9]

2. Investing in Japan: setting up an effective base, partnership or joint venture in Japan

3. Learning from Japan: the transfer of Japanese technology, techniques, and know-how to British companies

In Tokyo, the British embassy has two staff members whose time is devoted exclusively to promoting Japanese direct investment in Britain. All Britain's regional development associations have representatives in Tokyo. They invite projects in Scotland, Wales, Northeast United Kingdom, and the New Towns. The appeal for Japan's favor was further expressed by Foreign Secretary Douglas Hurd in remarks to a group of British parliamentarians and businessmen: "We believe," he said, "—I'll try to stress this—that we are Japan's best friend in Europe."[10]

As it happened, it was an opportune moment when Mrs. Thatcher approached the Japanese at the outset of her administration. Trade friction (*masatsu*) was rising to the boiling point between Japan and its major trading partners. Protectionists threatened to expel it from some of its export markets. The European Community was being rapidly integrated and formation of the world's largest single market was in prospect. Thus Britain's crisis was Japan's opportunity to expatriate its mature industries, to diversify its markets, and to reduce its overdependence on economic relations with the United States.

The stages of Japan's FDI entry abroad assume a familiar pattern. Typically, the Japanese head office begins by establishing a representative office abroad. The office surveys the market, makes contacts, and furnishes intelligence to its parent back home. It is not legally authorized to transact business, but it may refer business inquiries to its headquarters in Japan or elsewhere, which is almost as good. Second, a locally incorporated sales representative is appointed for distribution of imports from Japan. Next, a sales and service subsidiary of the Japanese parent is established to take over the distribution function. This is followed by construction of a screwdriver assembly plant, which procures a limited amount of local components. The enterprise may proceed to manufacturing activity that procures mainly local components and depends on local engineering and support facilities. Finally, local R&D activities may begin.

By type of industry, consumer electric and electronic products comprised the first wave of Japanese FDI in Britain. Electronic office equipment and related products were produced as well. The second wave was in motor vehicles. The third wave, now emerging, is in high-tech electronics. It is in this third area that technology transfer and local R&D become highly significant. Although no preconditions have been attached—and no quid pro quo has been demanded—as the price of admission for Japan's FDI in Britain, according to the DTI there is an understanding that Japan's R&D will be undertaken jointly with British firms. In the high-tech field, there are strong misgivings in Britain about Japan's performance of this understanding.

On the British side, another source of these feelings—which are rarely discussed—is the way in which some of the "empty spaces" in the U.K. economy were created. The indigenous consumer electronics industry was undermined by imports of Japanese high-quality, low-cost electronic products in the 1960s and 1970s. Lack of reciprocity in FDI is another source of British ambivalence. Britain is second only to the United States in the world league of outward direct investment.[11] Japan is certainly one of the prime candidates for inward investment. However, according to Japan's Ministry of Finance, Britain's FDI in Japan during 1950–1991 amounted to $1,083 million, as compared with $26,186 million invested by Japan in Britain. Total direct investment in Japan from all of Europe during the same period was only $6,347 million; from the United States, direct investment was $9,907 million. Japanese government restrictions on inward FDI largely account for these figures until the mid–1970s. Thereafter they are accounted for by institutional arrangements and restrictive practices in Japan's private sector.[12]

Beyond ambivalence, Britain itself has been the object of outright hostility on the part of its EC partners with regard to Japan's efforts to become an "insider" in the Community. In November 1990, Fujitsu purchased a controlling interest (80 percent) in ICL, the premier computer manufacturer in Britain. Shortly thereafter, in March 1991, on the ground that it was no longer a European company, ICL was expelled from JESSI (Joint European Submicron Silicon Initiative), a research group funded by European companies and the European Commission. It was later reinstated.

Discriminatory inconsistency between the EC's industrial and competition policies was illustrated by its response to American as opposed to Japanese FDI. With regard to Japan, for example, Canon's EC subsidiaries were treated by the EC Anti-Dumping Office as foreign companies, whereas in the case of the United States, Xerox's EC subsidiaries were considered to be EC companies. In anti-circumvention action, Canon's plants have been investigated for their local content, while Xerox's plants have not. "In sum, two similar companies were treated in an opposite way: the anti-dumping and anti-circumvention measures on Japanese copiers should be abolished."[13] The EC's perception of Japan's economic strategy probably had something to do with its inconsistent approach. There was, for example, the episode of 1984–1986 when "Japanese producers sold D-Rams in Europe at prices so far below costs as undoubtedly to constitute dumping. By this unfair trading they established market dominance and wiped out virtually all non-Japanese D-Ram producers both in the United States and in the European Community."[14]

The Impact of Japan's Direct Investment in Britain

Statistical Stock and Flow

The generally accepted definition of FDI is that of the IMF: "investment that is made to acquire a lasting interest in an enterprise operating in an economy other than that of the investor, the investor's purpose being to have an effective voice in the management of the enterprise."[15] In practice, however, for the purpose of collecting data, countries adopt more specific definitions, which differ in their scope and methodology. In contrast with direct investment, portfolio investment is performed without the purpose of acquiring a voice in management. In Britain, the threshold for classifying foreign in-

TABLE 2.1
JAPAN'S DIRECT INVESTMENT IN THE UNITED KINGDOM, BY INDUSTRY, BY JAPANESE FISCAL YEAR, 1977–1992 ($US million)

	Cumulative 1977–1992	1977	1978	1979	1980	1981	1982	1983	1984	1985	1986	1987	1988	1989	1990	1991	1992
Grand total	27,494	50	66	66	186	110	176	153	318	375	984	2,473	3,956	5,239	6,806	3,588	2,948
Manufacturing																	
Total	5,650	5	30	20	38	30	15	45	56	83	126	289	334	1,174	1,999	904	502
Foodstuffs	122	0	0	0	*	0	0	0	*	3	1	3	19	66	23	10	0
Textiles	253	1	*	4	1	1	*	*	1	1	*	1	16	9	157	29	33
Lumber and pulp	6	0	0	0	0	0	0	0	0	0	0	0	0	0	0	0	6
Chemicals	176	1	0	*	0	0	0	0	*	0	0	11	26	64	45	16	13
Iron and steel	115	0	12	5	10	0	0	0	0	2	0	7	21	{12	{15	{10	}21
Nonferrous metals																	
Machinery	721	2	7	9	6	5	1	4	10	15	19	38	45	335	66	140	19
Electric/electronic	2,264	*	7	2	19	23	12	39	17	24	28	121	132	347	1,161	180	153
Transport equipment	1,553	0	0	*	1	0	0	2	7	17	71	52	40	266	463	421	213
Other	435	1	3	*	1	1	1	*	22	21	7	56	35	75	69	98	44
Nonmanufacturing																	
Total	15,931	43	31	42	144	78	158	106	253	278	775	2,013	2,902	3,161	2,647	1,757	1,543
Agriculture and forestry	7	0	0	0	0	0	0	0	*	0	0	0	0	0	0	0	7
Fisheries	0	0	0	0	0	0	0	*	0	0	0	0	0	0	0	0	0
Mining	87	0	0	0	0	0	0	0	0	0	27	0	26	7	10	6	8
Construction	172	0	0	0	1	14	0	0	3	0	3	0	0	12	0	3	139
Commerce	2,272	5	17	13	40	24	73	19	119	73	86	193	193	335	284	580	218
Finance and insurance	11,845	6	7	27	46	35	83	80	122	193	644	1,709	2,634	2,535	2,109	889	726
Services	1,346	1	5	*	1	5	2	9	9	11	13	85	47	244	230	264	427
Shipping	103	0	0	0	0	*	0	1	*	*	1	26	1	28	13	15	18
Other	94	30	2	2	56	0	0	4	0	0	*	0	0	0	0	0	0
Branches	771	2	4	2	3	3	3	0	9	2	2	118	14	59	360	131	58
Real estate	5,141	*	1	2	1	0	0	0	0	11	81	53	706	845	1,800	796	845

NOTES: Statistics by industry are not available prior to 1977.

      * Less than $500,000.

SOURCE: Japanese Government, Ministry of Finance.

vestment as "direct" lies at the point where the investor acquires 20 percent or more of the capital stock of an enterprise. In the United States, in accordance with IMF and OECD guidelines, the threshold lies at 10 percent. Apart from this difference, U.S. and U.K. statistical practice with regard to FDI is almost identical. In Japan, the threshold has been at 10 percent since December 1980 in accordance with the revision of the Foreign Exchange and Foreign Trade Control Law that became effective then. (Before that, the Japanese threshold had been at 25 percent.)

In compiling statistics for outward direct investment, however, there is an important difference between the FDI data collected by Japan's Ministry of Finance as compared with data from the United States and the United Kingdom, where statistics concerning the position (stock) of outward direct investment are compiled from foreign affiliates'[16] accounts in terms of book value at a moment in time, namely year-end. In Japan, however, the stock of outward FDI is compiled by cumulating the annual outflow statistics over a period of time beginning with Japanese fiscal year 1951. These are unrevised; for example, the cumulative total reported by the Ministry of Finance is not adjusted for disinvestment. The statistics also exclude capital raised overseas by Japanese firms and invested abroad.

Moreover, Japan's annual statistics are based on "notifications" to the Ministry of Finance of the *intention* on the part of Japanese residents to conduct direct investment transactions. A notification contains all the details of a proposed transaction. Prior to December 1980, when revision of the Foreign Exchange and Foreign Trade Control Law became effective, prospective investors were required not only to notify the Ministry of Finance but also to obtain its approval of the proposed investment. It is noteworthy that for purposes of screening and administrative guidance, the Japanese government still requires submission of the notification document even though for statistical purposes it leaves something to be desired. In particular, Japanese FDI statistics have an upward bias because some transactions that are compiled by the Ministry as "notified" may never have been actually completed. The upward bias may be reduced, however, by another flaw in the statistics, namely that they do not include reinvested earnings of affiliates. (They also exclude FDI valued at less than ¥30 million.) This is contrary to statistical practice in Britain and the United States. As an alternative to the Ministry of Finance statistics, the balance of payments statistics from the Bank of Japan report FDI that has been completed. However, they include no breakdown of the industrial composition of these transactions. During the period 1984 through 1990, Japan's balance of payments statistics for total FDI from Japan to Britain were smaller than those of the Ministry of Finance by an annual average of $710 million.

As a result of these circumstances, the U.S. Department of Commerce statistics on the U.S. direct investment position in the United Kingdom on a historical-cost basis at year-end has no satisfactory counterpart on the Japanese side. Consequently the comparative positions of U.S. and Japanese direct investment in Britain can only be approximated. It is evident also, for example, that over time, with regard to the amount of Japan's FDI in Britain as expressed in terms of a common currency (dollars), the gap is increasing between Japanese and British statistics. During the period 1980 through 1986, the average annual excess of Japan's reporting on its FDI in Britain over that reported by Britain as an inflow from Japan amounted to $219 million. During the period 1987 through 1989, the average annual excess amounted to $2,282 million. In terms of stock statistics, in 1984 the total position of Japanese affiliates in Britain was reported by Japan's Ministry of Finance as $1,689 million larger than that reported by the U.K. Central Statistical Office (CSO). In 1989 the Japanese figure was $9,848 million larger. In that year, the Japanese position figure for FDI in Britain as reported by the Ministry of Finance was almost three times larger than that reported by the CSO. It may be noted that the U.S. FDI position in Britain as reported by the U.S. Department of Commerce is also somewhat larger than that reported by the CSO, but by a much smaller degree than the corresponding discrepancy between the reports of the CSO and the Ministry of Finance for Japan's FDI in Britain.

In terms of CSO statistics, it is evident that the position of Japan's affiliates in the United Kingdom is increasing faster than that of the United States. Prior to 1971, the volume of Japan's position was practically negligible. By 1984, Japan's FDI constituted 2.1 percent of total FDI in Britain. By 1989, it constituted 3.9 percent of the total. Correspondingly, the United States' share is shrinking. In 1984, it constituted 48.9 percent of total FDI in Britain. By 1989, its share had declined to 36.5 percent. In other words, the Japanese stock of direct investment in Britain, which in 1984 was only 4 percent as large as that of the United States, became 11 percent as large in 1989.

Obviously the U.S. position in Britain is much older, wider, and deeper than that of Japan. In volume, U.S. FDI is approximately ten times as great as Japan's, which dates largely from the mid-1980s. Why, then, has Japan's FDI created such a furor, especially in manufacturing, while that of the United States has not?

By the same token, while Japan's FDI in British commerce and finance is reportedly three times as great as in manufacturing, it has received much less attention. For one thing, it entered Britain earlier and more gradually, and the Japanese assumed a much lower profile in commerce and finance than in manufacturing. Moreover, in commerce and finance Japan did not threaten the established order—in Britain or elsewhere in the EC—with anything comparable to its "lean production" in the manufacturing sector. The speed and force of Japan's arrival in British manufacturing, however, staggered friend and foe alike and strongly influenced Britain's industrial structure, industrial practices, economic performance, and institutional arrangements and public policies.

The role of Japan's FDI in commerce and finance has nevertheless been extremely important behind the scenes. It recapitulates in Britain its role in Japan during the Occupation and in the early post-Occupation period. Banks and *sogo shosha* provided the foundation for Japan's economic rehabilitation and the economic "miracle." At that stage, as is well known, major manufacturing enterprises were dominated by their "main banks." In the small and middle-size sector of industry, *sogo shosha* served as financiers to many of their clients. Without their support much of Japan's postwar manufacturing progress could not have occurred.

Similarly, the first and predominant purpose of financial FDI abroad is to provide "supportive financial services for Japanese corporations engaging in overseas economic activities."[17] The expansion of Japan's financial FDI in the 1980s was performed by subsidiary finance companies, "most of which were set up by trading and manufacturing corporations."[18] Itochu, for example, one of Japan's leading *sogo shosha*, has greatly broadened its financial involvement and today performs many financial activities that augment the traditional scope of a trading company's operations. These include investing in European merchant banks, investing in venture business, establishing investment advisory services, and development and management of various financial products such as commodity funds. As of 1989, Japanese banks held 22 percent of all U.K. banking assets, as compared with 10 percent held by U.S. banks.

The bulk of Japan's manufacturing FDI in Britain came after the financial and commercial FDI (which accounted for about 90 percent of nonmanufacturing) had largely been put in place. According to the Ministry of Finance, during the period 1977–1991, manufacturing comprised 21 percent of Japan's total FDI in Britain. Within manufacturing, electric and electronic products accounted for 41 percent of the total; transport equipment, 26 percent; and machinery, 14 percent.

In overview, in the world at large, the crest of Japan's FDI occurred in 1989 coincident with the collapse of its "bubble" of the 1980s. Between 1989 and 1991, with the rise in the domestic cost of capital and the decline in its availability, Japan's FDI declined proportionally more in North America than globally, while its FDI in Europe declined proportionally less. The proportional decline in Britain was even less than in Europe as a whole. Between 1989 and 1991 the decline in Japan's FDI in Asia was likewise less than the decline in North America. These figures signify a shift in Japan's advance away from North America and in favor of Europe and Asia. They are also evidence of Japan's commitment to its strategy in Britain.

In comparing the Japanese position in EC with that of the United States, it has been observed from the start that Japan's FDI "has been oriented not toward any particular national market but to the EC market as a whole. This is in marked contrast to U.S. direct involvement in Europe in the 1950s and early 1960s, which was primarily geared to supplying the country in which production was undertaken."[19] Thus the statistics demonstrate that Britain serves as a fulcrum for Japan's exercise of leverage within the EC at large.

Consumer Electronics

The first wave of Japan's FDI in Britain was in consumer electric and electronic products. Like automobiles, this is a key industry with many upstream and downstream linkages, high income elasticity of demand, economies of scale, high export potential, high potential for technological advance, and externalities that enhance Japan's political relations in Britain. Altogether, these characteristics are basic to Japan's concept of a key industry. They create dependency relationships that can be manipulated in Japan's favor in the implementation of its industrial policy.

In accordance with its classic formula, Japan's domination of the consumer electronics industry began with exports of transistor radios to Britain in the early 1960s. During the mid-1970s through the end of the 1980s the indigenous industry was destroyed. Then Japanese firms came in to resurrect it with FDI. The pattern was repeated in the early 1970s when Japan waged a relentless drive in the export of television sets. British governments of all parties, however, were committed to free trade and relied on industry-to-industry talks between the U.K. Radio Industry Council (RIC) and the Electronic Industries Association of Japan (EIAJ) for the negotiation of a "voluntary" export restraint agreement. Beginning in 1973, meetings on this subject were held several times a year. Lord Arnold Weinstock described them as "a deer talking to a tiger," a simile that correctly anticipated the results of the conversations.[20] For example, although exports from Japan to Britain were moderated, the Japanese refused to discuss the matter of exports to

Britain from their plants outside Japan, such as Hitachi's plant in Singapore. In effect, this circumvented the understandings reached at the RIC/EIAJ talks. Consequently, indigenous British television firms failed to retain the 50 percent share of the market that was the minimum essential for a profitable level of production.

Japan's exports to Britain from its plants outside Japan made use of "third-country trade," an important tool in its economic strategy. Third-country trade is one of the chief instruments by which Japan orchestrates complementarities among regions in its global hinterland, thus implementing its industrial policy on the international plane. Another Japanese application of third-country trade is in its "outflanking" strategy, which I have discussed elsewhere.[21] As these examples demonstrate, third-country trade is a strategic complement to Japan's FDI. Japanese government collaboration with industry in the orchestration of third-country trade is described in the following dispatch:

> The Ministry of International Trade and Industry will urge consumer electronics makers to totally shift production of designated low-technology equipment to their Southeast Asian plants, a ministry source said Monday. By separating production lines in Japan and abroad, the ministry intends to avoid excessive increases in exports when domestic demand slumps.

> The ministry will form a study group with some ten major manufacturers in July to set guidelines on which consumer electronics should be manufactured at overseas factories and which should be produced in Japan.[22]

With regard to Japan's economic strategy, incidentally, it is significant that although third-country trade is a rising proportion of Japan's total trade—in 1991 it already constituted one-quarter of the total trade of the *sogo shosha*—statistics of the volume, commodity composition, and geographical distribution of this trade have not been published and are not public information.

In British consumer electronics, typical of Japanese competitive practice was its combination of both fair and unfair tactics. This is one of the reasons that both critics and apologists for Japan generally find it difficult to make a conclusive case in behalf of their respective positions. There is no single principle behind Japanese competitive practice, unless it is the principle of using whatever means are pragmatically effective in achieving a goal. In the early 1970s, Japanese competition in British consumer electronics was "fair" in that it offered value for money. However, it could also be "unfair." In 1974 in Japan, for example, Sony began producing the Trinitron tube, which was a radical improvement on existing television tubes and which by dumping soon dominated the market in Britain. The British response was academic. In October 1975, a British government investigation came to the conclusion that vertical integration in the Japanese television industry made it impossible to establish a Japanese "home market" price for tubes as compared with the export price; thus what was widely perceived as dumping provided no cause for action because it could not be quantitatively demonstrated.

Britain's reliance on Japan to pave the way to greater competitive power did not save the indigenous consumer electronics industry from extinction. Concerning labor productivity, for example, a report published in February 1979 by NEDO explained that although the Japanese hourly rate of pay was 72 percent higher than the British, the direct labor cost of a television set made in the United Kingdom was almost double that of one made in Japan because the Japanese set required 1.9 man-hours and the British set 6.1 man-hours. The difference was partly due to automation. NEDO also reported that the quality of components entering Japanese plants was an order of magnitude superior to those entering U.K. plants.[23] In publishing its report, the British government noted with approval that the situation was to be remedied by joint ventures between British and Japanese firms. Rank Bush Murphy Company had agreed to combine with Toshiba in a joint venture to be known as Rank Toshiba, and GEC (General Electric Company, Ltd.) had agreed to combine with Hitachi in a joint venture to be known as GEC-Hitachi. In the case of Rank Toshiba, the joint venture would be controlled and managed by Rank, which held 70 percent of the equity. Control of the GEC-Hitachi joint venture, with each party holding 50 percent of the equity, would ostensibly be shared equally; in this case again, however, it would be managed by the British partner with Hitachi controlling the technology.

These two cases are typical of other nonviable British-Japanese joint ventures in the consumer electronics industry in the 1980s. After they succumbed, they were revived as highly competitive Japanese wholly owned firms. A few details of this process are the following.

In the case of Rank Toshiba, it was totally obvious to Toshiba at the outset that the joint venture was not viable. As manager, Rank would persist in the management policies that had brought its predecessor firm to ruin. These included uneconomic vertical integration, acceptance of indifferent quality standards from suppliers, a workforce represented by seven different unions, and poor cooperation between departments. Toshiba correctly anticipated that upon collapse of the joint venture the remaining assets could be acquired cheaply and effectively reorganized under Japanese management.

Within two years, the Rank Toshiba Company announced that it would cease trading. In March 1981, three of its four plants were closed and the fourth was taken over as a Japanese wholly owned company known as Toshiba Consumer Products (TCP). With this takeover, the Japanese had become "farmers" instead of "hunters." Employing mainly British personnel, the management of the new company concentrated on quality control and relations with suppliers. Instead of patrolling inspectors, responsibility for quality checks was assigned to operators. Similarly, inspection of incoming components was terminated, but defective components were not tolerated. Various other innovations were also introduced that were significant examples of Japan's impact on institutional arrangements and management-labor practices in British industry. Among these was the "single status" policy. Rank Toshiba's six dining areas for various ranks of personnel were replaced by a single restaurant for all staff. TCP was managed by a Company Advisory Board drawn from employees at all levels. This was described by one British observer as "a dramatic advance on the usual phony system of consultation found in British industry." Meetings of the Company Advisory Board, moreover, were not precooked; they did not merely rubber-stamp decisions that had been taken in advance. Furthermore, the Company Advisory Board was given full information, including confidential data, about the firm's condition. One union, the Electrical, Electronic, Telecommunication, and Plumbing Union (EETPU), was given exclusive bargaining rights.[24] TCP made a no-strike agreement with the union, which attracted wide attention. More significant than the agreement itself were the procedures designed to insure that it would never be put to the test:

> Any problem not resolved by the COAB was to be negotiated directly between the union's full-time official and the Managing Director, and only if they failed to reach agreement would the matter go to arbitration. However, the arbitrator would not be allowed to recommend a compromise, but would be obliged to find for one side or the other; the object of this so-called "pendulum" arbitration was to encourage both parties to submit moderate proposals. . . . To date, it has never been necessary to invoke this procedure, let alone the "no-strike" agreement.[25]

The second case mentioned above was that of GEC, which in the late 1970s found itself with serious overcapacity and which was making unacceptable losses. Rather than close its factory, GEC arranged a joint venture with Hitachi, which had just been refused permission to establish its own TV-receiver factory in the United Kingdom. As in the Toshiba case, this was another example of adversarial investment by Japan. GEC-Hitachi was to be under GEC management, but its technology was to be controlled by Hitachi and the firm was to use a Japanese-designed chassis. A key element in the collapse of the joint venture was the following:

> Hitachi required twelve months' notice of any proposal to substitute a European component, which then had to be submitted to lengthy tests, so the chassis was often superseded before the change could be made. This situation tended to perpetuate the basic inequity that although the factory continued to operate at a loss, Hitachi were making profits on the imported tubes and other components whereas GEC were not.[26]

In March 1984, after friction between the parties and further losses by GEC, the latter sold out to Hitachi.

Altogether, powerful Japanese *keiretsu* firms, including Hitachi, Matsushita, Sony, and Sharp, as well as 21 other Japanese electronic companies, have taken over most of the British consumer electronics industry, including color television, its main product. (There are no U.S. audio or video manufacturers in Britain.) Fidelity, which was the last British-owned manufacturer of color television sets, was closed in July 1988.

Automobiles

In contrast with the consumer electronics industry, which collapsed under Japanese assault, Britain's indigenous auto industry collapsed largely of its own accord.[27] In the early 1980s, British cars were notorious for their poor quality. Ford and GM (Vauxhall) were supplying the British market chiefly from their continental rather than local sources. Prior to February 1994, the only indigenous British maker was the Rover Group (formerly British Leyland), which for survival depended heavily on its affiliation with Honda, the supplier of its technology. Rover and Honda owned 20 percent of each other's equity. (Honda decided to sever the cross-shareholding relationship when another foreigner, BMW of Germany, bought British Aerospace's 80 percent holding in Rover.) At the time of Mrs. Thatcher's appeal for Japanese FDI in 1979, the automobile industry was mature in Japan and ripe for expatriation to Europe as well as America. The British welcome was opportune for Nissan, Toyota, and Honda, which responded with speed and devastating force. News of their impending arrival set alarm bells ringing throughout the European Community, where in the midst of a recession automakers were already threatened with excess productive capacity.

Following and augmenting the impact of its entry into consumer electronics, the impact of Japan's auto production in Britain included operational, political, and institutional effects. Operationally, the Japanese brought changes in the production process, especially in the organization of production and management-labor relations. Second, they contributed to the politicization of Britain's economic relations within the EC. Third, they stoked the embers of industrial policy that remained from previous postwar and prewar eras in Britain.

Historically, it is ironic that Japanese automakers took out licenses from Austin soon after World War II. Subsequently, the first Japanese entrant into automaking in Britain was Nissan Motor Manufacturing (U.K.) Limited, which was established at Sunderland in April 1984. Production in a £900 million plant began in July 1986. It has 3,500 employees and an annual production capacity of 300,000 units. By the year 2000 it plans to produce 400,000 cars annually. Nissan was followed by Honda of the U.K. Limited, which inaugurated an engine plant at Swindon in February 1985. It commenced production in October 1989 in a plant with an annual capacity of 70,000 engines. Honda planned to employ 2,000 workers by 1995. In addition, with its minority interest in Rover, to which it supplies engines and transmissions, Honda, before severing its cross-shareholding relationship, in effect controlled Rover. By 1994, Honda committed to building 100,000 cars a year at its £300 million assembly plant at Swindon (next door to the engine plant), which began production in October 1992. Toyota Motor Manufacturing (U.K.) Limited, established at Deeside in north Wales in December 1989, began producing engines at a £140 million plant in September 1992. It began producing vehicles at a £700 million plant at Burnaston, Derbyshire, in December 1992. By the year 2000, Toyota planned to double its U.K. production to 200,000 cars annually. At full capacity there will be 3,000 employees at Burnaston and 300 at Deeside. The latter will supply the engines.[28]

In Europe as a whole, vehicle production during 1991 totalled 12.7 million cars, 160,000 of which were produced by Japanese transplants in Britain. According to a forecast, by 1999 Japan will have production capacity for 1.8 million vehicles in western Europe and a market share of 20 percent, up from about 12 percent in 1992.[29] In Britain during 1991, Japanese transplant production constituted 16.1 percent of the nation's vehicle output.[30] By the end of the decade Japanese transplants will have a 30 percent share of the U.K. market.[31] By the year 2000, Britain will be second only to Germany as a European automaker. The impact of Japanese producers, however, will be seen not only in the industry as a whole but also in the redistributed market shares of its members. Prospects for Ford, for example, which since 1977 has been Britain's leading car maker, are not bright. Ford's U.K. workforce fell from a peak of 80,000 in early 1980 to 33,000 by the end of 1992. At its peak in 1981, Ford accounted for one in three of all new domestic car sales in Britain. By 1992 its market share had declined to 22.2 percent. In that same year, Nissan and Honda were expanding their operations and Toyota was opening its new plant at Burnaston.

Technological exchange between Japan and Britain has been embodied both in Japan's export of management technology and in production line practice. Together their impact has been transmitted to British institutional arrangements. Toyota devised many of the practices that dominate Japanese automobile manufacturing. After being widely copied within Japan they were brought to Britain by the transplants and recopied by European competitors. As the first Japanese automaker to enter Britain, Nissan showed the way. According to Peter Wickens, Nissan's director of personnel, British management has learned four principles from the Japanese. First is an absolute commitment to quality at all levels of the enterprise. Second is the achievement of *kaizen* (continuous improvement) in the production process. Third is the resolve to plan and analyze every action in detail. Fourth is the application of a high level of engineering skill from the design stage through to final production.[32] These principles, however, are only an overview; they comprehend a complex system of techniques and relationships that have been synthesized in Japan over time. These include "lean production" (using less of everything), teamwork among multiskilled workers, highly flexible automated machines, and compression of bureaucracy by eliminating layers of management and maximizing contacts among employees at all levels . Decision-making and authority for incremental change has been assigned to autonomous work groups on the shop floor. In relations between assemblers and component suppliers, the policy of just-in-time delivery has the spinoff effect of imposing adherence to the criterion of zero defects (just-in-time delivery of junk would shut down production). Achievement of zero defects, in turn, depends upon stability and commitment in the labor force. Institutionally, the latter is conducive to the rise of the single union. These results of Japan's organizational genius have been transmitted to Britain along with its FDI.

Operationally, U.S. and other foreign car-makers within Britain have benefitted both directly and indirectly from Japanese innovations. Indirectly, for example, they have gained from the improved performance of component suppliers who have been trained by the Japanese.[33] Directly, following the Japanese example, European automakers have begun to rethink their customary practice of sourcing components on a cut-throat basis from multiple suppliers and instead are moving toward long-term contracts with a selected few. The result has been an improvement in component quality and a spirit of cooperation and mutual trust in place of defensive and adversarial relationships. The improved management of component suppliers has been one of the greatest innovations introduced by Japan's affiliates in Britain.

From their observation of what Japanese affiliates are doing in Britain, European automakers have drastically reformed other practices. In model changes, for example, instead of passing the blueprint from the design department to engineering, then to production, then to marketing, Renault and Peugeot have set up project teams that bring together all departments simultaneously at all stages of the development process. European automakers have flattened the structure of their traditional organizations and introduced Japanese-style project and production management teams. (Although there is vertical structure *within* departments of the Japanese firm, there are horizontal relationships *among* departments in the process of product development.) Mercedes-Benz, Volkswagen, General Motors, and Ford, among others, have all acknowledged their indebtedness to lessons from the Japanese. In Britain, the engineering group of the National Economic Development Council made a compilation of lessons from Japan that could be applied to the entire British engineering industry.

The picture, however, is mixed. The diffusion of Japanese management practices has indeed raised productivity and quality in British manufacturing. There has been progress in the utilization of human resources, plant organization, and organization of the supply chain. Thus, in maintaining its standards while producing abroad, Japan has demonstrated that performance depends on corporate culture rather than ethnic culture. Britain still has much to learn, however. In a study of the motor vehicle component industry, it has been found that representative firms (of unspecified national parentage) in Britain lag far behind world-class component suppliers in Japan.[34] The productivity of the world-class plants of Japan was found to be twice as great as that of the British plants; in terms of quality the astounding differential was 100 to 1. These results are important because, according to Daniel Jones, they may be taken as typical of the gap between British and world-class performance in U.K. manufacturing at large.[35] The results are important also because they emphasize the Japanese lesson that success depends on management of people rather than on robotics or automation. European producers, using the same machinery as the Japanese, achieve very different results. Indeed, even within Japanese plants, "expatriate Japanese managers gripe about how fully automatic machines installed in their British plants produce 40 percent less than the same tools back home."[36]

Although four or five large U.K. component suppliers survived the collapse of the indigenous motor vehicle industry, the British component industry is controlled by European rather than by British firms. In part this follows from the decision of Japanese automakers to heed one of the lessons of their experience in the United States. When they opened assembly plants in America, they brought with them their affiliated component suppliers from Japan. This aroused strong antagonism on the part of the American component industry. In Britain, therefore, "as a matter of policy," Japan's automakers have discouraged Japanese component makers from following them to Britain.[37]

Beyond operational and institutional matters, the politics of Japan's FDI in Britain are highly vexed. Japan has complicated Britain's problems by politicizing its economic relations within the European Community. At the outset in 1958, Britain had expressed its ambivalence toward Europe by choosing to place its "special relation" with the United States above adherence to the Treaty of Rome. It did not join the Community until 1973. As a member, it confronted other members with a second special relationship, namely that with Japan. To their dismay, it then brought the Japanese "Trojan horse" into their midst. In 1992, when Britain vacillated about ratifying the Maastricht Treaty and pulled out of the Exchange Rate Mechanism (ERM), its relations within the Community deteriorated further. Britain's relations with Japan also deteriorated because, for purposes of exchange rate stability, it is in Japan's interest that Britain should be a member of the ERM.

European Community authorities were resolved that Japan should not be allowed to become the main beneficiary of prospective growth and economies of scale in the single market. In 1988, a dispute arose between Britain and France when the latter refused to classify Nissan U.K.'s cars as EC products. France limited imports of cars from Japan to less than 8 percent of its domestic market.[38] Britain argued that inasmuch as Nissan's domestic content amounted to 60 percent, its cars should be classified as British. The French government insisted that they could not be considered British until their local content (defined as value added within the EC region as a whole) was 80 percent or more. The French, joined by Italy, argued that output exported by Britain from Japan's British transplants should be included in the quotas for exports to the Community from Japan proper. There was no dispute, however, about the local content of cars made by U.S. manufacturers in Britain.[39] The significance of this dispute was that if the French and Italian views prevailed, Britain's exports of cars from Japanese transplants to all other destinations within EC would be jeopardized. (Similarly, a problem could arise concerning whether cars exported to Europe from Japanese transplants in the United States were to be classified as of Japanese or U.S. origin.)

The argument between Britain and France had implications for another issue as well. According to the Single European Act, which was endorsed by Community heads of state in 1988, a deadline of December 31, 1992 was specified for establishment of an "area without internal frontiers in which the free movement of persons, goods, and services is assured." However, in 1990, the EC governments authorized the European Commission to negotiate "transitional" restraints on Japanese car sales to Europe after 1992. If Japanese transplants in Britain were to produce cars that were classified as "made in Japan," they would be subject to the transitional restraints.

After months of controversy, it was announced in July 1991 that a compromise entitled "Elements of Consensus" had been reached between the EC and Japan.[40] In accordance with the single market program, after December 31, 1992 all output from Japanese transplants in Britain would be exportable to other EC countries without restriction. France and Italy, however, disagreed with this interpretation of the "consensus." Furthermore, beginning January 1, 1993, there would be no national restrictions within EC concerning direct imports of cars or other light vehicles from Japan. However, an "understanding" added that direct exports of cars from Japan to EC would be limited by Japan to 1.23 million vehicles annually until the end of 1999, with subceilings for exports to five EC countries that had maintained national import restrictions prior to January 1, 1993, as follows: France, 150,000; Italy, 138,000; Spain, 79,000; Portugal, 23,000; and the United Kingdom, 190,000. Adherence to the ceilings was to be "monitored" by Japan. There were to be semiannual consultations between the Japanese and EC authorities until the end of the century, after which the EC auto market was to be completely liberalized for imports.

All of the "understandings," however, were based on highly arguable assumptions. Among these was a "working assumption" by the EC Commission concerning the volume of transplant output to be produced by the Japanese in Europe by the end of the century. The French insisted that the working assumption constituted a ceiling for Japanese sales; the British denied that there was a compulsory ceiling; and the Japanese simply took no cognizance of the Commission's assumption. Furthermore, there was no agreement between Brussels and Tokyo on how to adjust the share of future EC auto-market growth or decline between the European and Japanese auto industries. Instead there was only an "Internal Declaration" by the EC Commission in which it offered its own interpretation of these matters.[41] Britain was left in the middle. So much for the "consensus" of July 1991!

Performance Indicators of
Japanese FDI in the United Kingdom

Traditionally, foreign trade has been approximately twice as important in the United Kingdom as in the United States. However, Britain's share of world trade declined from almost 10 percent in 1956 to about 4 percent in 1984. Since then its share has been more or less stable. With the exception of 1980–1982, Britain's trade balance has been in deficit every year since 1978. The composition of the deficit is what attracts our attention; it consists primarily of an imbalance in manufactured goods. This is of central importance because, as mentioned above, although manufacturing constitutes only about 20 percent of national output, it produces over 60 percent of Britain's export earnings.

In 1983, for the first time since the Industrial Revolution, Britain's trade in manufactured goods fell into deficit, where it has remained ever since.[42] Within the total trade deficit, the largest single component is trade in passenger cars, which accounted for 21.3 percent of the total visible deficit during 1985–1990.

Accordingly, the answer to the question of whether Japan's FDI can overcome the British trade deficit lies chiefly with its automobile affiliates. Beginning in 1990, Britain's balance of payments deficit in visible trade began to decline, especially in automobiles. In that year, due primarily to Japanese car exports from Britain, the ratio of exports to imports in passenger cars rose to about 0.8, which was the same as the ratio in total manufacturing; prior to 1990, the ratio in automobiles had been about half the ratio in total manufacturing. By 1995, it was clear that this improvement was attributable to structural rather than cyclical factors.

Britain welcomed Japanese FDI in order to rebuild its competitive power—as reflected in exports—and to provide employment.[43] In analyzing the results of Japan's FDI, it is necessary first to specify the level of gross FDI output, the extent to which that output replaces imports, the extent to which it replaces domestic output, and the import content of FDI output and its components. The Nomura Research Institute (NRI) has attempted to answer these questions.[44] The NRI study makes various assumptions on these points, plus others on capital-output ratios, the export share of output, multiplier effects, productivity advances, technology transfer, and growth rates of British GDP. Nomura concludes that the improvement in the trade deficit beginning in 1990 reflected cyclical factors rather than structural change. However, they estimate that by 1995 Japanese FDI could add £4 billion to the trade balance, 2 percent to output, and over 400,000 jobs to employment. On average, Nomura expects Japanese plants in Britain to export 75 percent of their output. They are likely to eliminate the British deficit on cars by the mid-1990s. In 1991, Nissan exported 90 percent of its production in Britain. In 1992, Nissan Motor Manufacturing (U.K.) together with Kyushu Matsushita Electric (U.K.) and Yamazaki Machinery (U.K.) were each recognized by the Queen's Award for Export Achievement.

In color TV, a British trade deficit in almost every year of the 1980s was turned into a huge £446 million surplus in 1991, owing almost exclusively to factories owned by Japanese firms, principally the *keiretsu* firms of Sony, Mitsubishi, Hitachi, and Sanyo. According to the British Radio and Electronic Equipment Manufacturers' Association (BREMA), Japanese-owned consumer electronics firms in Britain export about one-half their output. In color TV and VCRs it is a bit less than one-half.

Concerning the employment performance of Toyota in Britain, it has been estimated that for every 100 jobs in automobile assembling or engine and component manufacture, an additional 22 jobs may be generated by backward linkages.[45] In the United Kingdom as a whole, in 1991 Japanese-owned firms provided direct employment for about 50,000 workers, or approximately 1 percent of the labor force in manufacturing. The indirect impact of these jobs was further employment of 50,000 to 100,000 workers. The total amounted to between 2 and 3 percent of all workers in manufacturing. These figures would seem to be minor except for the fact that Japanese manufacturing employment is concentrated within the key industries of electronics and motor vehicles.[46]

Japanese labor-management and production practices, as well as substitution of capital for labor, contributed to the dramatic improvement in British statistics for real value added per person in manufacturing during the 1980s. However, this should not disguise the fact that in absolute terms, having started from a low base, Britain's labor productivity is still low. Moreover, British labor is no longer cheap. Between 1980 and 1990, real wages rose by 42 percent in the United Kingdom. Including wage and nonwage costs, in 1991 British labor was receiving about $25 an hour, not much different from the cost of labor in France, Italy, Japan, or the United States.

Unfortunately, evaluation of the strategy, performance, and impact of Japan's FDI in Britain is hampered by the lack of official statistics on many of its dimensions. Such as they are, moreover, as mentioned above, British and Japanese statistics on Japan's FDI are not comparable. Data from trade or industry associations, such as the Society of Motor Manufacturers and Traders, fill in some of the gaps. There are no published government statistics, however, on the output of Japanese affiliates in Britain, broken down by type of commodity, by year. There are no statistics from either the Japanese or British governments on the commodity composition, value, and destination by country of exports—and similarly by country of origin for imports—resulting from Japan's FDI in Britain. According to the DTI, the British government does not compile separate reports from Japanese affiliates because it would be unwarranted to "treat them differently" from other foreign firms incorporated in Britain. Statistics are also lacking on the source of finance, by country, of Japan's FDI. This is difficult to track because much of it is arranged by foreign affiliates themselves rather than by parent companies in Japan. Often it is the purpose of such financing to deliberately conceal the nationality of the parent company. Even within Japan, the extent to which FDI has been financed by Japanese government agencies, such as the Export-Import Bank of Japan, is not public information.

Where Do We Go From Here?

The Prospect for Japan: A Scenario

"Restructuring" is a term often used as a euphemism for firing workers. It is more than that, however. Collectively, the following are a large component of the problem of restructuring Japan's overseas economy. First is the quintessentially Japanese problem of maintaining central control in an increasingly dense and diversified global network. Second is the politicization of Japan's economic relations within the European Community. Third is the problem of managing the complex transition between the sophisticated key industries of today and the supersophisticated key industries of tomorrow.

The organization of central decision-making in Japan is very much the story of the *sogo shosha* (general trading companies), whose name belies the extent of their diverse activities and enormous range of competence. At the close of the Occupation, the *sogo shosha* were chiefly importers of raw materials and exporters of finished products. Since then their evolution and structural change has paralleled that of the Japanese economy at large. They have become giant conglomerates involved in every sector of Japanese production, distribution, finance, and R&D. Together with their affiliated banks, they serve as eyes and ears, as well as operating partners, of the *keiretsu* that dominate Japan's economy. Their capability for performance depends on their raw business power—scale, diversity, and access to capital—but ultimately even more on their management and organizational competence and their information resources. Among these, information is provided by their field offices throughout the world, to which leading *sogo shosha* have instantaneous access by satellite communication.

Referring to these ingredients of central control, the president of a leading *sogo shosha* has described Japan's system for coordinating its MNEs: "At present," he said, "virtually all important decisions in connection with Japanese companies in Europe are taken in Japan. This is in sharp contrast to the policy of American companies in Europe."[47]

In the early days, when they were small, the *sogo shosha* developed their management style in terms of intimate relationships and personal networking. Formal tables of organization did not reveal the informal structure of function, responsibility, or power. In the headquarters, however, everyone knew what everyone else could do and what they were doing. The system has survived to the present day. Given a large and multiskilled management pool, such a system has advantages. Ad hoc task forces can be quickly mobilized to respond to any emergency that may arise. As coordinators, generalists have more expertise than specialists. However, this is not a system of "lean management." It is lavish and expensive in its use of personnel. As *sogo shosha* activities became more geographically and industrially diverse, the question of where to draw the line between central and local decision-making authority became more acute.

The *sogo shosha* have been flexible in coping with this problem. Notably, they have preserved their traditional system of management based on informal personal relationships and networking. The system retains a matrix arrangement with separate managers in charge of geographical regions and product groups. The chief innovation, however, is the establishment by major *sogo shosha* of subordinate management companies with regional jurisdiction. In the Mitsubishi organization, one of these subordinate headquarters is Mitsubishi Euro-Africa S.A., with offices in London. This is a company with control over both the regional and the product managers. Mitsubishi Euro-Africa is subordinate only to Mitsubishi Shoji, the top corporate headquarters in Tokyo. Its authority includes control of seven operating companies in its region, which in turn control 45 local offices in Europe and Africa. As a management company, it provides guidance, support, and strategic recommendations to the operating companies, but it is not responsible for sales or profits. The personnel of Mitsubishi Euro-Africa are veterans of diverse assignments throughout the world and within the Mitsubishi organization.

They are intimately acquainted with each other and with their colleagues in Tokyo, as well as with networks of colleagues in Mitsubishi offices throughout the world. The key element that makes the system workable, however, is that the chairman of Mitsubishi Euro-Africa is a senior managing director of Mitsubishi Shoji, the parent headquarters company in Tokyo. It is acknowledged by Mitsubishi Euro-Africa that without his presence in London, the management company would collapse.

A second difficulty concerns the increasing politicization of Japan's economic relations within the EC. On this score, a typical sequence of events suggests a scenario for Japan's strategy in seeking entry into markets that are already well supplied. As described above in the case of Britain's consumer electronics industry, the sequence begins with export dumping by Japan. If the industry in the target market is viable (which was not the case in Britain), Japan's trade partner may respond with severe anti-dumping regulations. At this point, the economics have already been politicized. Next, to overcome the anti-dumping regulations and to consolidate market share gained by previous dumping, Japan would respond with direct investment in the form of screwdriver plants. These would create excess productive capacity in the FDI host country and *domestic* dumping sustained by Japanese investment in losses. Host-country competitors would then receive assistance from their government in the form of comprehensive local content regulations. In the EC, local content demands by France and Italy have forced Japanese motor vehicle transplants in Britain to rely largely on British component suppliers. As described above, however, these are far from world-class in quality. They fail to meet the standards of Japan's lean production system and pose a threat to its competitive lead within the European Community. Furthermore, the FDI host country's retaliation may be imposed in a discriminatory manner. The host country may not enforce its rules equitably on all foreign producers. For example, it may allow non-Japanese firms to offer products containing a smaller proportion of local content than those of the Japanese. Moreover, discriminatory EC protectionism against Japan may favor competitive auto manufacturers who can procure superior components from Japan or from Japanese affiliates located in the United States. In sum, EC governments are intent upon helping their indigenous firms to catch up with the Japanese before they have become unassailable in EC markets.

Increasing politicization of Japan's economic relations implies that EC will be pushed into becoming a deeper—rather than wider—economic area in resisting Japan's adversarial advance. A deeper and more integrated EC could be protectionist. For this reason, the possibility of political integration within EC fills the Japanese with dread. It would have the further consequence of encouraging incipient regionalism and managed trade within the United States, which sees American firms being pushed out of EC markets by Japan. Even worse, EC and the United States could learn from each other in repelling Japan's exports and "economic colonialism." Japan would be forced back into a region of its own in East and Southeast Asia.

These apprehensions seem to have evoked some changes in Japanese policy. For political as well as for economic reasons (the post-bubble cost of capital has risen and its availability has declined), Japanese MNEs consider greenfield entry into the EC very expensive. Therefore, many of them have established positions in the EC by means of mergers and takeovers rather than by building new operations.[48] It is less politicizing to coopt the competitor than to (directly) drive him out of business.

Evidence of a change in policy concerning the deliberate construction of excess capacity for market entry by means of dumping is suggested by Isuzu's recent decision to stop manufacturing passenger cars and Nissan's announcing in February 1993 the closing of its plant at Zama in Kanagawa prefecture. In a further attempt to calm troubled waters, Takashi Ishihara, chairman of Nissan, made an interesting remark. In an interview, he said, "We have to *introduce* fair and open competition [emphasis added]."[49]

Politics may be pro- as well as anti-Japan. A new symbiosis may be implied by the visit of Germany's Chancellor Helmut Kohl to Tokyo for several days of talks in February 1993. The talks had clear overtones for Britain as well as for the next stage of Japan's industrial transition in Europe. Britain's fear that Japan might transfer its allegiance and its European headquarters to Germany is well founded. Germany is a better location than Britain for observing European business trends. Its workforce is more highly skilled than that of Britain. Germany is the most important nation within EC and would be a much more powerful ally for Japan than Britain. Its political favor would also be of prime help to Japan in future relations with Eastern Europe and in opening the way for the strategic alliances that will be fundamental in the next generation of super-high-tech industries.

The third restructuring problem of interest here concerns management of the transition between the sophisticated industries of today and the super-sophisticated high-tech industries of tomorrow. Japan has already developed three generations of industrial structure since World War II. It began the postwar period with emphasis on traditional labor-intensive, low-tech industries. Then it developed heavy and chemical industries. In the third generation these were superseded by high-tech industries on the knowledge frontier. In the fourth generation, Japan's strategy is *not* to break its way into markets already occupied by others, but rather to create new markets and establish large market shares. In the information field, the price of creating the industries of the future will be immense, and very likely potential competitors will be few. On Japan's part there might be no need to fight for market share, because only a few competitors will determine market shares and prices by collusive agreement. At the same time, the industries of the third generation of industrial structure will have matured and the market share gained by Japan's previous investment in losses will be producing profits.

Japan's future course will not lie exclusively in the domain of super-sophisticated products. It is already advancing in sectors such as advertising, retail industries, and service industries. As it diversifies its FDI in these sectors, however, it may find that it does less well in industries that are less homogeneous than autos and electronics, and less well in countries that are institutionally and culturally less congenial than Britain. As Japan branches out from manufacturing to industries that require non-Japanese networking, there may be frustrations in store. As one Japanese official remarked, "In manufacturing, you can show the worker a manual. We have no manual for networking."

The Prospect for Britain: A Challenge

In the spirit of whistling in the dark, a British bureaucrat remarked, "In Britain, there have been no complaints against Japan—as yet." This is not quite correct; moreover it ignores strong feelings of ambivalence and apprehension that lie below the surface in Britain.

At the official level, the first criticism of Japan occurred in March 1992, when Sony was accused of practicing transfer pricing as a means of tax avoidance. (Tax evasion was not mentioned.) In the private sector, at the annual convention of the Trades Union Congress in September 1991, a resolution was passed condemning what was described as the "alien approach" of Japanese companies in Britain. Their industrial relations system was described as "feudal." (Some of the constituent unions of the TUC opposed this resolution.)

Unexpressed ambivalence is more pervasive. It begins with the memory of how in the 1970s Japan's exports helped break the back of Britain's consumer electronics industry, which paved the way for the arrival of its FDI. When Japanese affiliates were established, they became members of British trade associations, in some cases forming a majority of the membership. By 1982, for example, Japanese firms were a majority among the members of BREMA. This is significant because, in contrast with the United States, there is no direct lobbying with legislators in Britain. Instead of personal approaches to Parliament, political pressure is applied by trade associations and professional groups such as BREMA and the Confederation of British Industry (CBI). In these organizations, Japan's substantial business lobby is conspicuous. In some cases the Japanese lobby is enthusiastically welcomed, in others it is abhorred. Within the SMMT (Society of Motor Manufacturers and Traders), for example, there are two classes of membership, component makers and car manufacturers. The component makers are delighted with the Japanese; the car makers dread their presence.

A profound source of ambivalence lies in the question, is it desirable that Japan should control key sectors of the British economy? Paradoxically, this is combined with apprehension that it may not choose to do so. Will Britain be bypassed in the process of Japan's transition from one set of key industries to another? Will Britain be left behind in a high-tech Europe? Will Britain eventually find itself in the worst of both worlds—abandoned by Japan and moldering in another misconceived industrial policy of its own?

As mentioned above, the Japanese have reservations about Britain both as a regional headquarters and as a location for high-tech production. One Japanese manager remarked, "You have to be on the continent in order to feel the pulse of change. In Britain you don't get the rhythm of European affairs." Thus there is a trend among EC transnational enterprises in favor of placing regional headquarters elsewhere than in Britain. Nissan, the most advanced and visible automaker in Europe, has set up its regional headquarters in Amsterdam. Toyota has its regional headquarters in Brussels. Mazda's regional headquarters for design and engineering is in Germany; its distribution management is in Belgium; it manufactures in Britain. Sony's regional headquarters is in Germany. GM, in 1986, decided to set up its European headquarters in Zurich. However, some headquarters remain in Britain. Toshiba's European headquarters is in London. Honda's European headquarters is likewise in England, at Reading. Ford, which depends heavily on the British market, has its headquarters at Brentwood, near London.

Britain is likewise threatened at the plant level. In inviting the entry of Japan's FDI, Britain's chief desiderata were an increase in employment, improvement in the trade balance, and the introduction of new technology. Japanese affiliates have contributed in each category—but these contributions have been pasted on at the top of a weak economy. They have not created self-sustaining growth within Britain. With regard to employment, for example, the leading principle of Japanese management has not been grasped. That principle has nothing to do with extracting a maximum from the workforce as it exists. Rather than "management procedures," it is *development* of the workforce through training and delegation of decision-making authority that promotes self-sustaining growth. The fundamental ingredient of reindustrialization, which Britain must supply on its own, is infrastructure for education, training, and R&D. In the absence of such infrastructure, Britain cannot absorb the lessons of Japan's experience or fully utilize the contributions of its technology transfer. To date, for example, according to Daniel Jones, the U.K. motor components industry has achieved average productivity levels of less than half its Japanese counterpart.

There are two apparently contrary arguments about skill requirements in Japanese manufacturing, both of which, paradoxically, have adverse implications for the employment spinoff of Japan's FDI in Britain. The first argument asserts that the industries most typical of Japan's FDI are increasingly footloose. These include "automobiles, electronics and electric appliances, office equipment, precision instruments, and machine tools."[50] According to the authority cited, to a significant degree the application of micro-electronic technology in these industries "emancipates them from dependence on a skillful and loyal workforce" and has increased the exportability of Japanese techniques. Consequently, "Japanese industries have become fundamentally footloose for the first time in their history." This argument suggests that the rising role of footloose industries in Japan's overseas economy will substantially increase the need for unskilled rather than for skilled workers in Britain. Even if true, however, the argument is offset by the fact that at present there is great competition in Europe for the capture of internationally mobile projects. Every country is trying to attract them. Their efforts are supported by MITI, which has advised Japanese investors to diversify the location of their FDI away from Britain. To the extent that this occurs, the prospect for employment of Britain's unskilled workers would not be improved.

Concerning the need for unskilled workers, the "lean-production" paradigm is contrary to the footloose-industry concept. Lean production portends the elimination of unskilled workers. This paradigm applies not only to automobile production where it originated but to other industries as well; thus its relevance is economy-wide. According to the paradigm, "As lean production replaces mass production . . . many jobs will disappear . . . [L]ean production displaces armies of mass-production workers who by the nature of this system have no skills and no place to go."[51]

Apart from the employment-generating potentiality of Japan's FDI, there is foreboding in Britain that it is indeed footloose. The chief indicator that prompts this feeling is the lack of significant Japanese R&D activity in Britain. Foreign investors who perform no R&D in a host country may not be committed to its economy and may eventually exit. According to a "List of Japanese Research and Development Companies in the United Kingdom" prepared by the Invest in Britain Bureau of the DTI, there were only seventeen Japanese research and development companies in the United Kingdom as of February 1992. In substance, according to a British authority, they are merely "window dressing." Likewise, a member of a Japanese research institute in London said that Japanese research agencies in Britain do no real research; they are created mainly as listening posts for their parent headquarters in Japan.

In the long run, Britain cannot rely merely on technology transfer; it must develop its own technology. Such as it is, moreover, technology transferred from Japan is largely concerned with *how* to produce (process technology) rather than *what* to produce (product technology). In any event, process technology is largely in the public domain—organization of assembly lines, methods of labor-management relations, and the like. Product technology, based on proprietary R&D, refers to the design of products and the development of new products. In a firm, control of product technology is intrinsic to control of management. Control, however, is precisely what Japanese firms are reluctant to share. Japanese design and development of sophisticated key components, for example, is performed almost exclusively in Japan. The result, according to a 1991 study of the consumer electronics industry commissioned by the DTI, is that these items are produced and available only from Japan or from Japanese affiliates abroad. The study showed that Japanese manufacturers in the United Kingdom bought only 15 percent of their electronic components from local suppliers. Local content in electronics reported by some Japanese companies consists largely of packing material, pressings and moldings, and mechanical parts.

Above all, Britain's greatest stake is in persuading indigenous U.K. firms to perform more R&D. In his 1991 presidential address to the British Association, Sir Denis Rooke reported that over the preceding forty years, economic growth in Britain was about the same as in the Soviet Union. He attributed this to "the cultural bias against industry which has long pervaded Britain" and the neglect of R&D it has induced. In urging U.K. companies to carry out more R&D, Sir Denis said, "This is an area where the United Kingdom is currently very weak; not only do the United States and Japan have a much greater scale of R&D financed by industry but so too do countries like Holland, Belgium and Sweden, as well as Germany and Switzerland."[52] According to a U.K. government-sponsored survey, 1991 statistics show that in every industrial sector, U.K. outlay on R&D is relatively low as compared with that of the United States, Germany, and Japan. This is the case "even [in] those few where Britain is, or has been, supposedly strong, such as chemicals and aerospace."[53]

On the frontiers of modern R&D, especially in the field of information technology (including semiconductors, computing, consumer electronics, and telecommunications), a new and daunting prospect confronts the United Kingdom. Information technology, following steam and electricity, is the bridgehead of the third industrial revolution. By the year 2000, industries in the information-technology field will be the largest in the world. The costs of development and the costs of building plants for manufacture of new products will be so great that no single firm, however large, will be able to afford the size and risk of the expenditure required. In each new generation of high-technology information products, the cost of R&D approximately doubles. It will cost over $1 billion for R&D and at least $1 billion more to build a manufacturing plant for the 256-megabit dynamic random access memory (DRAM) chip that may be developed by the turn of the century.

To share these expenses and risks, giant firms, including ostensible competitors, are already forming strategic alliances across national borders. In July 1992, IBM of the United States, Siemens of Germany, and Toshiba of Japan announced their alliance to develop and produce the 256-megabit chip.[54] In assessing the impact of these alliances, it should be noted that the technology required for production of the 256-DRAM microchip may be used for the production of other types of semiconductor chips as well. These will play a powerful role in other industries. Anticipated downstream spinoff and thus downstream control is central to the rationale of Japan's industrial policy.[55]

British R&D is not meeting this challenge. In the meantime, Japan's contribution to employment and export performance has been welcomed with rejoicing by the British government. Prospects in the high-technology information field, however, are seen with dismay by private observers. They anticipate that a cartel of three or four consortia, including Japan but excluding Britain, will eventually dominate information technology throughout the world. In the short run, it appears that the balance of benefits arising from Japan's industrial policy on the international plane may be somewhat in Britain's favor. In the long run, the prospect is problematical.

Notes

1. See Leon Hollerman, "The Headquarters Nation," *The National Interest,* No. 25, Fall 1991.
2. In Germany the national tax rate on undistributed corporate profits is 50 percent; in addition there is a local profits tax of 20.05 percent.
3. "[S]ince the early 1980s, labour costs in the United Kingdom were higher than in

France, Italy and the Netherlands, but below those in Japan, Germany and about [the same as] those in Belgium and the United States." OECD, *Economic Surveys,United Kingdom,* 1990/1991, p. 105.

4. Bill Emmott, *The Economist*, May 20, 1989.
5. The structural shift from manufacturing to services may be attributed partly to the statistical effect of vertical disaggregation in national enterprises that were privatized during the 1980s. Many activities that had been classified as manufacturing when they were part of a national enterprise were reclassified as services when they were spun off in the form of independent firms.
6. In the United States, manufacturing produced about 20 percent of national output in 1992. In Japan and Germany, manufacturing produced about 30 percent of GNP.
7. Japan's FDI has a good performance record in promoting third-country trade, which is at the core of that strategy. In the United States, for example, Honda (U.S.) is the largest "American" exporter of automobiles.
8. Unofficially, however, there have been clear overtones of industrial policy. For example, "Like Toyota in Derby, Honda was evidently offered its present 360-acre site—complete with an old wartime airfield for test-driving vehicles—at a price which it could not refuse." *Financial Times*, April 16, 1992.
9. The types of British exports that Priority Japan has attempted to promote in Japan include fine chemicals, construction equipment, designing services, semiconductors, financial services, pharmaceuticals, medical equipment, and ceramics.
10. Reuters, December 4, 1991.
11. In 1989, the stock of outward FDI of the United States was $376 billion. That of the United Kingdom was $213 billion. Japan's was $156 billion. United Nations, *World Investment Report,* 1992.
12. See Masaru Yoshitomi, "Foreign Direct Investment in Japan: What Accounts for Its Low Penetration?" Sumitomo-Life Research Institute, *Japanese Direct Investment in Europe* (Aldershot, England: Avebury, 1991).
13. Patrick A. Messerlin and Yoshiyuki Noguchi, "EC Industrial Policy: Worse Than Before," *Financial Times,* October 24, 1991.
14. Jörgen Knorr, president of the European Electronic Component Manufacturers' Association, "D-Ram Dumping Threatens Users Too," *Financial Times,* May 10, 1989.
15. International Monetary Fund, *Balance of Payments Manual.*
16. Affiliates include branches (wholly owned by the parent), subsidiaries (in which parent controls more than half the equity), and associate companies.
17. Sumitomo-Life Research Institute with Masaru Yoshitomi, *Japanese Direct Investment in Europe* (Aldershot, England: Avebury, 1990), p. 94.
18. Ibid., p. 96.
19. J. H. Dunning and J. A. Cantwell, "Japanese Direct Investment in Europe," in B. Burgenmeier and J. L. Mucchielli (eds.), *Multinationals and Europe 1992* (London and New York: Routledge, 1991), p. 158.
20. Keith Geddes and Gordon Bussey, *The Setmakers: A History of the Radio and Television Industry* (London: British Radio and Electronic Equipment Manufacturers' Association, 1991), p. 386.

21. Leon Hollerman, *Japan's Economic Strategy in Brazil: Challenge for the United States* (Lexington, Mass.: D. C. Heath & Company/Lexington Books, 1988).

22. *Nikkei News,* June 1, 1992.

23. Geddes and Bussey, *The Setmakers,* p. 198.

24. Most companies in the electronics sector have since opted for single union deals, mainly with EETPU. Peter Wickens, *The Road to Nissan: Flexibility, Quality, Teamwork* (London: The Macmillan Press, Ltd., 1987), p. 137.

25. Geddes and Bussey, *The Setmakers,* pp. 401–2.

26. Ibid., p. 403.

27. The British motorcycle industry, which until the late 1970s was dominated by indigenous producers, likewise collapsed. It was partly pushed and partly fell. Since 1979, the Japanese Big Four—Honda, Yamaha, Kawasaki, and Suzuki—have engrossed 90 percent of the industry's sales.

28. Data from Japan Automobile Manufacturers' Association, *The Motor Industry of Japan, 1992.*

29. Forecast by Ian Robertson, *Japan's Motor Industry: A Perspective on the Future,* Economist Intelligence Unit, Special Report No. 2200, May 1992.

30. Society of Motor Manufacturers & Traders, Ltd.

31. Forecast by Del Barrett at a meeting of the West Midlands Development Agency, April 15, 1992.

32. *Financial Times,* September 20, 1990, p. xiv.

33. European component manufacturers, including Robert Bosch of Germany and Valeo of France, have set up U.K. subsidiaries for the purpose of learning to improve their performance to the level of those suppliers who serve the Japanese.

34. Andersen Consulting, *The Lean Enterprise Benchmarking Project* (London), 1993. The project was performed jointly by Andersen Consulting, the Cardiff Business School, and the University of Cambridge. Participants in the project included Daniel Jones, coauthor of *The Machine That Changed the World* (1991) and Nick Oliver, coauthor of *The Japanisation of British Industry* (1988).

35. In another study, an IBM Consulting Group examined 202 manufacturing sites throughout the United Kingdom. Plants were rated on performance characteristics including lean production, quality of output, logistics, and manufacturing systems. The study concluded that only 2 percent of British factories are world-class. Britain's best performance was found in food manufacturing. Auto and aerospace components were found to be the worst. Professor Chris Voss of the London Business School was coauthor of the study. *Financial Times,* June 10, 1993.

36. *The Economist,* "A Survey of Britain," October 24, 1992, p. 12.

37. The Economist Intelligence Unit, *The European Automotive Components Industry,* Special Report 2107, December 1991.

38. Italy limited imports from Japan to no more than 3,500 cars annually. Complex rules in Portugal and Spain limited car imports from Japan to about 2 percent of their domestic markets. Since 1975, incidentally, Britain itself has had a VER arrangement with Japan that limits its share to no more than 11 percent of the British auto market.

39. In 1984, the local content of autos sold in the United Kingdom by Ford was 46

percent; the local content of General Motors autos was 22 percent. In these cases, however, local content was defined with reference to value added in the United Kingdom, not in the EC region as a whole. Allan Webster and John H. Dunning (eds.), *Structural Change in the World Economy* (London: Routledge, 1990), p. 176.

40. In describing the compromise as an "informal arrangement," EC intended to avoid conflict with GATT concerning the illegality of discriminatory bilateral deals.

41. Kevin Done, *Financial Times,* September 23, 1991.

42. Central Statistical Office, *Key Data,* 1991/92 edition. The deficit in manufactures increased every year from 1983 through 1989.

43. In the United States, *"The net impact of FDI on U.S. employment is approximately zero"* (italics in the original). Edward M. Graham and Paul R. Krugman, *Foreign Direct Investment in the United States* (Washington: Institute for International Economics, 1991), second edition, p. 61.

44. Nomura Research Institute, "Can the Japanese Eliminate the U.K. Trade Deficit?" October 1991.

45. "Toyota in Derbyshire: An Impact Study," prepared by the Research and Intelligence Unit, County Director's Department, Derbyshire County Council, September 1990.

46. Walter Eltis and Douglas Fraser, "The Contribution of Japanese Industrial Success to Britain and to Europe," National Westminster Bank *Quarterly Review,* November 1992.

47. Address by Tomio Tatsuno, president, Marubeni Corporation, "The European Market After 1992: Japanese Companies' Response to Unification," Tokyo, December 24, 1991.

48. During 1989–1991, Japanese M&A activity in the United Kingdom involved 102 cases with a total value of $5,582.1 million. Data from Daiwa Securities Company, May 26, 1992.

49. *Financial Times*, June 18, 1990.

50. Takashi Kiuchi, Managing Director, LTCB and F&C Investment Management Co., Ltd., "Europe and the United Kingdom: The Views of Japanese Investors," an address to the Cranfield Management Association International Conference, April 1991.

51. James P. Womack, Daniel T. Jones, and Daniel Roos, *The Machine That Changed the World* (New York: HarperCollins, 1991), pp. 235-36.

52. *Financial Times,* August 27, 1991.

53. *Financial Times,* October 9, 1992. Data from Company Reporting.

54. Other existing microchip partnerships include Toshiba-Motorola, Hitachi-Texas Instruments, Fujitsu-Advanced Micro Devices, Mitsubishi-AT&T, Oki-Hewlett Packard, and Sharp-Intel.

55. Collaboration between Japan's government and private sector in the promotion of these developments was announced in December 1992 when MITI inaugurated an "atomic-level manipulation technology" project, including plans to spend $208 million by 2001. The government money will be spent on a consortium including Hitachi, Toshiba, NEC, and Nippon Steel.

CHAPTER 3

Japanese Investment in Mexico
A New Industrial Nexus?

Terutomo Ozawa and Clark W. Reynolds

The first recorded contact between Mexico and Japan took place in 1609, when a ship bound for New Spain (Mexico) from the Philippines lost its bearings and was shipwrecked off the coast of Japan. The Mexican sailors on board were rescued and later given a new ship by a prominent Japanese lord. In 1613, Japan sent its first ambassador to Mexico, and in 1892 a treaty of friendship, trade, and navigation was signed between the two countries.[1] Except for such isolated historical events, economic relationships between the two countries remained relatively insignificant until after World War II. Since then, however, Mexico has played a modest but increasing role within the Japanese framework of world economic integration. With the passage of NAFTA, Mexico is now positioned to become a more significant component of Japan's expanding trade and production system.

Until now, Japan's economic relationship with Latin America has been most extensively cultivated with Brazil, especially through the medium of foreign direct investment (FDI) in manufacturing, notwithstanding Brazil's much greater distance from Japan. The more prominent position of Brazil is due to its relatively large size as a market, abundant and underutilized natural resource endowments, major production capabilities, and a large number of descendants of Japanese settlers who maintain personal and institutional ties with Japan and help to reduce the "familiarity gap" between the two countries. Panama is another key host economy for Japanese multinationals, notably in shipping, finance, and commerce. To date it has a larger number of Japanese overseas ventures than Mexico. When one includes financial services, the Cayman Islands and Bahamas have also received much more Japanese investment in both value and number of ventures than has Mexico. Insofar as manufacturing investment is concerned, however, Mexico at present stands second only to Brazil as a Latin American host country for Japanese FDI. As its economy integrates with those of the United States and Canada, while remaining open to the international economy, Mexico offers new possibilities for Japanese investment at all levels of trade and production.[2]

In what follows, we take a bird's-eye view of the post-World War II evolution of Japanese FDI in Latin America, and examine how Mexico stands as a host country relative to other Latin American countries. With this regionwide picture as a background, we then proceed to focus on Mexico, asking how and why Japanese industry has been attracted to that country as a site for overseas business activities. For this purpose, the push factors associated with the different phases of Japan's rapid structural transformation since the early 1950s are briefly described in order to see how they were matched by the pull factors on the part of Mexico, given the vicissitudes through which its economy has passed and its changing relationship with its regional partners. This chapter develops a rent-seeking approach to direct investment in the Americas in order to better explain and differentiate the Japanese role in that process. Finally, we assess the impact of Japanese multinationals' operations on Mexico, especially in the current phase of Japan's industrial upgrading and the evolution of its transnational activities.

Japan as Investor in Latin America and the Caribbean

As of 1990 the world's three major economic centers (United States, Europe, and Japan) had invested in Latin America and the Caribbean a total of $35.4 billion in direct investment (not including financial flows to offshore centers), of which $16.5 billion came from the United States, $14.9 billion from Europe,[3] and $4.0 billion from Japan, according to statistics prepared in 1993 by the Inter-American Development Bank (IDB) and the Institute for European-Latin American Relations (IRELA) (table 3.1).

The United Nations Economic Commission for Latin America and the Caribbean (ECLAC) provides comparable data, indicating that for the period 1980 through 1990 total Japanese investment flows to the five major

TABLE 3.1
OVERSEAS INVESTMENT FLOWS TO LATIN AMERICA AND THE CARIBBEAN, 1979–1990 ($US billion)

	1979–1982			1983–1986			1987–1990		
	Non-offshore investment (largely FDI)	*Offshore investment (largely financial)*	*Total overseas investment*	*Non-offshore investment*	*Offshore investment*	*Total overseas investment*	*Non-offshore investment*	*Offshore investment*	*Total overseas investment*
Europe	5,097	1,197	6,291	3,506	3,357	6,863	6,314	7,516	13,830
United States	8,524	5,732	14,256	–415	4,066	3,651	8,412	6,354	14,766
Japan	2,058	1,189	3,247	555	5,633	6,188	1,364	12,908	14,272
Total	15,679	8,115	23,794	3,646	13,056	16,702	16,090	26,778	42,868

	1979–1990		
	Non-offshore investment	*Offshore investment*	*Total overseas investment*
Europe	14,917	12,067	26,984
United States	16,521	16,152	32,673
Japan	3,977	19,730	23,707
Total	35,415	47,949	83,364

SOURCE: Inter-American Development Bank (IDB) Special Office in Europe (SOE)/Institute for European-Latin American Relations (IRELA) (1993), *Foreign Direct Investment in Latin America and the Caribbean: An Overview of Flows from Europe, Japan, and the United States, 1979–1990*, (Madrid/Paris: IRELA), p. 34.

countries of Latin America (Argentina, Brazil, Chile, Mexico, and Venezuela) amounted to $4.3 billion.[4] An additional flow of Japanese investment to tax havens over the same period in the amount of $26.6 billion led to a total amount of direct and indirect (financial) investment in Latin America of almost $31 billion during the 1980s (table 3.2).

Japanese Direct Investment in Latin America

The evidence from table 3.1 indicates that Japan's onshore investment flow to Latin America in the 1980s (for the most part corresponding to the more conventional definition of direct investment) was about one-quarter that of the United States. Japan's share stood at 11.2 percent for the 1979–1990 period as a whole, though the figure was somewhat higher in the earlier subperiods (13.1 percent for 1979–1982 and 15.2 percent for 1983–1986). The decline in the Japanese share during the course of the decade reflected a relatively much greater increase in investment of both European and American firms in comparison with their Japanese counterparts.

The attraction of Latin America for FDI has increased in recent years, as economies have progressively opened their markets, reducing obstacles to foreign ownership and increasing scope for the remittance of profits and the protection of intellectual property. However, past political problems and the perception, if not the reality, of potential instability continue to hinder Japanese FDI. In addition an all-important familiarity gap still exists for many Japanese investors in Latin America, vis-a-vis other regions such as Asia and the Pacific, North America, and Europe (the United Kingdom in particular). The one exception is Brazil, where a large community descended from Japanese settlers has gained experience working within the system over many years. Such considerations were of particular importance during past decades of import-substituting-industrialization, with its imposition of import barriers, subsidies, special preferences, and other privileges, since the securing of protection depended importantly on private contacts and political connections based on close ties with decision-making elites.

In the years before the liberalization, privatization, and increased attention to competitiveness of the mid-1980s, firms from Europe and the United States had a distinct advantage over those from Japan. The Japanese lack of experience in the region and unfamiliarity with its culture forced its investors to depend almost exclusively on compatriot trading companies for information and contacts about markets that were not readily accessible. The trading companies (information merchants) served as organizers of FDI and

TABLE 3.2

JAPANESE FOREIGN DIRECT INVESTMENT ($US million)

	1980	1981	1982	1983	1984	1985	1986	1987	1988	1989	1990
EC	527	698	774	932	1,680	1,725	3,250	6,211	8,277	13,799	13,177
France	83	54	102	93	117	67	152	330	463	1,136	1,257
Germany	110	116	194	117	245	172	210	403	409	1,083	1,242
Belgium/Luxemburg	77	211	191	391	386	384	1,142	1,834	821	979	591
Holland	41	138	73	313	452	613	651	829	2,359	4,547	2,744
United Kingdom	186	110	176	153	318	375	984	2,473	3,956	5,239	6,806
Spain	22	39	19	52	140	91	86	283	161	501	320
Italy	8	28	19	13	22	23	25	59	108	314	217
Other OECD	1,624	2,583	2,984	2,738	3,773	5,555	10,532	15,581	22,781	34,299	27,852
Canada	112	187	167	136	184	100	276	653	626	1,362	1,064
United States	1,484	2,329	2,738	2,565	3,360	5,395	10,165	14,704	21,701	32,640	26,128
Switzerland	28	67	79	37	229	60	91	224	454	397	660
Latin America/Caribbean	588	1,181	1,503	1,878	2,290	2,616	4,737	4,816	6,128	5,238	3,628
Argentina	7	9	10	2		2	6	15	24	3	213
Brazil	117	170	166	113	159	135	101	229	310	349	616
Chile	14	7	1	8	0.4	10	25	7	46	47	30
Mexico	329	212	66	4	36	79	146	28	87	36	168
Peru	2.7	7.1	4.5	2.8	2.4	2.1	2.1	-1.2	-9.4	0.1	0.1
Venezuela	1	61	2		-29	1	15	3	51	75	77
Financial havens	117	715	1,254	1,748	2,121	2,387	4,443	4,535	5,435	4,728	2,525
Middle East	158	96	124	175	4,273	45	44	62	259	66	88
East and S.E. Asia	1,188	3,338	1,384	1,847	1,628	1,638	2,327	4,868	5,569	8,238	7,053
Africa	139	573	489	364	326	172	309	272	653	671	551
Total FDI	4,222	8,447	7,258	7,934	13,970	11,548	21,199	31,810	43,667	62,311	52,289

SOURCE: Arahuetes, Alfredo (1993), "Relaciones Comerciales y Flujos de Inversion Directa entre España y America Latina en el Periodo 1980–1990" (Draft doctoral disseration Ch. III), Fundacion CEDEAL, Madrid.

helped to establish joint ventures with their affiliated compatriot firms. To-day, as Latin American economies open, and conditions facing newcomers improve, the region is gradually beginning to attract a wider range of inves-tors interested in new sources of supply and nontraditional markets. Venezu-ela, Argentina, and Chile—in addition to Brazil and Mexico—have been at-tracting Japanese FDI most recently, though the amounts invested remain relatively modest. For example, in 1991 Venezuela obtained Japanese FDI worth $102 million, Mexico $193 million, Brazil $171 million, Argentina $40 million, and Chile $75 million.[5]

In Venezuela, where foreign investment is again welcome in resource extraction, the Japanese trading companies Mitsui, Mitsubishi, C. Itoh, and Marubeni have recently become active in oil exploration and development. Toyota also expanded its Venezuelan assembly operations. In Argentina, Japa-nese banks engaged in debt-swaps to become shareholders in the newly privatized national telephone company ENTEL, and Japanese corporations invested in hotel construction, food processing, electric appliance manufac-turing, and real estate. In Chile, both Sumitomo and Mitsubishi groups in-vested in copper mining, and other Japanese firms became involved in for-estry development and salmon farming More developments in 1991 included an expansion of a joint auto-assembly venture by minority owners Toyota and Mitsui. In Colombia, there was a similar expansion of a joint auto-as-sembly project with Mazda and Sumitomo as minority owners in response to Andean Group trade liberalization. (These moves by Toyota and Mazda may also reflect strategic decisions to counteract the export drive of Nissan Mexicana, which will be described later.)

Along with these manufacturing activities, financial investments on the mainland of Latin America are increasing. The stock exchanges of Mexico and Argentina were approved in 1990 and 1992, respectively, by the Japan Securities Traders' Association as recommended overseas stock exchanges for Japanese securities trading. In short, Japanese investors are still cautious about the region, moving slowly and watching to see the effect of NAFTA on trade and investment prospects, along with the degree of success of other integration schemes and liberalization efforts including the G-3 (Colombia, Venezuela, and Mexico), Chilean accession to NAFTA, and developments in the Caribbean Basin and the Southern Cone.

Offshore Investment of Japan in the Caribbean

With regard to reported investment flows to offshore financial centers in Latin America, Japan was the top investor for the 1979–1990 period as a whole (table 3.1). Interestingly, the United States ranked first for the 1979–1982 subperiod, but was taken over by Japan from 1983–1986 and by both Japan and Europe for the 1987–1990 subperiod. The major offshore centers are Panama, the Cayman Islands, the Bahamas, and Bermuda.[6] According to Japan's official statistics, over the 1951–1989 period a total of $36,855 million (inclusive of investment in offshore financial centers) was invested by Japanese firms in the form of 6,858 investments throughout Latin America. Of this amount, Panama received $14,902 million with 1,051 investments; the Cayman Islands, $6,743 million with 6,743 investments; Brazil, $5,946 million with 1,446 investments; the Bahamas, $3,338 million with 106 investments; Mexico, $1,707 million with 260 investments; Bermuda, $1,219 million with 119 investments; and other countries, $3,000 million with 1,051 investments.[7]

Despite slow progress in direct investment onshore, why has Japan so suddenly achieved the status of the largest investor in Latin America's offshore financial centers, and what does this imply for future direct investment in the hemisphere? We will address this issue later in terms of Japan's structural paradigm of overseas investment as it attempts to recycle a huge trade surplus, find markets for an overhang of domestic savings, remove restrictions on finance, and provide a place for financial services as part of its overseas direct investment.

Further Patterns in the Recent Evolution of Japanese Investment

Another differentiating feature of Japan's direct investment in Latin America, as distinct from its European and American counterparts, is a much greater degree of fluctuation throughout the 1979–1990 period (figure 3.1). The status of Japan as a newcomer to the game of FDI, particularly in Latin America, is no doubt one important explanatory variable. Europe and the United States had long had both extensive and deep involvement in the Americas, which was a host region for European immigrants (and their former colonies), a major source of natural resources, and a key market for the United States and Europe. With a large accumulated stock of direct investment and well estab-

FIGURE 3.1

FOREIGN DIRECT INVESTMENT TO LATIN AMERICA AND THE CARIBBEAN

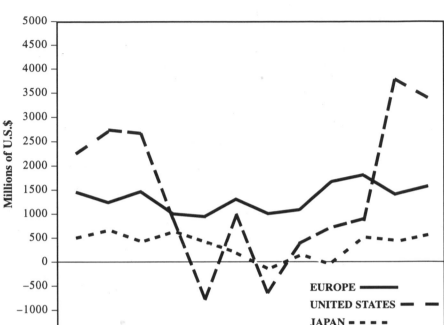

NOTES: Europe comprises Belgium, France, Germany, Italy, and the Netherlands, Spain, and
the United Kingdom. Flows to offshore centers and unallocated or unspecified
flows are excluded.

lished business relations throughout Latin America, the investments of the
United States and Europe in the region during the 1979–1990 period were
additive and incremental, whereas Japan's investments were a relatively new
experience. Even so, the observed intertemporal variability is perhaps too
large to be dismissed in such sweeping terms. Why did Japan's FDI in Latin
America fluctuate so widely, while European and U.S. investments exhibited a more stable pattern? The reason may lie in Japan's own economic
conditions, both internal and external, to be explored in the next section of
this chapter.

Looking specifically at Mexico as a host country, the IDB/IRELA report
describes the recent trend of FDI as follows:

Mexico has seen the most dynamic growth in foreign investment flows in

Latin America and the Caribbean. From 1987 to 1990, FDI from Europe, the United States and Japan rose *eight-fold* over the preceding four-year period: rising from $630 million to $5.1 billion. Much of the total entered Mexico in the latter part of this period: FDI inflows in 1990 alone were $2.4 billion. . . . Mexico received $3.6 billion in FDI during 1991. Around 67% of the total [came] from the United States, 20% from Europe and [only] 2% from Japan. . . .

. . . Total FDI stock in Mexico stood at just under $34 billion by end-1991. As is to be expected, the United States accounted for by far the largest share (63%). European countries provided a total of 24%, led by Germany (6%), the United Kingdom (5.9%), France (4.3%) and Switzerland (4.2%). Japan's participation amounted to 4.5%. By the end of 1991, slightly over half of total FDI stock was concentrated in industry and more than a third in services. Indeed, since 1988, the services sector has surpassed industry as the main destination for fresh FDI inflows.

In recent years, the climate for foreign investment has become increasingly favorable. This is due to the success of [the] Salinas Administration in stabilizing and radically deregulating the economy. The previously restrictive foreign investment legislation was liberalized in 1989. Certain sectors of the Mexican economy were opened up to FDI. These included the commercial banks (up to 30% ownership), insurance (up to 49%) and secondary petrochemicals (up to 40%). Foreign capital remains excluded from many parts of the economy, which are either a legal state monopoly (oil/gas extraction and basic petrochemicals) or limited to Mexican nationals (the media, gas distribution, forestry, etc.).

The North American Free Trade Agreement (NAFTA), signed on August 12, 1992 between the United States, Canada and Mexico, is expected to consolidate the current attractiveness of Mexico for FDI. Obviously, the NAFTA must first be ratified in all three member states. [*This took place in November 1993—ed. note*] Preliminary estimates indicate that foreign direct investment flows into Mexico during the first six months of 1992 exceeded $5.5 billion, significantly above the previous year. (Figures from Mexican Ministry of Trade and Industrial Development (SECOFI), as cited in IRELA (1993), pp. 14–15.)

Therefore the Japanese industrial presence in Mexico, viewed in terms of the total amount of inward FDI, is relatively insignificant (only 4.5%). Mexico is no South Korea or Thailand, in which Japanese multinationals are the leading players, accounting for as much as 45 and no less than 32 percent of total inward FDI, respectively. Mexico's internal FDI pattern thus far indicates a strong North American and Atlantic, rather than Pacific, orientation in its industrial linkups with foreign multinationals. There is still a huge familiarity gap across the Pacific between Japan and Mexico. Furthermore, Japan has been distracted from Mexico largely because of its ever-deepening involvement with the growing Asian Pacific region, and especially China, the next century's second-largest economy in the world. Yet as will be detailed below, Japan's impact on particular industrial sectors in Mexico, such as automobiles and consumer electronics, is already significant.

Push-and-Pull Factors: Japan's FDI as an Agent of Its Industrial Structural Transformation—and Mexico as a Host

Toward a Theory of FDI as Directly Productive Rent-Seeking Applied to Japanese FDI in Mexico and the Americas

Our analysis of Japanese FDI in the Americas is an effort to link microeconomic decision-making at the level of firm and industry to the interaction of market forces and government policies in both Japan and host countries during a time of sweeping international change. A rent-seeking approach of adjustment of decision-making from unproductive to productive investment, albeit general in nature, is shown to be particularly applicable to recent changes in Mexican and Latin American economic policy. These economies are in transition from regimes dominated by protected markets and state direction, with considerable barriers to entry, to ones favoring liberalization, privatization, and international opening. Our approach helps to explain why Japan's relative unfamiliarity with the region, even in recent years (with the exception of Brazil), has led to higher transaction costs and a more risk-averse response to the pull factors of protection and special privileges than those with a longer history in the region, leading to a lower and more fluctuating pattern of FDI than that of the United States or Western Europe. Our approach also suggests that as Mexico and other Latin American countries open their markets to the potential of international trade and technology, Japanese enterprise may well have a competitive edge. The new outlook for the Americas will favor those who depend less on privileged contacts, state protection, and financial subsidies and more on secure access to financial capital at competitive rates, managerial know-how, technical training, familiarity with the rapidly expanding markets of North America and the Pacific Rim, and proven innovative capability.

Since direct investment represents an entrepreneurial response to opportunities to earn profits over and above a normal return on capital, suitably discounted for risk and transaction costs, the policy environment affecting such opportunities matters importantly. We shall term such transitional profits *economic quasi rents* to facilitate their comparison with the various forms of rent-seeking application to Mexico and the Americas. Capital seeks economic quasi rents, whatever their source, reflecting market conditions, the social and institutional environment (including the organization of firm and industry) and policy regimes facing investors. The outcome of investment decision-making in terms of efficiency and equity may be positive or negative, productive or unproductive, dynamizing or favoring monopolistic and monopsonistic stagnation, depending on the relationship between market forces and the institutional and policy environment, subject always to consideration of private wants and the public interest.

One of the most fundamental sources of investment opportunities, especially in the first stages of economic development, represents the return on natural resources (*resource rents*). Resource rent-seeking is characteristic of investment in economies favored by nature and the adaptation of technology for raw material and primary product production, causing them to open to the international market. Since the Colonial period, the economies of the Western Hemisphere have been heavily dependent on resource rents and even today many depend on natural resources for important areas of comparative advantage. Japanese direct investment in Mexico and the Americas has been attracted by the search for resource rents and for secure sources of supply of raw materials and primary products not competitively available domestically. Resource-abundant economies face unusual challenges as well as opportunities, given the fact that part of their returns to investment reflect a natural bounty (return to naturally scarce factors of production such as mineral deposits, soil, climate, and location over and above the opportunity cost of labor, capital, technology, and other variable inputs.) These resource rents may be used for either productive or unproductive investment, consumption, or transfer payments motivated by political and other institutional factors. In such an economy there is the temptation to create barriers to exchange that protect certain sectors, institutions, and income groups. These have been identified by Anne Krueger and others as the result of directly unproductive rent-seeking (Krueger, 1974; Colander, 1984, protection rents).

In the area of international trade and investment, protection rents are created by tariff and nontariff barriers. Unfortunately in Latin America they have all too often arisen as a result of "import-substituting-industrialization" (ISI) policies and political favoritism, at the expense of competitive enterprise. In such cases, domestic and foreign investors (including U.S., Japanese, and other OECD interests) have taken advantage of such protective barriers through inward-looking investments within the countries. However, with hemispheric liberalization such protectionist measures have been curtailed, and policy now favors market-induced investment designed to compete in the international market. This has hurt the old ISI activities while creating new opportunities for productive profit-seeking. Hence today's investment in Mexico and much of the Americas pursues profits from trade as market barriers are reduced (*market penetration rents*) and from product and process innovations (*innovation rents*), and superior forms of institutional organization (*organizational quasi rents*), which characterize much of today's Japanese FDI.

As labor markets tighten, workers gain opportunities to share with capital in the rent-seeking process, earning returns to education, skill formation, and intellectual property. Rents that arise from the penetration of new markets and from product and process innovations and improved organizational forms are transitory. Schumpeter has shown that, unlike resource rents and other returns to factors that are in naturally inelastic supply, such abnormal profits ("rewards of entrepreneurship," in his nomenclature) may be expected to disappear through the normal process of competition. Hence it is necessary for productive rent-seeking to be flexible, always looking for new opportunities, since competition (itself spurred by the pursuit of rents from trade and investment flows) will eventually eliminate such transitional returns, at least in the absence of new protective measures. The imposition of new barriers to entry (although beneficial to innovation in the case of reasonable intellectual property rights) may lead from innovation rents to directly unproductive protection rents (in the case of unduly extended patents and copyrights). In short, productive rent-seeking is the dynamic of economic growth and development (Reynolds, 1989), just as unproductive rent-seeking can slow and distort growth.

In this chapter we argue that in the course of its domestic development and international expansion, Japanese direct investment (as well as that of any other country) has been a "rent-seeker," sometimes pursuing policies that have favored less productive import-substituting activities, but largely productive, as part of the diffusion of international development. Perhaps the most distinctive aspect of Japan's postwar FDI has been its responsiveness to market forces, often complemented by policies that appear to have "pushed" activities out of Japan both as a preparation for and as a consequence of the remarkable upgrading of Japanese industrial structure and its ever-rising international competitiveness.[8] Japan's FDI and trade with Latin America, and Mexico in particular, have reflected the changing structural requirements of Japanese industry. In other words, FDI and other forms of international business have been a critical instrument of Japan's economic developmental process, initially catching up with the more advanced industrial countries, but more recently representing "head-to-head" competition for leadership.[9]

Combined with factors specific to structural change in Japan, Japanese FDI in Mexico has also been sensitive to changing conditions in the host economy, including state-supported import-substituting industrialization before the oil discoveries of the 1970s and accelerating during the "oil boom" from 1978 to 1981; a dramatic reduction in the role of the state favoring structural adjustment, privatization, and debt renegotiation after the "crisis of 1982"; and stabilization, liberalization, and international opening in recent years, culminating in NAFTA. As a result, Mexico has participated with the rest of Latin America in six types of Japanese overseas investment that have been generated so far, coming in waves *pari passu* with the sequential industrial metamorphoses at home. This investment has been successively (1) *trade-supporting*, (2) *resource-seeking*, (3) *low-cost-labor-seeking*, (4) *trade-conflict-avoiding-assembly-transplanting* (which more recently also involves the *components-procurement* type of investment),[10] (5) *surplus-recycling*, and (6) *strategic networking*. In all cases there has been a tendency for the ex post appearance of a strategy to be consistent with ex ante profit expectations. However, as we shall see, for Latin America in general and Mexico in particular such expectations have not always been fulfilled, especially when sharp changes in public policy have given rise to a reversal of the fortunes of such ventures. There has been a correspondence between the sequential shifts in Japan's industrial structure and trade competitiveness, on the one hand, and its overseas investment activities, on the other, and conditions in host countries (pull factors) have played an important accompanying role, sometimes reinforcing and sometimes working against the push factors.

The Structural Transformation of the Japanese Economy after World War II

The Japanese economy has been characterized as passing through three historical stages before and since World War II, and is now seen to have entered a fourth industrial era (Ozawa, 1993). The sequence of development was from (1) the initial base in which labor and capital were applied to natural resources, (2) industries based on physical capital and scale economies, (3) industries based on scale and scope economies with product differentiation, and (4) industries based on innovative human capital. The first stage was represented by resource exporting and/or light manufacturing (e.g., textiles and sundries); the second, by heavy and chemical industries (steel, cement, glass, chemicals, etc.); the third, by components-intensive, assembly-based industries (automobiles and electronic goods); and the fourth, by high-technology industries (computers and software, innovative materials, biotechnology, etc.). The six types of investment that were described above have roughly corresponded with the stages of industrial transformation of the Japanese economy—but in all cases the actual decisions to invest depended on incentives in terms of profit (or rent-seeking) as presented at the outset. From a behavioral point of view, the stages approach to industrial structure, and the types of investment described above, take on their significance as they are reflected in the profit expectations of investors.

In the initial postwar period there was a replication of earlier development of Phases I (labor-driven industrialization) and II (modernization of heavy and chemical industries).[11] Japan had much catching-up to do, even in the conventional manufacturing sector, and was in no position to climb immediately to any higher phase. War-devastated Japan was initially labor-abundant and capital-scarce and had to export whatever it could manufacture competitively with its most abundant factor, labor, to earn scarce foreign exchange. In the early postwar stages, Japan's FDI was strictly limited to the *trade-supporting* type, mainly overseas investments by general trading companies for the purpose of restoring the prewar networks of commercial (sales/procurement) outposts.[12] As will be detailed below, Mexico then saw the arrival of only a handful of trade-supportive investments from Japan.

In the meantime, the modernization of heavy industries and chemicals in Japan's Phase II industrialization compelled resource-scarce Japan to seek stable sources of industrial raw materials and fuels abroad. This resulted in the *resource-seeking* type of FDI. In anticipation of an increased need to import industrial raw materials, Japanese industry, actively assisted by the Japanese government both financially and diplomatically, had actually begun to make resource-seeking overseas investments as early as the late 1950s.

The two oil crises of the 1970s, however, impelled Japanese industry and government to adopt in earnest an aggressive two-pronged policy for (1) securing Japan's own supply bases of overseas resources and (2) transforming its industrial structure away from resource/energy intensity into one that was more knowledge-based, with higher value-added. The structural need of

Japan to secure overseas resources coincided with the emergence of Mexico as a major oil supplier. Suddenly Japan's resource diplomacy began to be directed at Mexico. Both Japanese industry and government offered so-called "national projects" for implementation as close cooperative enterprises. This was the first time that Japan's industrial contact and presence became significantly noticeable in Mexico, particularly at the beginning of the 1980s, although the value and number of its investment ventures there remained comparatively insignificant.

As Phase I, closely followed by Phase II, successfully progressed, the very nature of labor-driven growth and capital intensification in Japan's industrial structure, successful as it was, led to upward pressure on wages and even labor shortages. It was against this background that the third wave of Japanese FDI (the *low-wage, labor-seeking* type) took place, during which Japan's low-wage-dependent light manufacturing sector (e.g., standardized textiles and sundries) began to migrate to neighboring Asian countries, notably Taiwan, Hong Kong, Singapore, and South Korea. Not only were Mexican wages higher than those prevailing in Asia, but transaction costs—economic, cultural, and psychological—for investing in Mexico were too high for the majority of Japanese firms starting out as novice multinationals.

The social costs of chemicals and other heavy industries increasingly aroused public concern in Japan.[13] In addition, the first oil crisis of 1974 and the subsequent resource nationalism revealed Japan's vulnerability to its resource dependency. Japanese investors were compelled to shift their industrial structure away from heavy and chemical industries to less pollution-prone, higher value-added, assembly-type industries. Automobiles and consumer electronics thus emerged as more attractive sectors for development. What emerged was the well-known story of how Japanese companies such as Toyota, Nissan, Honda, Sony, and Matsushita succeeded in innovating and implementing the techniques of so-called "lean" or "flexible" manufacturing, which dramatically improved their competitive position in world trade. (The actual and potential impacts of this Japanese-originated new industrial paradigm on Mexican industry are explored in the final section of this chapter.)

Ironically, the more successful Japan's trade-based strategy was at both the national and corporate levels, the greater the political and economic pressure to shift from trade to overseas production through FDI. These pressures intensified when Japanese industry succeeded in transforming itself into a Phase-III structure, in which the "components-dependent, assembly-based" industries, notably automobiles and consumer electronics, emerged decisively as the dominant sectors both in industrial production and exports. Japanese

FDI first began to exert a modest impact on Mexican industry when Phase III (assembly-based industrialization) progressed and deepened in Japan and some techniques and institutional arrangements of Japanese-brand flexible manufacturing started to be applied in Mexico, not only by Japanese multinationals but also by U.S. firms—often acting in collaboration.

Japanese Transformation and Recycling Investment Flows Abroad

The success of Japanese export-led growth pursuing the stages of transformation described above was associated with a large and steadily rising trade surplus. In part the surplus reflected an international balancing mechanism in which Japan's relatively high rate of domestic savings helped to offset lower rates of saving (including fiscal deficits) in its OECD partners (including the United States). The resulting imbalances between domestic absorption (aggregate demand) and production (aggregate supply) led to a demand for capital account transfers from Japan, which were offset in real terms by its current account surplus. As Japan's trade surplus swelled throughout the 1980s, a transfer problem arose, necessitating the recycling of foreign financial assets. This gave rise to considerable cross-border financial activities, leading to huge outflows of capital, especially to the United States, which increasingly found it necessary to finance its burgeoning federal deficit with money borrowed from overseas.

A theoretical argument that reconciles the use of debt finance to level equity investment, in order to concentrate the "excess profits" (or quasi rents as we have called such transitional profits) in the hands of ownership of the enterprise, was presented in a path-breaking 1960 MIT thesis by Stephen H. Hymer, *The International Operations of National Firms: A Study of Direct Foreign Investment* (MIT Press, 1976). The argument is that since debt capital can be obtained at a "normal" rate of interest, reflecting competitive financial markets, additional returns (quasi rents) can be retained by equity holders through the use of financial capital as much as possible. In this regard, Japanese (and other) FDI would be expected to take full advantage of the international liquidity available during times of "transfer problems," such as those induced by Japan's significant trade surplus in the 1980s, to permit the greatest possible concentrating of rents in the hands of equity investors.

Part of this "recycling" money entered Mexico as commercial bank loans, making Japan Mexico's number-two creditor by the 1980s. However, in the Mexican case, especially after the 1982 debt crisis, the funding from Japan

represented a shift from private-sector to public-sector commercial bank lending and increased government loans. For Mexico, as with most of Latin
America, the debt crisis of the 1980s happened to coincide with Japan's period of recycling-based FDI. As a result, the region did not receive a proportional share of the explosive increase in financial investment from Japan
during those years as did the United States and other regions. In fact, Japanese private-sector commercial bank claims on Mexico actually fell from
1982 to 1990, while the public sector commercial bank claims provided an
offsetting increase through 1988 (see table 3.3).

It was during the phase of debt restructuring after 1982 that some Japanese multinationals, including Nissan Motor Co., were actively involved
in debt-equity swap deals with debt-ridden Mexico and other developing
countries.

The New Phase of Japanese Strategic Networking Investments

The latest phase of Japan's overseas business operations, associated with the
most recent stage of industrial upgrading (the growth of innovative human-
capital-intensive industries), is most strongly characterized by the *strategic
networking* type of multinational business activities. Such a shift is especially evident in joint research and development, product development, and
marketing. Up to now, however, there has been relatively little of this type of
networking activity between Japanese multinationals and Mexican interests.

TABLE 3.3

JAPANESE PRIVATE AND PUBLIC LOANS TO MEXICO:
COMMERCIAL BANK CLAIMS ($US billion)

	Public sector	*Private sector*	*Total*
1982	8.1	19.1	27.2
1985	10.7	16.7	27.4
1988	15.3	7	22.3
1990	13.4	5.5	18.9

SOURCE: Export-Import Bank of Japan and Mexico's Ministry of Finance as presented in Szekely,
Gabriel (1993), "Japanese Investment in Mexico," Table 2; paper presented for conference,
*Integrating the World Economy: Japanese Direct Investment During the Late Twentieth
Century,* Hoover Institution and Japan-U.S. Friendship Commission..

Strategic networking relationships are at present more pronounced among Japanese multinationals and their Western counterparts—notably the United States—that operate in Mexico, especially in the automobile sector. With the successful entry of Mexico into NAFTA, new networking relations are likely to be more actively pursued between Japanese and Mexican business interests.

Both the industrial and regional focuses of Japan's FDI have shifted, reflecting the postwar stages of Japan's structural upgrading and its changing trade requirements. The *trade-supporting* type of FDI was globally scattered, as Japanese industry first endeavored to regain its former export markets and then to capture new ones. For obvious reasons, the *resource-seeking* type of FDI was centered on the resource-abundant countries in Latin America, Asia, North America, and the Middle East. The *labor-seeking* type of FDI was initially most intensively clustered in East Asia, but later extended to Southeast Asia—and currently to China. Initially, North America and then Europe hosted the *assembly-transplanting (trade-conflict-avoiding)* type of Japanese manufacturing FDI. In addition to financing the United States' federal deficit, the *surplus-recycling* type of investment in banking and finance motivated to earn higher rates of return on Japan's excess savings was headed to the world's financial centers, notably London and New York, as well as to the so-called offshore financial centers including those in the Caribbean.[14]

Phases of Japanese FDI in Mexico

The Period Before the First Oil Crisis: Mexico as a Host Country in the Americas and Resource-Access-Based Investment

Although Japan's overseas investment in Latin America has been on the wane as a proportion of its total global investment (for example, a mere 8 percent in 1991), the region early played a relatively more important role as a host for Japanese ventures, especially in resource extraction and manufacturing. For example, for the period of 1951–1970 (Japan's early stages of FDI involving the resource-seeking and the trade-supporting types), Latin America received 28.4 percent of Japanese manufacturing investments (amounting to $273.7 million), next to 34.7 percent for Asia ($334.3 million), while North America attracted 24.9 percent ($239.4 million), Oceania 5.2 percent ($49.7 million), and Europe only 3.8 percent ($36.6 million).[15]

One major reason for the attraction of Latin America for Japan's early FDI was the relative abundance of mineral resources, notably copper, lead, zinc, and iron ore. Despite the paucity of capital at home, Japanese industry was encouraged—in terms of subsidies—by its government to secure the supply sources of industrial minerals abroad for which it expected an increasing need as resource-intensive heavy and chemical industries (Phase II industrialization) were promoted as part of Japan's industrial policy.

The ventures established in the region before 1970 included:

- Chacarillia, Bolivia (1959): 100% Japanese-funded (via a loan) by Nitto Metal Mining to develop a copper mine

- Cia-Mirerde Atacama Ltd., Chile (1959): 100% Japanese-owned by Mitsubishi Metal Mining and Mitsubishi Corporation to extract iron ore

- Compania Minera Candesiable S.A., Peru (1963): 100% Japanese-owned by Japan Mining Co. and Mitsui Bussan to develop copper mines

- Compania Minera Santa Luisa S.A., Peru (1964): 100% Japanese-owned mining company (by Mitsui Metal Mining, 70%, and Mitsui Bussan, 30%), to extract copper, lead, and zinc ores

- Minas de Cobre de Chapi S.A., Peru (1964): 100% Japanese-owned by Japan's Overseas Mineral Resources Development Corporation to explore and develop copper mines

- Compania Frinro Santa Lucia S.A., Peru (1966): 100% Japanese-owned by Mitsui Metals to mine lead and zinc ores

In addition, Japanese investment was aimed at securing wool and marine products. For example, in 1957 Taiyo Argentina S.A. was established in Argentina by Taiyo Fishery to engage in squid and shrimp fishing (initially, an annual catch of 5,000 tons). Also in Argentina, Nihonkeori Argentina S.A. was set up in 1956 by Nippon Woolen Spinning, C. Itoh (trading company), and Kanematsu Kosho (trading company) for making woolen yarns.

The early arrivals of Japanese ventures in Latin America were thus clearly focused on natural resources and they were normally wholly owned by Japanese interests. In addition to direct investment (equity ownership), Japanese investors extended a large number of loans to the local suppliers of resources to be used for the purpose of raising output for shipment to Japan. The latter form of approach may be described as the "lend-and-import" formula; the former, the "invest-and-import" formula; both were designed to secure overseas resources to be shipped back to Japan. For example, during the 1950s and 1960s, Latin America hosted fifteen "invest-and-import" ventures in mining with equity ownership totaling $4.3 million and nineteen "lend-and-import" ventures with loans worth $83.2 million in total.[16]

Throughout the 1950s and 1960s (that is, prior to the oil crises of the 1970s), however, Mexico had not been looked at by Japanese industry as a potential supplier of natural resources. In other words, the *resource-seeking* type of investment was completely absent. Although Japan was importing silver from Mexico, the silver mines had been already well developed and, furthermore, Mexico did not allow any foreign ownership of its natural resources (with the exception of salt, as will be described below). The attraction, if any, of Mexico in those days lay in a relatively large internal market, which was heavily protected under its import-substitution policy. *Protection rent* was thus the major attraction for foreign multinationals. Moreover, such rent was magnified because during the 1950s and 1960s the Mexican economy remarkably grew at annual growth rates of almost 7 percent.

Therefore, as might well have been predicted by the paradigm of Japan's postwar overseas investment set forth in the previous section, the very first investment was the *trade-supporting* type made by a Japanese general trading company, Marubeni Corporation, in 1950 with a total capital of $200,000 to set up a locally incorporated venture, Marubeni de Mexico. Other general trading companies also moved into Mexico in a similar manner; C. Itoh de Mexico S.A. (1955) by C. Itoh with a capital of $3.1 million, Bussan Mexico S.A. (1956) by Mitsui Bussan with a capital of $113,000, Mitsubishi de Mexico S.A. (1964) by Mitsubishi Corporation with a capital of $80,000. Four of Japan's then top-ten general trading companies thus had made advances by the early 1970s. As can be easily surmised from the very small amounts of capital invested—even by then international standards—to set up these trade-supporting type of ventures, they were initially meant to restore as much as feasible the prewar networks of information-gathering and marketing outposts in order to facilitate trade between Mexico and Japan—as well as between Mexico and third countries.

In addition to the general trading companies, Japan's major manufacturers established sales offices and limited local productive facilities targeted mostly on the Mexican markets. For the 1951–1970 period, however, only fourteen such ventures were opened in Mexico. They are:

- Ajinomoto de Mexico S.A. (initial capital of $48,000 in 1968), a soda-making venture majority-owned by Ajinomoto

- Fibras Acrilicas S.A. ($1.6 million in 1967), a minority-owned joint venture (15.6%) of Asahi Kasei to produce acrylic fiber; Ciapaperia Kino

Cia ($60,000 in 1962), a venture 84%-owned by C. Itoh and Kyokuto Notes to produce stationery goods

- Kyoritsu de Mexico S.A. ($52,000 in 1964), a sales/service office 77%-owned by Kyoritsu Farm Equipment and Mitsui Bussan to market farm equipment; Rimsa Saginomiya S.A. ($159,000 in 1969), a refrigerator-parts-making venture 49%-owned by Saginomiya Works

- Suntory de Mexico S.A. ($159,000 in 1963), a whisky-making/sales venture 40%-owned by Suntory; Citizen de Mexico S.A. ($800,000 in 1968), a wristwatch-making/sales venture 49%-owned by Citizen Tokei (Timepiece)

- Laboratories Takeda de Mexico S.A. ($450,000 in 1961), a pharmaceutical manufacturing venture wholly owned by Takeda Pharmaceuticals; Delsa Toshiba S.A. ($450,000 in 1966), a semiconductor manufacturing venture 49%-owned by Tokyo Shibaura Electric

- Nissan Mexicana S.A. ($400,000 in 1961), initially a sales office 100%-owned by Nissan Motor Co. to market its trucks and cars; Yamaha de Mexico S.A. ($160,000 in 1958), an assembly operation of motorcycles and pianos, wholly owned by Yamaha; Industries Rangon Business S.A. ($20,000 in 1968), a calculator-making venture 20%-owned by Nippon Keisanki Hanbai

- Maekawa de Mexico S.A. ($100,000 in 1961), a refrigerator-making venture 49%-owned by Maekawa Seisakusho; and National Mexican S.A. ($480,000 in 1965), a radio/TV-manufacturing venture 49%-owned by Matsushita Electric Industries[17]

Many of these ventures did not last long and were later closed. For example, Ajinomoto de Mexico, Fibras Acrilicas, Laboratorios Takeda, and Ciapaperia Kino Sia pulled out of Mexico. They were actually the ventures set up by those Japanese corporations that had existed in the prewar period; that is, they were in rather conventional manufacturing industries (such as glutamine, acrylic fiber, standardized pharmaceuticals, and office stationery supplies)—relatively low value-added industries (of the "undifferentiated Smithian" type) that would soon be overshadowed in Japan's industrial activity by its new growth industries of the "differentiated Smithian" type, such as automobiles, electronics, and machine tools, which came on stream later.

Nissan Motors, one of the earlier investors, turned out to be an exception. Nissan Mexicana remained in Mexico and began to transform itself into a local assembly operation in the mid-1970s, initially to assemble small trucks, from its original sales office status. It received a special investment loan from Japan's Export-Import Bank when it built the first assembly facilities. Moreover, Nissan—and, for that matter, Japan's automobile industry as a whole—came to gradually develop firm-specific and firm-differentiated *process* technologies in the form of "lean" or "flexible" production. This development quickly endowed Japanese manufacturers with strong ownership-specific advantages, corporate assets that could be appropriated by way of direct overseas production. In other words, not only did Nissan build its unique ownership advantages but Japan later moved into the full-fledged stage of industrialization characterized by the dominance of "components-intensive, assembly-based" industries (Phase III type), as described earlier. The same thing can be said about Yamaha's local production in Mexico. Pianos and motorcycles belonged to the assembly-based industries that grew quickly and became dominant in Japan's industrial structure during the Phase-III economic growth. *Pari passu* with industrial upgrading, Yamaha's operations expanded in the local production of new products such as pianos, outboard motors, and recreational boats.

Interestingly enough, just prior to the first oil crisis of 1974 two resource-based investments were made by Japanese industry in the form of capital participation in existing local enterprises. The first was a salt-making venture in Baja California, Exportadora del Sal S.A. de C.V., in which Mitsubishi Corporation (a general trading company) began to participate in 1973 by acquiring a 49 percent interest. This unique venture was arranged in partnership with the Mexican government, which retained 51 percent. Mitsubishi Corporation as a general trader known for its business acumen in cultivating business connections was clearly motivated to build goodwill with the Mexican government, which then had extensive involvement with state-run enterprises. As a result of this joint venture, salt eventually became Mexico's second most important export to Japan, next to petroleum. The Mitsubishi group also made a successful bid to supply electric machinery and equipment (motors and control devices) for the new subway cars in Mexico City in 1978.

The second investment was a manganese-ore-extracting/alloy-producing enterprise in which Sumitomo Corporation (a general trading company) acquired a minority ownership (5.7%). It is majority-owned by local interests: Autlan S.A. de C.V. (38%), Metlan Trading (13%), and the rest by other local investors. These ventures had actually remained the two largest employers among the Japanese-affiliated enterprises in Mexico—until other big investments were made in the early 1980s by Japanese manufacturers in consumer electronics and automobiles, as will be discussed below. Japan's interest in securing access to Mexican resources by way of investment did not really appear until after Mexico's emergence as a major oil producer and especially until after the second oil crisis of 1979. Japan's significant involvement in Mexico's local manufacturing had not materialized either until after Japan reached the phase of *components-intensive, assembly-based* industrialization and some export-replacing *trade-conflict-avoiding* type of investments began to show up in the Americas.

It should be noted in passing that Brazil as a Latin American host was clearly an exception in terms of Japanese industry's early advances in the local manufacturing sector. Just to cite some major manufacturing investments[18] as early as the 1950s:

- Toyobo do Brasil (cotton textiles): 100%-owned by Toyo Boseki, with an initial capital of $2,420,000 in 1955

- Ishikawajima do Brasil (ships and machinery): 90%-owned by Ishikawajima-Harima, with an initial capital of $14,296,000 in 1956

- Yanmar Diesel Motors Brasil (motors): 95%-owned by Yanmar Diesel, with an initial capital of $2,500,000 in 1957

- Usinas Siderurgicas de Minas Gerais (USIMINAS) (steel): 21%-owned by Nippon USIMINAS (a consortium of Japanese firms) and the rest by the Brazilian government in 1957

- Toyota do Brasil (utility vehicles): 100%-owned by Toyota Motors, with an initial capital of $5 million in 1957

These early Japanese manufacturing ventures in Brazil exhibited two features looked upon at that time as rather exceptional or unusual. First, they were large-scale by then-prevailing Japanese standards; second, they were wholly- or majority-Japanese-owned. Indeed, Brazil was the very first host country for Toyota's overseas investment. Japan had then barely recovered from the war damage and was in the midst of a national struggle to build its own industrial capacity. Why, then, was Japan so much attracted to such a distant country as Brazil and on such a large scale? Although there are several important reasons, it suffices here to point out that at that time Brazil already had become a key export market for Japanese manufactures, notably textiles, and that the future of Brazil looked particularly promising because of its rich endowment of natural resources. Moreover, Brazil's hospitality in accepting a large number of Japanese immigrants in the early postwar years and the presence of prewar Japanese descendants served as a powerful magnet for Japanese investments.[19] Mexico likewise might have attracted a much larger amount of Japanese FDI if it had opened its doors earlier to Japanese immigrants. With a growing familarity of Japanese investors with Latin America as a whole and a shift away from directly unproductive forms of rent-seeking, which required a special knowledge of conditions in the host country, Mexico promises to compensate in the future for this lag.

Japan's Resource-Securing Diplomacy Toward Mexico: The First and Second Oil Crises and Resource-Supply Uncertainty (1970s and Early 1980s)

Mexico's position in its external commercial relations changed suddenly after the first oil crisis of 1973–74—and particularly after the second oil crisis of 1979—because of the discovery of huge oil reserves in the mid-1970s and the industrial world's (particularly the United States') desire to reduce dependence on Middle East oil and import from more friendly oil-producing countries, notably United Kingdom (North Sea oil), Canada, Mexico, and Venezuela. For example, in 1979, Saudi Arabia was America's largest seller, supplying 16 percent of U.S. oil imports, followed by Nigeria (13%), Libya (8%), and Algeria (8%). By 1985, however, Mexico had emerged as America's largest supplier (16%), Canada the second (15%), Venezuela the third (12%), and United Kingdom the fourth (6%).[20]

It was against this background of the increased importance of natural resources, especially oil, during the decade of the 1970s, that Mexico started to subsidize its protected industries with oil revenues—plus the money it borrowed heavily from the multinational banks of the United States, Europe, and Japan. The decade of resource-supply uncertainty was a troublesome period, particularly for resource-scarce economies such as Japan. Having already built up resource-intensive (particularly petroleum-based) heavy and chemical industries, Japan was then desperate to secure the stable supply bases for oil. In particular, it had been largely dependent for the bulk of its oil imports upon on-the-spot market purchases and upon supplies from the Western oil majors. In fact, Japan was once able to purchase oil in ever-growing amounts at relatively advantageous prices.

Lulled into the initial period of oil abundance, which facilitated the rapid development of heavy and chemical industries at home, Japan then became all the more dependent on oil and on imported rather than domestic coal, which had been a major source of energy until about 1960. For example, in 1953, no less than 46.8 percent of Japan's national energy requirements were met by domestic coal, only 6.0 percent by imported coal, and 17.7 percent by oil. Twenty years later, however, the share of domestic coal declined to a minuscule 3.8 percent, that of imported coal nearly doubled to 11.7 percent, and that of oil rose to as much as 77.6 percent.[21] It was against the backdrop of this heightened uncertainty that Japan launched a so-called "resource diplomacy," a resource-securing joint effort pursued by *both* government and industry as an economic diplomatic unit, in which certain types of resource-related projects (for exploration, development, expansion, and their supportive activities) were to be collaboratively organized between the government of a host country as a key partner and a consortium of Japanese companies with the active participation of the Japanese government as a majority investor—and a provider of foreign economic aid.

The Japanese government channels public funds through the Overseas Economic Cooperation Fund (OECF) and the Japanese International Cooperation Agency (JICA), two major aid agencies, as well as through the Export-Import Bank (EXIM) of Japan, which offers concessionary loans. To facilitate this flow of financial assistance, the government encourages the major users of a particular overseas resource to form an investment consortium simultaneously with their affiliated companies, usually along the lines of Japan's industrial groups (the Mitsubishi, the Mitsui, and the Sumitomo groups, etc.)—a practice that would almost surely violate U.S. antitrust regulations if American companies followed suit. The investment by the group (whose membership ranges anywhere from five to more than fifty companies) is designed, among other things, to disperse financial risks, to increase bargaining strength, to internalize business linkages (e.g., newly created demands for plant machinery and equipment, construction workers, etc.) and to make it politically palatable to disperse subsidies. Once a consortium is organized, and once the overseas venture involved is designated as a "national project," the OECF becomes the major shareholder of the Japanese group and often extends long-term loans to its overseas joint ventures.[22] The JICA extends technical assistance (surveys and feasibility studies) and provides loans and grants for the development of natural-resource-related infrastructure in the developing countries. The EXIM Bank of Japan extends to Japanese investors large loans they can use for overseas ventures in three ways: (1) to finance their equity ownership, (2) to provide debt capital, and (3) to finance the export of plants and equipment from Japan to be installed in their ventures. The bank also makes concessionary loans to those overseas ventures organized as national projects.

As for the host countries, resource-extractive ventures have great potential as a vehicle of regional development because they normally require provision of the necessary infrastructure (such as roads, railways, harbor facilities, and communications), which can be used for other industrial activities, and the developing host countries often demand the participation of foreign investors in the development of this necessary infrastructure. It was indeed at the height of Japan's resource diplomacy that Mexico was approached by the Japanese government and industry, acting in unison with an eye to Mexican oil and natural gas in the mid-1970s and especially after the second oil crisis of 1979. In 1979, Japan's powerful *Keidanren* (the Federation of Business Organizations whose membership includes all Japan's major corporations)—powerful in terms of its influence on government industrial policies—sent a special mission (with the representatives from Japan's five leading steel makers) to discuss with the Mexican government the possible ways of extending economic cooperation. Then, on the occasion of Japanese Prime Minister Ohira's visit to Mexico in May 1980, three big national projects were initiated. They were (1) the Large Steel Pipe Project (2) the Iron and Steel Casting and Forging Project and (3) the SICARTSA Steel Works Second-Expansion Project. All these projects were designed to strengthen the capacity of Mexico's steel industry to produce steel products, notably pipes, that were required to transport oil and natural gas to the Pacific coast and store them for shipping.[23]

In November 1980, the Large Steel Pipe Project specifically set up a joint venture, Productora Americana de Tuberia S.A de C.V., with an initial capital of ¥13 billion, 60%-owned by SIDERMEX and NAFINSA and 40%-owned by the Japanese consortium. A new steel mill capable of producing 290,000 tons of large pipes (originally scheduled to start in 1983) was built in a steel mill complex on the Pacific coast. In addition to the equity participation of OECF, Japan's EXIM Bank extended a series of special loans (initially, ¥20 billion).

The Iron and Steel Casting and Forging Project was actually a supplement to the first project. Under this program, a new mill was established at the same location with an annual capacity of two tons each of cast and forged products. The parties involved were exactly identical; SIDERMEX and NAFINSA acquired 67% interest, the Japanese consortium acquired 33% interest (which was in turn 30% owned by OECF), and Japan's EXIM Bank extended special loans worth ¥37.8 billion.

The third project, again supplementary with the first and second, was to modernize the existing SICARTSA Steel Works by expanding its annual capacity of 1,300,000 tons of crude steel to that of 3,300,000 tons. For this purpose, special loans (¥8,889 million for electric furnaces and ¥8,917 million for continuous slab forging) were offered by the Japanese government.

The increasing importance of Mexican oil was well reflected in Japan's rising trade deficit with Mexico in the early 1980s: $595 million in 1982, $1,122 million in 1983, and $1,303 million in 1984.[24] Further, the improved transportation and port facilities on Mexico's Pacific coast were clearly in the interests of both countries.

These national projects did not proceed smoothly, however, after the weakening of the world oil market, subsequent upon the second oil crisis of 1979, which caused a drastic decrease in the Mexican government's revenues. The sharp devaluation of the peso in 1982 and its continued decline in value—plus the rising interest rates in the global financial market—most importantly raised the cost of servicing debts, about $90 billion of external debts Mexico had by then come to accumulate. Hence, the 1982 debt crisis for Mexico. By then, Japan had become Mexico's second-largest creditor (accounting for about 15% of Mexico's total debt) next to the United States (30%)—followed by the United Kingdom (10%).[25] The Japanese official loans given to the national projects (so-called "sovereign loans") were denominated in the Japanese currency, yen, which began to appreciate sharply in 1985 vis-a-vis the dollar, hence against the Mexican currency. This inevitably strained the two countries' relationship.

In the meantime, Japanese commercial banks, which had actively extended loans to Mexico's state-owned enterprises and private industrial groups up until the debt crisis of 1982, often in cooperation with Japan's EXIM Bank in the form of syndicated loans, eventually had to write off as much as $4.3 billion on their loans to Mexico. The collapse of the world oil price and the phenomenal appreciation of the yen (a more than twofold rise against the dollar between 1985 and 1990) gave Japanese industry an unprecedentedly sharp windfall discount for imported oil, abruptly turning the terms of trade in favor of Japan. As a result, the urgency for resource diplomacy evaporated. More fundamentally, by the end of the 1980s Japan had succeeded in transforming its industrial structure away from the resource-intensive, heavy and chemical industries (Phase II growth) into a less energy-intensive, higher value-creating one, in which "components-intensive, assembly-based" (Phase III) industries, notably automobiles and electronic goods, became the dominant industrial sector.

Mexico's Move Toward Export-Promotion and the Maquila Program (mid-1980s onward): Mexico as an "Export Platform" for Japanese FDI

Throughout the 1970s, the Mexican federal government started to use subsidies paid out of oil revenues and money borrowed from abroad to support an inward-looking import-substituting regime, a regime that eventually came to be confronted with the crises of federal budget deficits, arrears in debt servicing, and a worsening inflation. In 1982, Mexico nationalized virtually all commercial banks in order to stem capital flight and speculative investment.

In 1985, President de la Madrid finally began to reverse some of the worst excesses of the past policies by moving away from state control and adopting the market principles to rebuild the Mexican economy (Aspe, 1993). Mexico was admitted into the GATT in 1986 and began to remove import barriers and simultaneously to promote export expansion. "When Carlos Salinas replaced him in 1988, the new PRI-sponsored president continued tearing down the old statist foundations. Thanks to the reforms of de la Madrid and Salinas, more than 80% of the 1,155 state-run Mexican enterprises have been sold, merged, or closed to date. These include Telmex, the national telephone company; Aeromexico and Mexicana, the two national airlines; 18 commercial banks, and extensive holdings in food processing, fishing, automotive products, textiles, petrochemicals, paper products, and construction materials." (Hecht and Morici, 1993, p. 38)

Along with the move toward privatization and deregulation pursued throughout the 1980s, the so-called "maquila program" of free zone assembly plants also saw phenomenal expansion, especially in the latter half of the decade. Although the real origin of the maquila industry is somewhat complicated because of the prior existence of free trade zones along the border with the United States, especially in Tijuana, Baja California Norte, it is generally claimed that in 1964, Campos Salas, Mexican Treasury Secretary, made a tour of the Far East where he witnessed how U.S. manufacturers were creating local employment in labor-intensive manufacturing activities involving the traditional apparel industry as well as the newly booming electronic goods.[26] The latter, in particular, usually used U.S.-made parts and components.

Whatever the true provenance of the maquila, four key factors prodded Mexico to introduce the maquila industry: (1) Mexico's eagerness to create employment (initially for low-skilled manpower), (2) Asian competition that compelled U.S. manufacturers to seek low-wage labor as a way of cutting production costs, (3) U.S. tariff items 806/807 that tax only foreign value-added, and (4) the prior experience with the free trade zones in Mexico. These factors saw their timely convergence in 1965 when the Border Indus-trialization Program was introduced.

The expansion of Mexico's maquila program has gone through three phases.[27] The first phase was from the mid-1960s to the crash of 1973–1974 the second from 1975 to the collapse of the peso in 1982, and the third from 1982 onward. The transitions from the first to the second, and from the sec-ond to the third, were accompanied by the drastic devaluations of the peso to adjust the overvalued status caused by domestic inflation. The first phase ended with militant labor strife, the second with the increasing misalignment of the real value of the peso caused by a lag of devaluation behind inflation. President Lopez Portillo's decision to finally devalue the peso in 1982 and thereafter had a decisive impact on the competitiveness of the maquila in-dustry—in a way to place Mexico in a position as a viable substitute for Asian host economies. As Sklair (1989) incisively observed:

> Before 1982, there was always the feeling that maquila wages were, how-ever inadequately, related to U.S. minimum wages, but after the devalua-tions of 1982, maquila wage rates seemed much more related to those pre-vailing in Asia and other competing offshore sites in the Third World. When the new president, Miguel de la Madrid, widely seen as technocratic and pro-U.S., took office, he continued the peso devaluations, mainly to stimu-late exports to service foreign debt. One immediate effect, of course, was to relieve the wage pressure that the maquilas were finding so intolerable. Mexico was once more competitive. The maquila industry again was saved, and in 1983, the biggest annual rise in maquila employment— almost 24,000 jobs—was recorded. (pp. 66–67)

In other words, through the aggressive use of exchange-rate policy Mexico began, for the first time, to pit itself against low-wage Asian manu-facturers in the race for FDI-sponsored, labor-driven industrialization. Mexico thus presented itself as an alternative location for offshore manufac-turing, relative to low-wage Asian countries. For American multinationals, in particular, the "Mexico-vs.-Asia" option became a serious decision-mak-ing factor in setting up labor-intensive facilities.

Although it is not widely known, Japan was initially the largest "benefi-ciary" of the U.S. tariff provisions 806/807, under which U.S. parts, compo-nents, and materials were imported into Japan and fabricated or processed into finished goods that were in turn exported back to the United States. Throughout the 1960s and the 1970s (until the first sign of the yen's appreciation), Japanese industry was definitely a low-cost processor/fabricator, in terms of real wage rates and real productive efficiency and capacity, far more cost-effective in a wide range of manufacturing activities than Mexican producers. In a sense, it can be said that Japanese industry as a whole served as a maquila for American industry. In fact, in those days some detractors pointed out that Japanese industry was turning into America's subcontractor.

The U.S. provisions 806/807 actually involved three types of trade:[28]

- 806.20: Articles previously exported for *repair or alteration*

- 806.30: Articles previously exported for *processing* and returned to the United States for further processing

- 807.00: Articles previously exported for *assembly* abroad

Repair/processing-based 806 trade has been much smaller, ranging anywhere between 2 and 11 percent of assembly-based 807 trade. What is more, "When the 807 provisions were first enacted, the primary sources of 807 products were developed countries. In 1966, 807 imports from the DCs totaled $829.3 million, over 93 percent of the total for that year. Since then, the DC portion has steadily declined, as LDCs have taken advantage of the 807 provisions in increasing their exports to the United States. . . . By 1983, the LDC share of total 807 trade had risen from less than 7 percent in 1966 to over 44 percent."[29]

In 1983, Japan accounted for as much as 53.1 percent of total 807 imports from developed countries, followed by West Germany (22.7%) and Canada (9.9%), and motor vehicles were responsible for America's 807 imports, especially from Japan, West Germany, and Sweden. "Because of the motor vehicle component, a relatively high proportion of U.S. imports from these three developed countries entered under 807. About 15.6 percent of imports from Japan entered the United States under the 807 provisions. Similarly, 21.3 percent from West Germany and 34.5 percent from Sweden entered the United States under 807. The U.S. component, however, was small since motor vehicles constituted a large percentage of these imports."[30]

It cannot be overemphasized that Japan's 807 exports to the United States were promoted during the very transitional period when Japan's industrial structure shifted from heavy and chemical industrialization (Phase II) to components-intensive, assembly-based industries (Phase III). In its effort to develop the automobile and electronics industries, Japanese industry actively imported not only U.S.-made components, at least initially, but also—and more importantly—U.S. technologies under licenses. For example, in close collaboration with their major assemblers, Japanese auto-parts makers avidly absorbed the latest technologies and made continuous improvements on what they had learned from the West. In fact, the major assemblers and their parts suppliers, in close cooperation with each other, made their own organizational (shop floor- and procurement-related) production innovations that came to constitute the core of Japanese-style flexible manufacturing.

It was toward the end of the second phase of the maquila industry (i.e., the end of the 1970s and in the early 1980s) that Japanese manufacturers in the components-intensive, assembly-based industries, notably automobiles and consumer electronic goods, began to transplant some of their production to Mexico. By then, however, they had already succeeded in cultivating on their own the new techniques of flexible manufacturing (multi-variety, small-lot production) to such an extent that they began to dominate in the world market, causing severe trade frictions. In other words, these Japanese manufacturers started to possess formidable firm-specific, as well as industry-specific, advantages that enabled them to produce competitively even in the high-wage countries such as the United States. Hence Mexico's wages were less of an advantage during the 1970s, until the same techniques began to be transplanted to Mexico as well. For example, by the end of the 1970s all Japan's seven major producers of color TV sets had set up shop (of the *trade-friction-avoiding* type) in the United States (table 3.4).

It was mostly as an *extension* of these investments in the United States that some of those assemblers, having gained experiences with North American production, began to look at Mexico as an additional offshore production site supplementary/complementary to their U.S. operations. In 1979,

TABLE 3.4

JAPANESE PRODUCERS OF COLOR TV SETS

Sony	New investment	San Diego, Calif.	1972
Matsushita Electric Ind.	Acquisition	Franklin Park, Ill.	1974
Sanyo Electric	Acquisition	Forest, Ark.	1977
Mitsubishi Electric	New investment	Los Angeles, Calif.	1978
Toshiba Electric	New investment	Lebanon, Tenn.	1978
Sharp	New investment	Memphis, Tenn.	1979
Hitachi	New investment	Compton, Calif.	1979

Matsushita Electric Corporation of America (Matsushita's wholly owned subsidiary in the United States) built a new plant in Baja California to produce TV chassis to be shipped out to its American color TV plant. This plant was opened in a new and less crowded industrial park, Ciudad Industrial Nueva Tijuana, prepared by the state government to attract more FDI. Matsushita's plant presently employs 1,770 local workers, and is one of the largest Japanese employers in Mexico.

Similarly, Toshiba International Corp. (U.S.A.) followed suit by establishing a TV chassis plant in Chihuahua as a supplier to its U.S. plant. Partly abetted by Matsushita's success in Mexico, Sony also set up a wholly owned venture, Magneticos de Mexico, in Nuevo Laredo, in 1980 to produce audiocassette tapes; it was Sony's very first overseas plant so far as audiocassette tapes are concerned. Hitachi is an exception; as early as 1972 it acquired 30% interest in Television del Distrito Federal, S.A. de C.V. to assemble TV sets—ahead of the opening of its U.S. plant.

In the automobile industry, too, Nissan Mexicana's decision to assemble light trucks and passenger cars in Mexico led to the opening of new plants by its affiliated Japanese suppliers. In 1979, Atsugi Motor Parts Co. (the primary supplier of engine and transmission parts and other auto parts for Nissan Motors) set up a 40%-owned joint venture, Atsugi Mexicana, in Lerma, with the Borg and Beck of America (60%) to produce auto pumps for Nissan Mexicana—and also for GM's and Ford's Mexican plants. Nissan Mexicana itself started to run a new plant in 1983 to produce aluminum engines locally and to ship some of them to its American plant in Tennessee. At about the same time (1982), Yazaki Sogyo, a major Japanese auto-wire-harness maker, set up across-border twin plants—a Mexican plant, Auto Partes y Arneses de Mexico, in Cd. Juarez, Chihuahua, and an American plant, ELCOM Inc., in El Paso, Texas. Later on, Yazaki also opened two more harness plants in Mexico in 1987 and 1988—Axa-Yazaki S.A. de C.V. in Nuevo Leon and Buenaventura Autopartes S.A. de C.V. in Chihuahua. These three Mexican plants of Yazaki's together now employ as many as 7,485 local workers.[31]

Other Japanese suppliers of parts and accessories are also attracted to Mexico's expanding automobile industry. Perfek S.A. De C.V. is a small-scale joint venture 88.7%-owned by Metalsa S.A. and 11.4%-owned by Japan's Miyazu Works and Sumitomo Corp., which was set up in 1988 to produce metallic molds for cars. Japanese makers of air-conditioners, car radios, and car stereos likewise advanced into Mexico. Clarion Co., Japan's top maker of auto audio equipment, opened two minority-owned (40%) plants, Electronica Clarion and Dispositivos de Precision Electronica, in 1984 and 1986, respectively. Sanden International set up a joint venture, Sanden Mexicana, to produce car air-conditioners and parts in 1984.

These Japanese investments, many of which are closely affiliated with their ventures in the United States, clearly marked the beginning of a subregionally focused integrative type of investment by Japanese multinationals. Soon, however, their ventures in the maquila industry, in particular, began to be criticized as a "Trojan horse" designed to camouflage their exports to the United States. Hence, Japanese industrialists became increasingly wary of too large a Mexican presence and cautious about connecting Mexican ventures with the U.S. market.

So far as Japanese investments in maquilas are concerned, they numbered only 14 as recently as 1985, despite the devaluation of 1982. Ever since Mexico began to dismantle trade restrictions and was admitted into GATT in 1986, Mexico has become increasingly attractive to foreign multinational corporations. Many foreign direct investments in recent years have been made in anticipation of the successful conclusion of NAFTA. According to the official statistics of Mexico, its stock of inward FDI expanded 10.4 percent in 1989, 14.0 percent in 1990, and 11.8 percent in 1991. By 1987, Japanese maquilas jumped to 31, 41 in 1990, and 62 as of May 1992. They are mostly in electric/electronic goods and auto parts, and the majority of them are located in Baja California and Chihuahua.

Another example of the trilateral integrative type of foreign investment, though not in manufacturing but in resource-processing activities and targeted not at the U.S. market but at the Japanese market as exports from Mexico, is a joint venture set up by Japan's C. Itoh & Co., a major Japanese trading firm, and Tyson Foods Inc., America's leading chicken-processing firm, and a Mexican firm. The venture was designed to take advantage of high-quality chickens and low-cost labor in Mexico. Basically, Mexico produces chickens and processes them into frozen meat, with the technical expertise of Tyson, and C. Itoh takes charge of marketing in Japan.[32] This type of investment is aimed solely at the Japanese market, a reversal of marketing orientation from Japan's traditional targeting of the North American market. This may be a harbinger of what may be called "a reverse maquila," the *new* form of trilateral economic integration in which Japan plays a role of consumer (demand) as well as that of manufacturer (supply). An argument for the establishment of reverse maquilas in Mexico as intermediaries in the production-sharing between the United States and Japan, as a complement to Japanese FDI that has been accustomed to facilitate flows in the other direction (from Japan to the United States, processing intermediate goods in Mexico), was made by Ozawa and Reynolds (1991). The new post-maquiladora investments that are being made by Japan appear to have that potential, leading to a more complementary and bidirectional interlocking of production-sharing and market-sharing between Japan and NAFTA. In fact, some auto parts and electronic goods also began to be shipped back to Japan.

Japanese FDI and Post-NAFTA Mexico: Trojan Horse or New North American Tiger?

The Challenge of Japanese FDI Under "Open Regionalism"

With the passage of NAFTA, two fundamental questions arise regarding the role of Japanese FDI in Mexico. The first is whether such investment will respond to new regional preferences (such as somewhat higher local-content requirements in the auto sector—as opposed to electronics, where NAFTA negotiations led to greater external liberalization), locating within Mexico to take advantage of special preferences favoring those within the North American market. For some this might be interpreted as a Japanese "Trojan horse" strategy, by which Mexico becomes a base of operations for Japan to take advantage of existing competitiveness by setting up activities within the region. A different and more realistic view, given the relatively open character of NAFTA as a "GATT-plus" agreement, is that Japanese FDI in Mexico could be expected to increase as a natural response to market forces, in order to take advantage of new "market penetration rents" available to capital willing to participate in the integration of the North American market. From the latter viewpoint, any investor should be able to have the same benefits as Japan (or for that matter the United States and Canada and Mexico), making the Trojan horse an inappropriate metaphor for the free operation of competitive markets—in which convergence in productivity, profits, and wages will result from the flow of new investment.

The second question is related to the first—will the incentivation of Japanese FDI in Mexico, as a result of NAFTA and regional market-completion, improve the productivity and competitiveness of the Mexican economy, possibly creating a new "tiger" in North America that would increase its own, as well as regionwide, competitiveness in the global market, following the pattern associated with Japanese FDI in the Asian NICs? The tiger effect also challenges producers in competition with the new Mexican activities (fueled by Japanese FDI), as would the Trojan horse effect, but the former refers more to the legitimate growth of *Mexican* competitiveness under a liberalized trade regime, whereas the latter refers to potentially improper *Japanese* utilization of implicit NAFTA preferences to increase its own competitive edge.

Both issues have important implications for both Mexico and its North American partners as well as for Japan and other third countries. To understand the problem, it is necessary to revert to the model of progressive rent-seeking referred to in the earlier sections of this chapter, in order to determine whether Mexico, within the framework of NAFTA, offers equal opportunity to all comers, including Japanese investors, to earn transitional (above normal) profits reflecting *resource rents, market penetration rents,* and *innovation rents,* and to benefit from Japanese institutionally specific *organizational quasi-rents,* for activities within the new North American framework, or whether that framework will give rise to *protection rents* (from directly unproductive rent-seeking) by the creation of regional market shelters.

A "closed regionalism" approach to NAFTA would lead to trade and investment diversion, with adverse consequences for more efficient suppliers outside the region. Such an approach to the formation of new blocs might be countered by Trojan-horse strategies of Japanese and other foreign investors, as opposed to North American investors who would be in a favored position to reap protection rents. The answer to the Trojan horse question depends upon the strategy of the NAFTA laws and institutions and whether they represent "closed" or "open" regionalism. The results of the agreement and its supplements (dealing with labor and the environment) suggest strongly that NAFTA is with few exceptions an open-regionalism agreement combining a reduction in internal barriers among the three signatories with increased external liberalization. An open-regionalism approach focuses on the reduction of transaction costs through regional cooperation (including removal of barriers to transport and communications and improved information about the regional market as well as greater freedom of exchange of goods, services, and factors of production) that improve the competitiveness of the region's comparative advantage-based industries vis-a-vis the rest of the world than before. Hence an open-regionalism strategy is consistent with GATT (GATT-plus) and favors increased global liberalization and trade creation.[33] (The appearance of "trade diversion" under the open-regionalism approach is in fact the result of trade pursuing more competitive regional avenues rather than a loss of efficiency through higher levels of external rather than internal protection.) Open regionalism by this definition is very different from more traditional closed-regionalism approaches (employed in practice in earlier decades and described in customs union theory), which widened national market shelters by combining internal liberalization with increased external barriers, giving rise to trade and investment diversion as well as creation.[34]

Why Mexico's Dynamic Comparative Advantage Is Not Based on Cheap Labor

Although Mexico is usually depicted as a low-wage country, the dollar value of its wage rates (unadjusted for productivity) is currently much higher than, say, that in Thailand, Indonesia, or the Philippines—not to mention China—and may even be higher than that in Malaysia, which has recently risen very rapidly. True, all the Asian NICs (Hong Kong, Singapore, Taiwan, and South Korea) presently have higher wages than does Mexico, but back in the 1960s when they first took off, they offered much lower-wage labor. The successful labor-driven, export-oriented policies pursued by the Asian NICs inevitably drove their wages up by increasing the demand for labor, raising the standard of living, widening the scope of the domestic market, and permitting industries to benefit from the home market as well as from exports. The rising incomes, savings, and induced investments subsequently helped shift their economies to higher phases of industrialization. Mexico is in a position to pursue a similar course of development—taking advantage of the initial impetus of exports to the United States, Japan, and other OECD countries as well as with its NIC partners. Its own latent market potential will depend on the gains from productivity diffusing through the work force in the form of rising real wages as the labor market tightens and skill formation accompanies export growth.

Given the diversity of levels of development in which NICs find themselves, it is necessary to consider the particular stage of industrialization Mexico is in, as perceived by potential foreign direct investors. This is particular relevant vis-a-vis Mexico's Asian competitors, to whom Western and Japanese multinationals often turn for offshore manufacturing. Here the stages paradigm for Japan's structural upgrading in the post-World War II period referred to earlier might well apply to Mexico. This sequence essentially describes a longitudinal process through which a developing country can upgrade itself, step by step, from the initial stage of labor-intensive, low-skill-based industrialization to the stage of physical-capital-intensive expansion and finally toward the more advanced stage of human-capital-intensive growth.

As seen in the former policies of Latin America, an inward-looking orientation based on import-substituting industrialization (ISI) was employed in Mexico in an attempt to bring about and even accelerate the transformation that might normally have been expected to occur through the operation of market forces and government policies that were more consistent with competition. Unfortunately, however, all too often the ISI strategies led to directly unproductive rent-seeking (as referred to by Krueger and others), which gave rise to a structure of inefficient protected industries. Although ISI was a part of the Mexican industrialization "miracle" of rapid growth during the entire postwar period, the distortions increased particularly rapidly during the oil boom when growth was 8 percent per annum (1978–1981). This growth was largely due to the expectation of *future* oil revenues and associated external borrowing rather than oil rents actually being earned during the "boom" period, which were far more modest.

Since 1982 Mexico's policies have undergone a 180-degree change toward liberalization and international competitiveness. This has forced severe cutbacks on production of the previously protected industries (including those in which FDI was involved).[35] On the other hand, a number of more capital-intensive industries are demonstrating a significant degree of competitiveness. For example, glass and cement producers VITRO and CEMEX have become nascent Mexican multinationals along with the national oil monopoly PEMEX, which enjoys a unique position of resource-rent intensity but is not notably competitive in terms of cost efficiency. In recent years, these firms have started their own subsidiary ventures in the United States, sometimes (as in the case of VITRO) making use of U.S. loan capital to complement Mexican equity. Mexico appears to be entering the third stage of industrialization (as was Japan in the late 1960s and the Asian NICs in the early 1980s).

Transference of Flexible Manufacturing in the Assembly-Based Industries

It is important to keep in mind that Japan is structurally in the stage of the "assembly-transplanting" (trade-conflict-avoiding) type of overseas investment, although it still continues to make investments of other types (i.e., "resource-seeking" and "low-cost-labor-seeking"), which once dominated its pattern of FDI at the previous stages of development—further, it also has just begun to weave out a new modality of FDI, the "networking" type. *Thus in terms of structural compatibility in home-host relations between Japan and Mexico, the push factor emanating from Japan's current stage of outward FDI perfectly matches the pull factor of Mexico in attracting FDI into this phase-specific type of industry.* Indeed, the components-intensive, assembly-based industry (auto assembly, auto parts, and consumer electric/ electronic goods) is the very type of industry on which Japanese ventures in Mexico have been centered. Interestingly enough, Western multinationals' operations in Mexico are likewise concentrated in Phase III industries.

In fact, assisted by FDI inflows, Mexico seems well on its way to building an automobile industry. Above all, it has discovered a new advantage in the currently prevailing institutional characteristics of its labor force, the characteristics that are rather specific to the early stages of economic development and are almost serendipitously compatible with the car-assembly-operations of Japanese-style flexible manufacturing. Nissan represents well over 50 percent of total Japanese investment in Mexico, and its operation reflects the new approach that one would expect future Japanese and other FDI investors to take, in which Mexico is regarded as part of the broader North American market for production-sharing in an integrated fashion in which the highest possible technology and skills are employed.[36]

In the past, the conventional wisdom held that Mexican workers were much less productive (usually cited as about 20%) than American workers. Hence it was argued that the latter did not need to worry about any decline in their wages even under free trade with Mexico. Yet Mexican auto workers have proved equally or more productive, efficient, and quality-conscious compared to their American counterparts. In the recent past, evidence to this effect has emerged, especially in those sectors of the Mexican economy that have assimilated the most advanced technology and provided on-the-job training for Mexican workers. In such cases, particularly in the auto sector, Mexican labor is shown to have equal or superior productivity to its U.S. counterpart.[37]

Nissan Motor Co. will construct a center to design and develop automobile parts in Toluca, 50km west of (Mexico City), at a cost of around ¥2 billion ($18 million). Construction will begin in March and is scheduled for completion by year-end.

Nissan now has around 500 workers for components design, purchasing and quality control scattered throughout Mexico. They will be brought together at the center to be constructed on a 90,000-sq.-meter site adjacent to the foundry plant of Nissan Mexicana S.A. de CV, Nissan's local manufacturing unit.

The center will have design rooms and laboratories available for use by *around 170 local parts makers*. The company said it hopes to shorten the time required for development of components for its Mexican-built cars.[38]

No wonder, then, that it was reportedly the Big Three that the Clinton Administration first approached in its rather misdirected effort to urge U.S. firms to pledge not to move jobs to Mexico for the purpose of pacifying labor unions prior to the House vote ratifying NAFTA.[39] The perceived threat of more competitive Mexican workers (with lower productivity-adjusted wages) had led observers such as Shaiken (1993) to strongly oppose the NAFTA agreement, along with many in the labor unions. The proponents of NAFTA often agreed with the Shaiken argument about worker productivity being as positive or even better than that of U.S. counterparts. The disagreement was not about the present observations, but in the dynamic perception of Mexico as a new partner in a growing North American economy in which all parties would gain, provided that investment in the United States increased despite any amount diverted to Mexico in a hypothetical zero sum game. This more dynamic viewpoint, which also saw Mexico as a future partner in competitiveness with the United States and Canada, facing a widening world pool of productive wage-labor, won the day in the ultimate bipartisan support for NAFTA.

The transformation of the Mexican economy, as one that would sustain a workforce with rising productivity and expanding domestic market, is supported by trends in the auto industry experience, just as with the Canada-U.S. Auto Pact of the 1960s both countries gained in productivity and employment in that sector by cooperating through trade and investment liberalization. Mexico is perceived by post- NAFTA investors (as reflected in the auto sector) as far more than a low-wage source of labor or convenient location for assembly plants. Indeed, if that were the case, NAFTA would not have been needed, since the incentives for cheap labor assembly plants were already largely in place and maquiladoras had even greater incentives before NAFTA because Mexican law had then permitted them to import from Japan and other third countries for re-export.

The recent experience of Japanese FDI in Mexico involves the transformation of production techniques going well beyond assembly activities to fully integrated components of the Japanese global industrial structure and its North American base. This has been possible in part because of the receptivity of local labor to the assimilation of Japanese-style production techniques, as exemplified by the rapid emergence of Mexico's automobile industry. The Mexican government's foresighted policy and Ford Motor's decision to transplant Japan's new industrial paradigm are credited for starting this auto boom in Mexico. Reversing its past restrictive import-substituting policy, the government allowed Ford to build in a desert cow town, Hermosillo, a brand-new $500-million plant modeled on Mazda Motor Corp. of Japan, its business partner. Being near the west-coast port of Guaymas, the town was chosen since it would facilitate the "quasi-just-in-time" importation of the transmissions from Japan (that is, with the minimum inventory of imports).

The Mexican government imposed no local-content requirement as long as the great majority of its output was exported. Ford found "lots of young, educated workers with no auto experience,"[40] but they were sent to Japan for training. By late 1987, Ford's plant was producing Mercury Tracers, a clone of Mazdas, which later won quality awards—and the plant itself became rated as one of the best plants in North America.[41] The parts originally imported from Japan—engines, transmissions, and other key components—gradually came to be produced locally because of the suddenly risen value of the yen. In addition, the Mexican government extended the same liberal policy on local-content requirements "not just for Hermosillo but for the entire Mexican motor-vehicle industry."[42] GM, Ford, Chrysler, Nissan, VW, and even Mercedes-Benz all stepped up production. Simultaneously, a large fraction of the parts began to be manufactured in northern Mexico, turning the region into quasi-Detroit South.

Thus *the impact of Japanese industry on Mexico's newly emerging auto industry is quite considerable, going far beyond Nissan Mexicana's own effort to introduce Japanese-style manufacturing techniques thanks to the successful application of such techniques by U.S. automakers to their Mexican operations.* The fact that American automakers are adopting Japanese-style flexible manufacturing as eagerly and as effectively as at Nissan Mexicana's plants is a strong indication that institutional compatibility exists between the Mexican labor force and the requirements of the new industrial paradigm.[43] The U.S. auto industry has itself gone through an impressive process of transformation, regaining market shares vis-a-vis Japanese imports, with a particular increase in the share of Mexican production in that recovery. It appears that the North American integrated economy is positioned to maintain and even enhance its role in global competitiveness together with Japanese and other FDI that have contributed to the transformation process. The complementary nature of Mexico's inroads into flexible manufacturing, with regard to U.S. and Canadian industry, is becoming increasingly evident, even to those observers who were highly skeptical in earlier years.

Summary and Conclusions

The changing pattern of Japanese FDI in Mexico has reflected an interaction of push and pull factors in which firms have hesitantly responded to what were perceived to be limited opportunities, in a region that was relatively unfamiliar and considered to be unstable. Only since the mid-1980s have those perceptions begun to change, and with them evidence of the determination to include Mexico within Japan's international industrial structure. In the initial postwar years Japanese investment in Latin America tended to follow trade, in response to its own resource needs and limited marketing opportunities. Its regional investment in manufacturing was minimal and largely inward-looking, reflecting the limited size of protected local markets and the dominance of U.S. and European ventures, with the possible exception of Brazil. In the 1970s there was some recycling of Japanese trade surpluses in the form of commercial bank lending to the region, often as part of international consortia loans to governments and state enterprises, with limited impact on Japanese activities in the Americas.

By the 1980s much of this debt turned out to be nonperforming, discouraging further private investment and requiring the Japanese government to step in as lender of last resort. Despite expectations, which in retrospect appear to have been unrealistic, Japan's heralded financial surpluses, generated by successful export-led growth and high rates of private savings, did little to alter its FDI relationship with Mexico and Latin America. Instead, the surplus was used to acquire assets including real estate in the United States and other OECD countries and to invest in the newly industrializing economies of Asia and the Pacific rather than elsewhere in the developing world. The fact that a huge flow of Japanese financial capital found its way to offshore havens in the Caribbean appears to have had little impact on physical investment on the mainland of Latin America, although the use of those funds for the acquisition of financial assets may well have contributed to the boom in the region's securities markets since the mid-1980s. Latin America's prolonged debt crisis and restructuring of hemisphere economies away from import-substituting-industrialization toward open markets and the challenge of international competitiveness proved too great a risk—at least until recently. Partly because of the need to repay foreign borrowing, the region's terms of trade for basic commodity exports were depressed, alleviating Japanese insecurity about the supply of natural resources and investments related to that concern. As a result there was little push or pull in the 1980s that propelled Japanese FDI toward Latin America. Indeed one reason given for the reversal of course on the part of Mexico's leaders, who sought out a NAFTA agreement with its North American partners in the 1990s, was the lackluster response from Japanese and European investors to Mexico's FDI overtures, even after its impressive unilateral opening and successful stabilization program.

Only in recent years have perceptions of Mexico's investment potential begun to change. New pull factors have arisen and with them evidence of the determination to include Mexico within Japan's international industrial structure. The slow but stable recovery of the Mexican economy since the mid-1980s has finally attracted the interest of investors in its large potential market, linked to the United States and Canada through NAFTA, as well as its proven ability to network with hemispheric neighbors north and south through a series of ad hoc free trade agreements. Mexican government programs such as PRONASOL, which use fiscal resources to diffuse purchasing power and productivity to previously marginal regions and income groups, are expected to have a widening impact on the domestic market. Popular protests radiating from Chiapas since the beginning of 1994 are serving to reinforce the rethinking of Mexico's policy regime toward more political and economic inclusiveness, spreading from the grassroots to the highest levels of government. The commitment of the three North American countries to a more socially equitable NAFTA, once accepted and implemented, is likely to reinforce the disposition of investors and their financial institutions to find a new place for Mexico in their long-term corporate strategies. In the auto sector farsighted firms like Nissan have already taken the lead.

There are major quasi-rents to be earned in the form of transitional profits and rising real wages for those willing and able to take advantage of production-sharing and market-sharing within a newly integrating North American market. It is no longer necessary for such investments to rely on the privileged legal and institutional shelters and personal politicking that characterized the directly unproductive rent-seeking of earlier years and tended to discourage those without special contacts in the region, such as the Japanese. Earlier Asian concerns to the contrary, evidence now emerging that NAFTA is predicated on "open regionalism" and "GATT- plus" approaches to integration makes it likely that Japan's wait-and-see attitude of the past will give way to a major thrust of trade, investment, and technology transfer to Mexico. From the viewpoint of the host country and its partners, a growing Japanese presence in Mexico offers a complement to the greater participation of North America in the dynamic development of the Pacific Rim. Flows of goods and services through Mexico toward Asia and the Pacific, facilitated by Japanese direct investment, will help to balance trade and investment in the opposite direction. Mexico is ahead of the curve for Latin America as a whole, and its experience offers a useful testing ground for Japanese and other OECD involvement in what is expected to become a robust Americas-wide market.

Notes

1. These and other contacts are briefly described in Scott and Worley (1990), p. 161.
2. Events in Chiapas reflect repercussions of the uneven incidence of economic adjustment and have had an offsetting effect to NAFTA on investor perceptions of Mexican political and economic risk, but such concerns have been tempered by subsequent accords between the government and opposition parties, intensified efforts of regional agreements, the promise of greater commitment on the part of the national leadership to growth with equity (that would also have the effect of widening domestic markets), and the positive macroeconomic impact of U.S. economic recovery.
3. Among the European countries, the United Kingdom was the largest investor in Latin America, accounting for around a third of total flows (the data exclude Switzerland). The second was Germany, which supplied a quarter of European investment, and the third France (14%). IDB/IRELA (1993), p. 33.
4. Data from the Japanese Ministry of Finance and the World Investment Directory—Developed Countries, United Nations provided from Alfredo Arahuetes, draft of Chapter III of doctoral dissertation, "Relaciones Comerciales y Flujos de Inversion Directa entre España y America Latina en el Periodo 1980–1990." Fundacion CEDEAL, Madrid (1993).
5. The specific figures and information cited are from JETRO, *1993 JETRO Hakusho: Kaigai chokusetsu toshi* (1993 JETRO white paper: Overseas Direct Investment), Tokyo (1993).
6. All of the flows presented in table 3.1 by IRELA/IDB (1993) are designated "Foreign Direct Investment" (FDI) in the original source. However, the authors of this chapter have been advised that even for specific new investment projects or the formation of new enterprises in the region, a significant portion of the so-called "direct investment" of Japanese firms reported in this and other statistical sources is in fact debt-financed, often from the banks associated with Japanese industrial groups, the funds being used to lever a much smaller share of owner-equity capital in the enterprise. For this reason there may be double counting where indirect financial capital provided to the Japanese parent firm and its partners and "direct investment" are summed to equal "total Japanese direct investment" in the figures reported, and while offshore investment is largely financial in nature, some of it may be used to fund onshore "equity" investments. It is not possible to make the functional breakdown necessary to differentiate direct and indirect investment totals from the reported figures. Hence we have relabeled the data in table 3.1 "overseas investment flows" and divided them into "onshore" and "offshore" investments. The former may be regarded as primarily direct investment and the latter as primarily financial (indirect) investment, only a fraction of which is likely to end up in Latin America. Presumably figures for "medium and long-term loans" such as those reported separately from "foreign direct investment" by the Japanese Ministry of Finance (*Annual Report of*

International Finance Bureau) do not face such definitional problems. (See thesection, "Offshore Investment of Japan in the Caribbean," below.) The IMF definition for FDI is wider than other conventional economic definitions of investment. The IMF definition includes (1) equity capital, (2) reinvestment of earnings, (3) other long-term capital, and (4) short-term capital. (In U.S. Commerce Department reporting, profits of U.S. corporations abroad not remitted to the United States are also accounted as "foreign direct investment" in the host country, which is more inclusive than the conventional economic definition of direct investment.)

7. MITI, *Kaigai toshi tōkei sōran (Report #4)*, Tokyo, 1992, p. 50.

8. This theme is the basic proposition used in the "industrial restructuring" (macro-developmental) paradigm of FDI. See Ozawa (1991a, 1991b, 1992, and 1993).

9. For the consequences of this altered pattern of competition from the "niche" type to "head-to-head" type, see Thurow (1992).

10. Type 4 FDI (*trade-conflict-avoiding-assembly-transplanting*) corresponds to quid pro quo investment à la Bhagwati, as discussed by Wong and Yamamura in chapter 1. Their analysis, dealing with the 1980s, also covers our Type 5 (*surplus recycling*) investment.

11. Japan had actually moved into Phase II (heavy and chemical industrialization) before World War II and had continued in this phase during the war, but in the immediate postwar years pressures were applied to dismantle and remove heavy machinery and equipment and ship them to other Asian countries as part of war reparations. This would have left the Japanese economy with only a light industrial base. The immediate postwar Communist takeover in China led to a dramatic reversal of the allied occupying force's (U.S.) policy toward Japan. Japanese industry was now encouraged to rebuild heavy and chemical industries to serve as a bulwark against Communism in Asia, particularly in the wake of the Korean conflict. Japan took full advantage of the new American policy, and subsequently pursued an earlier prewar strategy of absorbing state-of-the art technologies, improving them, and adapting them to Japanese conditions, in order to catch up with and eventually compete with the West, moving in the direction of Phases III and IV.

12. Japan's overseas investment was initially controlled and subject to case-by-case screening and approval by the Ministry of Finance, which made decisions in close consultation with other government agencies, especially the Ministry of International Trade and Industry. Although no requirements for approval were officially announced, it was generally understood that FDI must either promote exports from Japan or lead to the overseas development of natural resources vital to Japanese industry and that overseas production must not jeopardize the competitive position of other Japanese firms at home. In this sense, as with internationally oligopolistic investment from other sources, there may well have been barriers to the fully competitive flow of FDI to Mexico. However, since the spread of competition among multinational enterprises in recent decades, FDI has become an increasing element in domestic as well as international competitiveness, improving the opportunities for NICs such as Mexico.

13. Throughout the 1950s and 1960s and up until the early 1970s (i.e., the pre-oil-crisis postwar period that corresponded to Phase I and Phase II), Japan's catch-

up development efforts were basically aimed at industrial expansion based on trade. Japanese industry was designed to operate as *trade-supported* workshops that imported raw materials, processed them, and exported finished goods. Yet the successful build-up of energy-intensive, resource-dependent heavy industries and chemical plants, in a resource-scarce and geographically confined small country like Japan, had quickly caused two serious problems by the early 1970s; one was the ever- worsening environmental decay and pollution, and the second was the ever-rising dependency on overseas resources.

14. It should be noted that the sequential emergence of these different types of overseas investment is nothing particularly peculiar to Japan. In fact, the advanced Western countries have gone through the similarly different stages of economic development but over a much longer span of time—say, in Britains' case, well over one century. But Japan's uniqueness lies in that the sequence has been highly time-compressed as it has occurred in only four decades. And the Asian NIEs (the newly industrializing economies of Hong Kong, Singapore, Taiwan, and South Korea) are, indeed, currently in the "elementary manufacturing/labor-seeking" stage of FDI as they shift low-wage-based, labor-intensive industries to the ASEAN and China.

15. JETRO, *1972 Kaigai shijō hakusho: Wagakuni kaigai toshi no genjō*, Tokyo, 1972, p. 3.

16. Ibid.

17. These data are from *Jūkagaku kōgyō tsūshinsha, kaigai toshi-gijutsu yushutsu yōran* [Japan's Overseas Investment and Technical Exports], Tokyo: 1970.

18. These examples are from Ozawa, Pluciennik, and Rao (1976).

19. For other reasons, see Ozawa (1979), pp. 124–28.

20. Energy Information Administration, *Monthly Energy Review*, February 1986, as cited by Gerald H. Anderson and K. J. Kowalewski, "Implications of a Tariff on Oil Imports," *Economic Commentary*, Federal Reserve Bank of Cleveland, September 1, 1986, p. 2.

21. MITI, *Tsūshō sangyō gyōsei shihan seiki no ayuki* [A Quarter Century of Trade and Industrial Administration], Tokyo, pp. 302–5.

22. These references to institutional arrangements for Japan's resource diplomacy are based on Ozawa, 1992.

23. The information about these three projects in this section is drawn from MITI, *Keizai kyōryoku no genjō to mondaiten, 1982,* Tokyo.

24. MITI, *Keizai kyōryoku no genjō to mondaiten, 1985,* Tokyo, p. 742. The deficits have subsequently become surplus as Mexico's economy has opened and it has reversed the debt crisis.

25. Scott and Worley (1990), p. 162.

26. Sklair (1989), pp. 44–45. "A different account of the origins of the maquila industry involves an attorney in Ciudad Juarez, Javier Alvarez Moreno, who was approached in 1962 by two Boston lawyers on behalf of a U.S. client who wished to utilize Mexico's pool of cheap labor to set up a factory. Alvarez researched the problem and came up with the idea of taking advantage of 806/807 to assemble U.S. parts with cheap Mexican labor for re-export to the United States. Eventually his idea came to the attention of the President, Diaz Ordaz, and Campos Salas, and they built the BIP [Border Industrialization Program] and

the maquila industry around it." Others attributed Mexican maquiladora origins
to the success of Puerto Rico's "operation bootstrap."

27. This chronological demarcation is presented in Sklair (1989), pp. 43–76.
28. Mehl (1985), p. 71.
29. Ibid., p. 74.
30. Ibid., p. 75.
31. Information about these Japanese operations in this section is from Toyo Keizai
    (1990).
32. *Japan Economic Journal,* Oct. 15, 1988, p. 18.
33. There is some debate as to whether NAFTA, with its telephone-book-sized report
    (Governments of Canada, the United Mexican States, and the United States of
    America, *North American Free Trade Agreement,* Oct. 7, 1992) is in fact truly
    "open." The treaty appears to be a heavily liberalizing document. In it
    regionwide tariffs are phased out over a period of from one to thirteen stages
    between Jan. 1, 1994 and 2008 (the longest phase-outs being those for basic
    agricultural commodities such as maize where important segments of the rural
    population are affected). There are few exceptions to most favored nation
    treatment, principally for aviation, fisheries, maritime, and telecommunications
    transportation networks and services. Third-country tariffs in important areas
    such as electronics have been lowered in the process of negotiation. Increases in
    domestic content requirements, such as for autos and auto parts, were modest
    and the final outcome reflected Canadian as well as Mexican pressures for a
    more open relationship, aimed at increasing regionwide trade through lowering
    of costs rather than increasing external protection or voluntary trade restrictions
    of third countries. (The preceding commentary benefited from observations by
    Ronald Wonnacott, reflecting positively on the NAFTA outcome from a trade
    liberalization perspective in lectures at Stanford in 1993.)
35. The open-regionalism concept is based on an Asia-Pacific term that has been
    formalized by one of the authors of this chapter for application to the Andean
    region and other Latin American regional groupings, but which offers a generic
    approach of much wider applicability. Reynolds, Thoumi, and Wettmann (1994),
    *A Case for Open Regionalism in the Andes: Policy Implications of Andean
    Integration in a Period of Hemispheric Liberalization and Structural Adjust-
    ment,* Report for USAID-ILDIS, draft Stanford, 1994, esp. Chap. 3, "New
    Approaches to Market Integration: Open Regionalism." An earlier version of this
    approach was prepared by Clark W. Reynolds for a conference of INCAE, Quito,
    Ecuador, spring 1992, entitled "Open Regionalism in the Andes," draft Stanford
    North America Forum, rev. June 1992.
35. "For example, Mexican toy companies, which once averaged 30% profit margins
    behind a 40% tariff on imports, now face stiff foreign competition. By 1990, the
    tariff had been cut in half, and 80 of the 265 members of the Mexican toy
    industry association vanished in one year. In the past, the Mexican government
    protected garment producers from foreign imports in the hopes of building up an
    aggressive domestic industry. . . . Foreign clothes [mostly from Asia] clutter
    Mexico City's downtown markets, while in nearby Puebla, domestic textile
    plants remain idle—or shut down for good." (Hecht and Morici, 1993, p. 36)
36. One informed Mexican observer, who interviewed many of the main Japanese

firms in Mexico just before NAFTA was completed, pointed out the prominence and importance of Nissan in this regard (Rubio, 1992). ". . . Nissan's investment would represent 75 percent of all Japanese direct investment in Mexico by the end of 1991; what they do will obviously matter much more than the 150 other little Japanese firms with presence in Mexico. This fact notwithstanding, as a global competitor in the auto industry, Nissan is following the logic of a global firm that is behind its foremost rival in the international arena, Toyota. . . . Some Japanese observers believe the Nissan strategy has been changing as Mexico's policies have changed, the investment becoming ever more relevant to the firm's global strategy, i.e. production-sharing, where part of their production would be located in Mexico, typically the more labor-intensive parts of it, and Japanese components and parts would be used. In this context, Mexico would have duplicated in North America the role that Indonesia, Thailand, or Malaysia play for Japanese firms in Asia. . . . In the context of a NAFTA, however, the new plant could be a major component of a new, North American strategy. This could well imply integrated production across the United States-Canada-Mexico borders for the region only. In fact, Mexico has rapidly become one of the largest manufacturers of cars and auto parts and components in the world, relative to its GNP." (pp. 89ff.)

37. "Mexican auto workers, it seems, not only are dirt cheap but can also deliver quality. In Detroit's view, Mexico's young work force adapts more quickly to new industrial regimes than entrenched workers in the Rust Belt. The workers in GM's Ramos Arizpe plant, for example, quickly mastered Japanese-style manufacturing techniques to become GM's No. 1 plant, setting companywide quality records . . .

"[U.S. auto workers] see themselves pitted against a young, malleable work force amenable to the manufacturing revolution. This Japanese-style system, which has caught on in Mexico, calls for a flexible labor force, where highly trained workers in small teams can jump into each other's jobs and monitor quality each step of the way. Some workers have taken to quality programs with a near-religious zeal. Singing groups at Ramos Arizpe have even recorded odes to quality manufacturing. In *planta mia,* workers sing, 'ay, dear assembly plant, with your people so united and responsible. . . .' Although workers at GM's Saturn and Ford's Wayne (Mich.) Escort factory have adopted this nimble approach, many U.S. plants are still hobbled by *rigid work rules.* Now, Mexico's success gives carmakers leverage to push changes back home" (emphasis added). (*Business Week*, March 16, 1992, p. 100)

Another journal reports; "The Big Three own other manufacturing facilities besides the maquilas to serve the Mexican market. Ford, GM, and Chrysler have all found that the quality in their best Mexican plants is equal to or better than the quality in many U.S. plants. For obvious reasons, workers in these auto plants are conscientious and pay attention to detail: they're paid much more than maquila employees. What's more, in a country with high unemployment, they have steady jobs. Donald Hilty, Chrysler's corporate economist, notes that the quality of interior trim for Chrysler convertibles produced in Mexico is *higher* than in the United States. Meanwhile, Volkswagen, Nissan, and Mercedes have joined the U.S. Big Three in ambitious expansion programs that take advantage of this quality-oriented work force" (emphasis added). (Hecht and Morici, 1993)

38. *Nikkei Weekly,* (January 24, 1994, p. 24).
39. *Wall Street Journal,* November 1, 1993, p. A2.
40. *Business Week,* March 16, 1992, p. 100.
41. Ibid., p. 102.
42. Womack, Jones, and Roos (1990), pp. 265–66.
43. When flexible manufacturing came to be recognized as a new form of production, two opposing views emerged as to whether it is compatible with low-cost labor locations such as Mexico. (These opposing views are surveyed and analyzed in Wilson (1990), pp. 140–43.)

References and Bibliography

Arahuetes, Alfredo (1993), "Relaciones Comerciales y Flujos de Inversion Directa entre España y America Latina en el Periodo 1980–1990" (doctoral dissertation draft), Fundacion CEDEAL, Madrid, Spain.

Aspe, Pedro (1993), *Economic Transformation the Mexican Way.* Cambridge, Mass.: MIT Press.

Colander, David C., ed. (1984), *Neoclassical Political Economy: The Analysis of Rent-Seeking and DUP* [directly unproductive profit-seeking] *Activities.* Cambridge, Mass.: Ballinger Publishing Company.

Energy Information Administration (1986), *Monthly Energy Review* (February), as cited by Gerald H. Anderson and K. J. Kowalewski, "Implications of a Tariff on Oil Imports," *Economic Commentary* (a newsletter). Federal Reserve Bank of Cleveland, September 1, 1986.

Gilpin, Robert (1987), *The Political Economy of International Relations.* Princeton: Princeton University Press.

Governments of Canada, the United Mexican States, and the United States of America, Oct. 7, 1992, *North American Free Trade Agreement,* Washington, D.C., eight parts and annexes.

Hecht, Laurence, and Morici, Peter (1993), "Managing Risks in Mexico," *Harvard Business Review,* Vol. 71, No. 4 (July–August), pp. 32–40.

Hymer, Stephen H. (1976), *The International Operations of National Firms: A Study of Direct Foreign Investment* (publication of 1960 MIT dissertation by MIT Press).

Institute for European-Latin American Relations (IRELA)/Inter-American Development Bank (IDB), Special Office in Europe (SOE) (1993), *Foreign Direct Investment in Latin America and the Caribbean: An Overview of Flows from Europe, Japan and the United States, 1979–1990.* Madrid/Paris: IRELA.

JETRO (Japan External Trade Organization) (1972), *1972 Kaigai shijō hakusho:*

Wagakuni kaigai toshi no genjō [White Paper on Overseas Markets: Current Status of Japanese Overseas Investment]. Tokyo: MITI.

Jūkagaku Kōgyō Tsūshinsha (1970), *Kaigai toshi-gijutsu yushutsu yōran* [Manual on Japan's Overseas Investment and Technical Exports]. Tokyo: Jūkagaku Kōgyō Tsūshinsha.

Komiya, Kazuyuki (1990), *Kume-san, orenimo iwasero* [Mr. Kume, Let Me Tell You Something]. Tokyo: Tōyō Keizai Shimpōsha.

Krueger, Anne Osborne (1974), "The Political Economy of the Rent-Seeking Society," *American Economic Review* 64 (June): 291–303.

Mehl, G. M. (1985), "Trade in Item 806/807 Goods," in U.S. Department of Commerce, *United States Trade: Performance in 1984 and Outlook.* Washington: U.S. Government Printing Office.

MITI (Ministry of International Trade and Industry) (1992), *Kaigai toshi tōkei sōran* [Statistics on Overseas Investments], Report No. 4. Tokyo: MITI.

MITI (Ministry of International Trade and Industry) (1982), *Keizai kyōryoku no genjō to mondaiten* [Present Status and Issues of Japan's Overseas Economic Cooperation]. Tokyo: MITI.

MITI (Ministry of International Trade and Industry) (1978), *Tsūshō sangyō gyōsei shihan seiki no ayumi* [A Quarter Century of Trade and Industrial Administration], Tokyo, pp. 302–5, as cited in Chalmers Johnson, *Japan's Public Policy Companies.* Washington, D.C.: American Enterprise Institute, 1978, p. 122.

MITI (Ministry of International Trade and Industry) (1992), *Wagakuni kigyō no kaigai jigyō katsudō* [Overseas Business Activities of Japanese Enterprises], Report No. 22. Tokyo: MITI.

Ozawa, Terutomo (forthcoming), *In Search of Flexibility in the Industrial Milieu: The Developing Countries and Japanese-Style Flexible Manufacturing* (tentative title). Paris: OECD.

Ozawa, Terutomo (1993), "Foreign Direct Investment and Structural Transformation: Japan as a Recycler of Market and Industry," *Business & Contemporary World,* Vol. V, No. 2 (Spring), pp. 129–50.

Ozawa, Terutomo (1992), "Foreign Direct Investment and Economic Development," *Transnational Corporations,* Vol. 1, No. 1 (February), pp. 27–54.

Ozawa, Terutomo (1991), "The Dynamics of Pacific Rim Industrialization: How Mexico Can Join the Asian Flock of 'Flying Geese,'" in Riordan Roett, ed., *Mexico's External Relations in the 1990s.* Boulder; London: Rienner, pp. 129–54.

Ozawa, Terutomo (1989), *Recycling Japan's Surpluses for Developing Countries.* Paris: OECD.

Ozawa, Terutomo (1979), *Multinationalism, Japanese Style: The Political Economy of Outward Dependency.* Princeton: Princeton University Press.

Ozawa, Terutomo, and Reynolds, Clark W. (1991), "La Nueva Conexion Estados

Unidos-Mexico-Japan: Interaccion Economica Trilateral e Integracion Regional en la Cuenca del Pacifico," in A. A. Bejar and John Borrego, eds., *La Insercion de Mexico en la Cuenca del Pacifico.* Mexico City: Universidad Nacional Autonoma de Mexico, pp. 170–236. (English version available from North America Forum, Stanford University.)

Ozawa, Terutomo, Moyses Pluciennik, and K. Nagaraja Rao (1976), "Japan's Direct Investment in Brazil," *Columbia Journal of World Business,* Vol. 11, pp. 107–16.

Reynolds, Clark W. (1989), "The Political Economy of Interdependence in the Americas: Toward a Generalized Approach to Rent-Seeking," Americas Program Working Paper 89-7, Stanford University.

Rubio, Luis (1992), "Japan in Mexico: A Changing Pattern," in *Japan and Latin America in the New Global Order,* ed. Susan Kaufman Purcell and Robert M. Immerman. Boulder, Colo.: Lynne Rienner Publishers.

Scott, Richard C., and Joel K. Worley (1990), "The Use of Maquiladoras by Non-American Companies: The Case of Japanese Multinationals," in Khosrow Fatemi, ed., *The Maquiladora Industry: Economic Solution or Problem?* New York: Praeger, pp. 159–70.

Shaiken, Harley, and Stephen Herzenberg (1987), *Automation and Global Production: Automobile Engine Production in Mexico, the United States, and Canada,* Monograph Series, No. 26. La Jolla, Center for U.S.-Mexican Studies, University of California, San Diego.

Shaiken, Harley (1994), "Advanced Manufacturing and Mexico: The Auto and Electronics Sectors in U.S.-Mexico Trade and Investment," *Latin America Research Review,* Vol. 29, No. 2.

Sklair, Leslie (1989), *Assembling for Development: The Maquila Industry in Mexico and the United States.* Boston: Unwin Hyman.

Szekeley, Gabriel (1993), "Japanese Investment in Mexico," essay presented at conference, *Integrating the World Economy: Japanese Direct Investment During the Late Twentieth Century,* Hoover Institution and Japan-U.S. Friendship Commission.

Thurow, Lester (1992), *Head to Head: The Coming Economic Battle Among Japan, Europe, and America.* New York: William Morrow.

Toyo Keizai (1990), *Kaigai shinshutsu kigyō sōran* [Data Bank on Japanese Overseas Ventures]. Tokyo: Tōyō Keizai.

Wilson, Patricia A. (1992), *Exports and Local Development: Mexico's New Maquiladoras.* Austin: University of Texas Press.

Wilson, Patricia (1990), "The New Maquiladoras: Flexible Production in Low-Wage Regions," in Khosrow Fatemi, ed., *The Maquiladora Industry: Economic Solution or Problem?* New York: Praeger.

Womack, James P., Jones, Daniel T., and Roos, Daniel (1990), *The Machine That Changed the World.* New York: Macmillan.

Chapter 4

Japanese Direct Investment in Australia in Comparative Perspective

• • • • • • • • • • •

PETER DRYSDALE

Foreign direct investment (FDI) has had an enormous impact on the economic development of Australia; significantly contributed to capital formation; played a large role in introducing modern industrial and commercial management know-how to Australia; served as an important vehicle for the import of new technology, especially with the establishment of new industrial activities in Australia; and originated in the foreign enterprises that operate in almost all sectors of the Australian economy.

First the United Kingdom and then, in the early postwar period, the United States dominated FDI activity in all sectors of Australian industry. The United Kingdom and the United States were also the primary sources of portfolio and other capital imports into Australia.

The United Kingdom and the United States still hold the largest share of FDI in Australia, but Japan is rapidly catching up with these traditional suppliers of foreign capital to Australia. In 1991, the United States held 26.9 percent of the total stock of FDI in Australia, the United Kingdom accounted for 25.2 percent, and Japan's share was only 16.2 percent (see table 4.1). Japan's share rose very rapidly, however, especially since the mid-1980s, when it was only 7.5 percent. Throughout the 1980s the flow of investment from Japan began to rival or exceed that of the United Kingdom and the United States and, in 1991, Japan was Australia's largest source of direct capital inflow.

The remarkable thing about the role of Japanese investment in Australia is not so much how it grew in importance over the last decade but rather why it remained relatively unimportant for such a long time. Economic links between Australia and Japan were well established almost thirty years ago. The Agreement on Commerce between Australia and Japan was ratified in July 1957 and paved the way for Australia and Japan to develop a very strong bilateral trading relationship based on the economic complementarity (and proximity) of the two countries. Both Australia and Japan benefited enormously from the growing interdependence. Japan, entering a period of rapidly expanding industrial growth, found in Australia a stable supply of industrial and agricultural raw materials. Australia, on the other hand, had the opportunity to access this rapidly growing market. The proportion of Australian exports going to Japan increased from 14 percent in 1957 to 31 percent in 1974. Japan has been Australia's largest export market since the late 1960s and Australia's second largest source of imports, after the United States, since the first half of the 1970s. The strong trading links were built on Australian exports of wool, wheat, and beef and Japanese exports of labor-intensive manufactures such as textiles and plastic materials. However, the changing industrial structure of the Japanese economy opened new opportunities for trade between the two countries. The demands of the growing iron and steel industry in Japan encouraged the development of Australia's mineral resources. By the mid-1960s, iron ore and coal accounted for 20 percent of Australia's exports to Japan, and this grew to nearly 50 percent by 1975. A growing proportion of imports from Japan were in the form of capital-intensive and technology-intensive manufactures. Although it has narrowed in recent years, Australia has been one of few nations to maintain a bilateral commodity trade surplus with Japan, and, since the 1970s, the structure of trade has diversified beyond the traditional reliance on raw materials exports. Australia's exports of manufactures to Japan are now greater than its exports of all commodities to the United Kingdom. With nearly 30 percent of Australia's exports going to Japan and 17 percent of imports coming from there, Japan is by far Australia's most important trading partner. One might have expected the intensity of trade links between the two countries to have encouraged strong investment links sooner. Japanese trading and commercial houses have had a long and active presence in Australia, dating back over more than a century—yet it is only in the last decade that Japan has become a significant investor in Australia.

TABLE 4.1
SHARES IN LEVEL OF DIRECT INVESTMENT IN AUSTRALIA, 1981–1991[a]
(% share and value in $US millon)

	Japan		United States		United Kingdom		Total
1981	5.0%	1,480	35.5%	11,136	36.5%	10,779	29,532
1982	6.1	1,828	37.0	11,049	33.4	9,978	29,853
1983	6.9	1,917	39.5	10,832	32.6	8,956	27,456
1984	7.5	2,159	36.1	10,405	30.9	8,915	28,790
1985	7.5	2,139	33.6	9,558	31.3	8,893	28,430
1986	10.2	2,892	33.3	9,431	30.3	8,580	28,335
1987	10.9	3,283	34.7	12,570	29.3	10,581	36,145
1988	10.9	5,156	30.5	14,494	31.6	14,993	47,443
1989	13.2	8,218	26.6	16,565	30.7	20,676	62,365
1990	14.3	9,929	26.9	18,764	28.7	19,978	69,582
1991	16.2	12,397	26.9	20,568	25.2	19,271	76,421

NOTES: [a]Year to 30 June.
In 1985–1986 the definition of direct investment changed from 25% equity to 10% equity. Therefore, entries from years prior to that are not strictly comparable with the entries of subsequent years.

SOURCE: Australian Bureau of Statistics (ABS) Catalog No. 5305, *Foreign Investment—Australia*, 1985/86, 1987/88, 1988/89, 1990/91. Canberra: ABS.

The new wave of Japanese investment, like U.S. and U.K. investment in earlier periods, has not been absorbed entirely without controversy. Perhaps, however, there has been much less controversy accompanying the rising share of Japanese investment in Australia than might have been expected. British and U.S. investment (although less so) both come from familiar cultural and institutional climes. The concentration of Australian trade, particularly exports of raw materials, on the Japanese market made it seem likely that the growth of Japanese corporate ownership, especially of export activities, would generate concern about economic and political domination. These elements have been present but not at all prominent in attitudes toward development of investment ties between Australia and Japan. One reason is that the appearance of Japanese investment in Australia, alongside the established operations of European (mainly British) and U.S. investors represented a welcome diversification of foreign investment activity and increased investment competition (Drysdale, 1972). Another reason is that Japanese FDI did not dominate the development of the raw materials trade with Japan; U.S., European, and Australian investors initiated this trade and they remain the principal players. Concern about transfer pricing, for example, remained muted. A further reason is that the rapid growth of Japanese investment capacity coincided nicely with strong growth of Australian demand for foreign capital as economic expansion promoted a larger role for it in public and private spending and as economic reform widened the opportunities for participation in the Australian economy by foreign enterprise. Much more so than in the United States, this conjuncture of events was viewed as a happy coincidence.

But issues there have been.

The principal complaint about Japanese FDI in Australia has not been that there has been too much of it, but that there has been too little of it. Even at the height of the boom in real estate investment in Australia in 1989, when there was some public outcry in the areas in which Japanese and other foreign investment in real estate was concentrated (mainly in Queensland tourism locations and in Sydney), there was no general reaction against Japanese investment in Australia. Rather, it was urged, there should be less speculative investment in real estate and related developments (*Time Australia,* 11 July 1988) and more Japanese investment directed toward making the Australian manufacturing sector more productive and internationally oriented. There was a growing mood to attract Japanese investment into high technology, research and development intensive activity, a mood quintessentially expressed in the joint government commitment to the development of an international science city in Australia (the Multifunction Polis project).

Foreign direct investment became a much more important element in

Japan's capital exports to Australia through the 1980s. Manufacturing activity, however, was not the principal target of Japanese investors in this period. British and U.S. companies are still more strongly represented in Australian manufacturing than are Japanese companies, despite the competitive strength and global reach of Japanese industrial corporations. There are exceptions—for example, in motor vehicles—but they are notable as long-standing exceptions and are not the product of the recent expansion of Japanese corporate activity in Australia.

Why is this so and are there any changes under way?

Another complaint is that Japanese firms operating in Australia have an unusually strong preference to buy from Japanese rather than local or other non-Japanese foreign suppliers in their purchases of capital equipment, materials, and components or services.

The most telling criticism of Japanese manufacturing companies in Australia, Edgington asserts (1991, p. 73), has been their tendency to engage in enclave operations. Kreinin's (1989) much-cited survey of Japanese, as well as U.S. and European, manufacturing operations in Australia suggests that the vast majority of capital equipment used by Japanese subsidiaries in Australia is "of Japanese origin [whereas for] U.S. and European investors . . . there was . . . no preponderance of equivalent purchases from any one source" (Edgington, ibid.).

Interestingly, this complaint about Japanese manufacturing activity has not been widely heard in Australia. It has, however, attracted much attention in the North American debate about the closed nature of the Japanese market for manufactured goods and the role of Japanese corporate practices (*keiretsu*, or corporate affiliations) in limiting market access for non-Japanese corporations in the Japanese market (Lawrence, 1991, p. 21).

A related issue has received more public attention in Australia. The debate about the upsurge of Japanese investment in tourism and resort development has suggested exclusionary behavior by Japanese operators in this sector. Because of the consortium-style of Japanese business activities, Edgington (1991, p. 74) observes, there was concern that here too Japanese-oriented tourist developments would be dominated by a network of Japanese construction companies, banks, trading companies, hotel groups, and airlines.

Is there evidence that Japanese investors are exclusionary in their purchasing practices, technology policies, or employment practices in a way that is different from U.S. or other foreign investors—and is this changing over time?

This chapter provides an overview of the development and role of Japanese FDI in Australia. By exploring the structure of Japanese capital exports to Australia and trends in FDI over the past decade, I also compare the performance of Japanese and U.S. FDI over the same period and in earlier times. As for Japanese investment in Australia in general, what has determined its size, its timing, and the activities into which it has been directed? Does it really have characteristics that are distinctive from other FDI in Australia?

Japan as a Source of Capital

The strength of Japan's savings base and the progressive liberalization of the Japanese capital market saw Japan's emergence as a major supplier of international capital in the 1980s. The reform of Japan's foreign-exchange-control laws encouraged the rapid diversification of Japan's capital exports across the entire range of financial instruments, rapid growth of net capital outflows, and a vast increase in the acquisition of foreign assets and international financial intermediation. By 1989 Japan generated 26.74 percent of the world's savings, greater than that of any single country.

It is not surprising that capital flows from Japan to Australia rose sharply over this period (Australia-Japan Foundation, 1991, p. 4). Australia's status as a long-term capital importer and the added requirement for public borrowing in the early 1980s saw both the scale and composition of Japan's capital exports to Australia change dramatically, although these changes were roughly in line with the changes then taking place in Japan's investment abroad more generally.

The upsurge of Japanese investment abroad in the 1980s was led by the growth of portfolio investment. Japanese banks, securities companies, insurance and pension funds, corporations, and individuals sought to increase sharply their stock of foreign financial and other assets following foreign exchange decontrol in 1980, the steady explosion of asset prices in Japan, and the appreciation of the yen after 1985. Excess domestic savings in Japan, given the opportunity, sought relatively cheap assets overseas, with the focus in turn on bonds, stocks, and real estate. This process continued until the sharp falls in Japanese asset prices in the late 1980s brought them into line with international asset prices as the emphasis in long-term capital outflow shifted to direct investment.

Japanese capital exports to Australia in the first half of the 1980s, in the form of Australian bond purchases, eased the burden of financing Australia's public deficit. As these deficits were eliminated, the structure of borrowing from Japan and other countries also shifted toward direct investment.

Japan's direct investment abroad rose from $US 12 billion in Japanese fiscal year 1985 to $US 42 billion in 1991. The rush by Japanese corporations to establish operations abroad was driven by the impact of the yen appreciation and inexorably changing cost structures on the competitiveness of home-based operations, the effect of trade restrictions in North America and Europe on market access for goods made in Japan, and the massive liberalization of financial and related markets in industrial countries (notably also in Australia), which encouraged the expansion of service activities abroad.

The growth of Japan's FDI in the 1980s was accompanied by a considerable change in its direction and sectoral distribution. Japanese policies and corporate strategies in earlier years were heavily influenced by Japan's trade and resource procurement needs. Investment in trade and upstream resource and manufacturing activities was an important priority (Hamada, 1972, pp. 173–200). What funds were available for investment abroad were directed toward commerce, the resource industries, and manufacturing. During the 1980s Japanese investment rapidly shifted toward banking and insurance, real estate, and other services (table 4.2).

Japan's traditional interests in direct investment abroad were heavily represented in the Australian activities of Japanese corporations. The new direction of Japanese investment in the 1980s dovetailed closely with the financial market deregulation in Australia and other developments that opened opportunities for foreign participation in the service industries, especially tourism, tourism-related projects, and other real estate development projects at this time.

How did Australia fare in attracting Japanese investment interest relative to other potential destinations? The same pressures saw North America and Europe become increasingly important destinations for Japanese direct investment abroad. There was also expansion of Japanese production facilities in lower-labor-cost destinations, although East Asian and Latin American shares in Japan's FDI both fell in this period. The important facts are that, contrary to perception, Japanese investment in Australian activities was always relatively high and that, in the past decade, it grew significantly relative to Japanese investment activities in other countries.

Australia has long had a relatively large share in Japan's direct investment abroad, accounting for 4–5 percent of the total over the past forty years, a share that places Australia as the fourth largest single destination for Japanese direct investment after the United States, the United Kingdom, and Panama, still ahead of Indonesia, Hong Kong, and China. Australia's importance as an investment outlet for Japanese corporations has risen in the past ten years, exceeding 6 percent of all Japanese investment abroad in recent years (table 4.3).

TABLE 4.2
COMPOSITION OF JAPANESE INVESTMENT TO REST OF WORLD
(% share and $US million)

	Cumulative 1950/51–1980/81	1980/81	1984/85	1987/88	1988/89	1989/90	1990/91	1991/92	Cumulative 1950/51–1991/92
Manufacturing	34.4	36.4	24.7	23.5	29.4	24.1	27.2	29.6	26.7
	12,573	1,706	2,505	7,832	13,805	16,284	15,486	12,309	93,924
Mining and agricultural	21.9	13.6	5.3	1.9	2.7	2.2	2.2	3.2	5.7
	7,981	638	534	652	1,269	1,460	1,542	1,351	19,987
Banking and insurance	6.6	8.1	20.5	32.0	27.9	22.8	14.1	12.0	19.9
	2,426	380	2,085	10,673	13,104	15,395	8,047	4,972	70,290
Real estate	na	14.4	4.2	16.3	18.4	20.9	19.5	21.4	15.5
	na	675	430	5,428	8,641	14,116	1,107	8,899	54,748
Other services	37.04	29.1	45.3	26.3	21.6	30.0	36.4	33.8	32.2
	13,517	1,367	4,601	8,780	10,204	20,256	20,731	14,052	113,414
Total	36,497	4,693	10,155	33,364	47,022	67,540	56,911	41,583	352,392

NOTES: na Not available.
Japanese fiscal year ends in March

SOURCE: Ministry of Finance, Japan, *Monthly Finance Review*, 1980–1991, Information Systems Department, Institute of Fiscal and Monetary Policy, Tokyo.

When these relative investment shares are compared with Australia's much lesser importance in world production and trade and the world market for investment funds, they suggest unusually strong investment links between Australia and Japan. Australia is more than four times as important to Japan as an investment partner than it is in world economic activity.

Strong investment links between Japan and Australia are a product of the exceptionally strong and well-established resource trade links between the two countries, and they have strengthened further in recent times by the new links that have developed in the service sector, in tourism, finance, and real estate development. Earlier, Australia also induced Japanese producers of automobile and electronic products to locate in the Australian market, well over a decade ahead of their move into the North American market, behind high tariff and other barriers to trade. Despite the steady reduction of protection and the rationalization of these industries begun in the 1980s (and the exit of Nissan from Australian automobile production in 1992), these investors remain the largest Japanese manufacturers operating in Australia.

Hence, the most impressive change in the 1980s was not so much the intensification of investment ties between Australia and Japan as the impact of the growth in the scale of Japanese investment overseas upon the scale of investment flows to Australia. This surge of Japanese investment had almost no precedent, except that of the growth of U.S. foreign investment in the 1950s and 1960s.

Japanese Investment in Australia: Trends and Structure

Trends in Japanese investment in Australia and changes in the structure of Japan's investment portfolio in Australia reflect developments in Japanese investment globally. Some sectors of direct investment, of course, are more strongly represented in Australia than they are in other countries, both because of underlying complementarities in investment interests and because of the policy environment.

Until the 1980s the overall level of Japanese investment in Australia was much lower than that of the United States or the United Kingdom. Table 4.4 sets out the shares of Japan, the United States, and the United Kingdom in total foreign investment in Australia through to 1991. In the past decade Japan's share in this total leapt from 8.7 percent to 17.9 percent.

In the 1970s Japanese investment was fairly evenly spread between di-

Table 4.3

Japan's Annual Direct Investment Abroad: Ranking of Major Recipient Countries (%)

FY1980		FY1981		FY1982	
Country	*Rank*	*Country*	*Rank*	*Country*	*Rank*
United States	31.6	Indonesia	27.3	United States	35.5
Indonesia	11.3	United States	26.2	Panama	9.4
Australia	9.2	Panama	6.9	Liberia	5.6
Panama	4.7	Liberia	5.2	Indonesia	5.3
United Kingdom	4.0	Australia	3.9	Hong Kong	5.2
Brazil	3.6	Hong Kong	3.7	Australia	4.8

FY1983	
Country	*Rank*
United States	31.5
Panama	15.0
Hong Kong	6.9
Brazil	5.0
Indonesia	4.6
Liberia	4.0
Singapore	4.0
Luxembourg	3.3
Australia	2.0

FY1984		FY1987		FY1989		FY1991	
Country	*Rank*	*Country*	*Rank*	*Country*	*Rank*	*Country*	*Rank*
United States	27.9	United States	44.1	United States	48.2	United States	43.4
Indonesia	11.2	United Kingdom	7.4	United Kingdom	7.8	United Kingdom	8.6
Panama	6.9	Panama	6.9	Holland	6.7	Australia	6.1
Brazil	6.0	Luxembourg	5.3	Australia	6.3	Holland	4.7
Australia	4.4	China	3.7	Panama	3.0	Panama	3.8
		Australia	3.7	Singapore	2.8	Indonesia	2.9

SOURCE: Australia-Japan Economic Institute, various newsletters, Sydney.

TABLE 4.4
SHARES IN LEVEL OF TOTAL INVESTMENT IN AUSTRALIA, 1981–1991[a]

(% share and value in $US million)

	Japan		United States		United Kingdom		Total
1981	8.7%	4,749	27.6%	15,162	30.8%	16,895	54,861
1982	9.9	6,020	27.3	16,695	27.8	16,958	61,066
1983	13.1	8,683	24.9	16,504	26.5	17,579	66,395
1984	13.2	9,756	24.8	18,353	25.2	18,634	73,948
1985	14.5	12,519	24.0	20,726	23.7	20,431	86,258
1986	15.2	14,844	22.7	22,192	21.3	20,846	97,792
1987	12.5	14,839	23.1	27,437	21.3	25,217	118,537
1988	14.9	21,583	20.1	29,231	22.1	32,120	145,151
1989	16.3	29,207	19.8	35,376	20.2	36,310	179,558
1990	18.0	35,468	18.0	35,648	17.9	35,376	197,572
1991	17.9	39,142	19.3	42,299	17.2	38,330	219,015

NOTES: [a]Year to 30 June.
In 1985/1986 the definition of direct investment changed from 25% equity to 10% equity; therefore, entries from years prior to that are not strictly comparable with entries of subsequent years.

SOURCE: Australian Bureau of Statistics (ABS) Catalog No. 5305, *Foreign Investment—Australia*, 1985/86, 1987/88, 1988/89, 1990/91. Canberra: ABS.

FIGURE 4.1

LEVEL OF U.S. INVESTMENT IN AUSTRALIA BY TYPE OF INVESTMENT, 1990

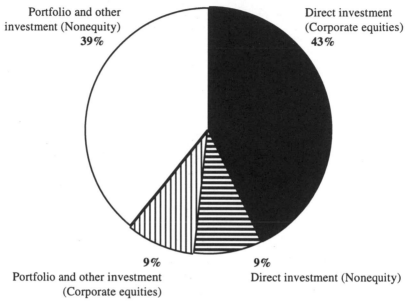

Portfolio and other
investment (Nonequity)
39%

Direct investment
(Corporate equities)
43%

9%
Portfolio and other investment
(Corporate equities)

9%
Direct investment (Nonequity)

SOURCE: ABS Catalog No. 5305, *Foreign Investment—Australia*, 1990/91. Canberra: ABS.

rect and portfolio investment, primarily because policy and administrative guidelines limited Japanese institutional investment in bonds and equities abroad. United States investment in Australia was highly concentrated in direct investment in this period. There was a sharp change in the structure of these capital flows to Australia at the end of the 1970s. From 1979 to 1980 Japanese portfolio investment began to rise strongly: In that year direct investment from the United States totaled $772 million (U.S.), and portfolio investment was only $113 million, whereas portfolio investment from Japan had risen to $656 million and direct investment was $242 million.

The growth of portfolio investment in the 1980s, despite the large fall in purchases of Australian securities in 1985–86, left Japan with a larger stake in Australian securities and equities markets than in direct investment at the beginning of the 1990s (see figure 4.1). Japanese direct investment continued to grow relative to portfolio investment (especially through the second half of the 1980s) but the surge of direct investment has not yet overwhelmed the earlier growth of portfolio investment in Japan's investment portfolio in Australia.

FIGURE 4.2

LEVEL OF JAPANESE INVESTMENT IN AUSTRALIA BY TYPE OF INVESTMENT, 1990

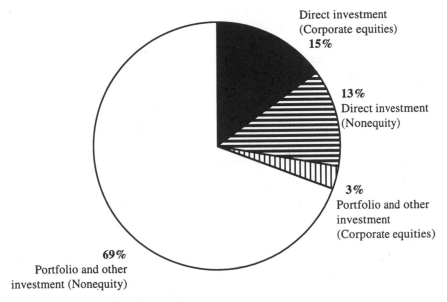

SOURCE: ABS Catalog No. 5305, *Foreign Investment—Australia*, 1990/91. Canberra: ABS.

Figure 4.2 depicts the structure of American total investment in Australia in 1990 and may be compared with figure 4.1, which presents the same data for Japan. These graphs show that 72 percent of the stock of Japanese investment was portfolio and other investment, and 28 percent was direct investment in 1990. By contrast, only 48 percent of the total stock of U.S. investment in Australia in 1990 was portfolio and other investment, whereas 52 percent was direct investment. For Japan, 33 percent of all this investment had gone into the Australian government sector, 51 percent into industrial and commercial enterprises, and 16 percent to banks and other nonbank financial institutions. The destination of U.S. investment was very different; only 10 percent went to the Australian government sector, 14 percent to banks and other nonbank financial institutions, and a massive 76 percent went into industrial and commercial enterprises. Further, a larger proportion of Japanese direct investment (46 percent) was financed in the form of loans rather than through equity investment, compared with U.S. direct investment (of which only 17 percent was loan financed).

Japanese firms in Australia have relied heavily on borrowing from parent firms and Japanese-based financial institutions. In 1989, only 16 percent of long-term funding was secured from local banking establishments (Ministry of International Trade and Industry, 1991). This pattern is long-established. Hamada and Nishimura (1975) report that 40.7 percent of Japanese affiliate funding in Australia was drawn from Japan in 1972. This pattern of financing Japanese direct investment in Australia is consistent with observations about the role of the main banks (Sheard, 1992) in funding long-term corporate investment by Japanese affiliated manufacturing and commercial firms and about the role of the Japanese trading companies in coordinating investment and trade in the resources sector through financing from affiliated banks (Ozawa, 1979).

At 16.2 percent in 1991, Japan's share of total direct investment in Australia was still less than its share in total foreign investment (17.9 percent in the same year). The high proportion of loans and portfolio investment in total Japanese investment also means that Japanese ownership and control of Australian industry is less than implied by looking at Japan's share of total investment in Australia. Capital flows from Japan have been mobilized significantly by Australian governments, institutions, and enterprises to finance public and private investment as well as for direct investment by Japanese enterprises, much more so than was the case for capital flows from the United States.

Access to the Japanese capital market from Australia is now open to many channels and is not dominated by any particular channel of funding or investment.

Sectoral Distribution of Japanese Direct Investment in Australia

As of March 1992, the bulk of Japanese direct investment was in commerce (trading company activity) and real estate, which together accounted for 41 percent of total Japanese FDI in Australia, according to Japanese data (see table 4.5). This pattern of investment flow to Australia is not greatly different from the sectoral pattern of Japanese FDI globally.

Compared with all FDI in Australia, Japanese FDI appears heavily concentrated in agriculture, mining, transport equipment, and finance. The share of Japanese investment in these sectors exceeds Japan's share in total direct investment in Australia, most markedly in agriculture and transport

TABLE 4.5
JAPANESE DIRECT INVESTMENT IN AUSTRALIA BY SECTOR, 1980–1991
(% share and $US million)

	1980/81	1983/84	1984/85	1985/86	1986/87	1987/88	1988/89	1989/90	1990/91	1991/92	Cumulative 1950/51– 1991/92
Manufacturing	28.3	9.03	27.6	2.8	14.0	20.8	8.7	3.7	9.8	13.4	10.5
	122	15	29	13	123	254	211	159	360	342	1,948
Mining and agricultural	53.1	31.9	4.8	5.3	22.1	9.5	7.7	12.1	21.0	11.4	18.4
	229	53	5	25	195	116	186	516	769	291	3,418
Banking and insurance	2.6	1.2	8.6	52.1	10.4	17.0	15.0	12.8	5.5	2.8	9.8
	11	2	9	244	92	208	363	545	200	72	1,819
Real estate	0.0	1.2	5.7	12.0	14.4	33.6	52.6	38.1	36.4	49.2	32.7
	0	2	6	56	127	411	1,270	1,623	1,333	1,255	6,095
Commerce	12.3	53.0	25.7	12.4	8.7	8.9	3.8	7.0	8.9	8.0	8.2
	53	88	27	58	77	109	92	296	326	204	1,528
Other services	3.9	3.6	29.5	15.6	30.1	10.3	12.1	26.2	18.5	15.1	20.4
	17	6	31	73	265	126	292	1,117	679	385	3,804
Total	431	166	105	468	881	1,224	2,414	4,256	3,667	2,549	18,612

NOTE: Japanese fiscal year ends in March.
SOURCE: Ministry of Finance, Japan, *Monthly Finance Review*, 1980–1991, Information Systems Department, Institute of Fiscal and Monetary Policy, Tokyo.

equipment. The financial sector which includes real estate and tourism, is underestimated in Australian data, but in this sector also, Japanese investment share is higher than average.

The focus of Japanese direct investment in agriculture, mining, basic metals, and, in recent years, tourism and real estate appears closely related to Australia's strong comparative advantage and the extensive trade links between Australia and Japan in those sectors. An important question is whether direct investment flows promote these strong trade links. To what extent is Japanese investment in Australia export-oriented?

Direct investment in the manufacture of transport equipment in Australia is a prominent example of investment aimed initially not at promoting exports but rather at protecting shares in the Australian market. Investment in this sector was the strategic response by Japanese producers to heightened trade barriers and local-content requirements, aimed at protecting their growing sales of Japanese motor vehicles in Australia through the 1960s, 1970s, and 1980s.

Table 4.5 sets out changes in the sectoral distribution of Japanese direct investment in Australia over the past decade, as recorded in Japanese data. These data show more clearly the recent growth of real estate and tourism investment and the growth of investment in finance activities through the 1980s. Surveys of the establishment of Japanese enterprises in Australia and Oceania by the Australia-Japan Economic Institute and MITI underline the importance of investment in commerce, the recent growth of real estate and tourism ventures, and the stronger growth of manufacturing activities in the past few years.

Table 4.6 records the period of establishment of 610 Japanese companies surveyed by the Australia-Japan Economic Institute in 1992. These data reveal that, in the early 1970s, most companies were involved in mining or commerce, but by the late 1980s nearly half of Japanese establishments in Australia were in finance, insurance, property, and the business service sector. A similar pattern can be observed in a MITI survey of 382 Japanese companies in Oceania, in which manufacturing investment activity rapidly increased in the past few years.

Figure 4.3 compares Japanese direct investment by major sector in Australia with Japanese investment by sector worldwide. Although the sectoral distribution of Japanese investment in Australia and globally are similar, this figure demonstrates the relatively high proportion of direct investment in Australia going into mining and agricultural activities and real estate development.

TABLE 4.6

JAPANESE SUBSIDIARIES IN AUSTRALIA BY YEAR OF ESTABLISHMENT
(Number of companies and percentage share in each period)

Industry	Pre-1970 No.	Pre-1970 %	1970–1979 No.	1970–1979 %	1980–1984 No.	1980–1984 %	1985–1991 No.	1985–1991 %	Total
Automotive	8	20.5	10	25.6	8	20.5	13	33.3	39
Banking and finance	6	8.7	10	14.5	14	20.3	39	56.5	69
Business services	1	5.0	5	25.0	4	20.0	10	50.0	20
Cement	3	75.0	0	0.0	0	0.0	1	25.0	4
Communications	0	0.0	1	33.3	0	0.0	2	66.6	3
Construction	1	8.3	2	16.7	3	25.0	6	50.0	12
Education	0	0.0	0	0.0	1	20.0	4	80.8	5
Electrical and electronic	3	7.1	19	45.2	7	16.7	13	31.0	42
Food and catering	5	1.0	6	19.2	4	15.4	11	42.3	26
Forestry	1	50.0	0	0.0	1	50.0	0	0.0	2
Insurance	3	20.0	4	26.7	2	13.3	6	40.0	15
Machinery	11	26.2	15	35.7	11	26.2	5	12.0	42
Other manufacturing	6	18.8	6	18.8	10	31.3	10	31.3	32
Media	1	16.7	3	50.0	1	16.7	1	16.7	6
Medical	2	28.6	2	28.6	0	0.0	3	42.9	7
Mining and energy	19	21.6	18	20.5	27	30.8	24	27.3	88
Miscellaneous	0	0.0	0	0.0	0	0.0	1	100.0	1
Pastoral	4	14.3	9	32.1	4	14.3	11	39.2	28
Real estate	0	0.0	4	10.0	1	2.5	35	81.5	40
Tourism	1	34.5	3	10.3	2	6.9	23	79.3	29
Trading companies	12	66.7	3	16.7	1	5.6	2	11.1	18
Transport and storage	6	20.7	2	6.9	6	20.7	15	51.7	29
Wholesale and retail	5	14.7	12	35.3	7	20.6	10	29.4	34
No response									19
Total	98		134		114		245		610

NOTES: The companies are grouped into 22 categories (23 including miscellaneous) according to the main activity of the parent companies.
It is often difficult to distinguish between real estate and tourism because of overlap.
Some of the categories listed can include both manufacturing and distribution.

SOURCE: Australia-Japan Economic Institute, *Japanese Business Activity in Australia*, 1992, Sydney.

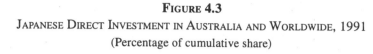

FIGURE 4.3

JAPANESE DIRECT INVESTMENT IN AUSTRALIA AND WORLDWIDE, 1991
(Percentage of cumulative share)

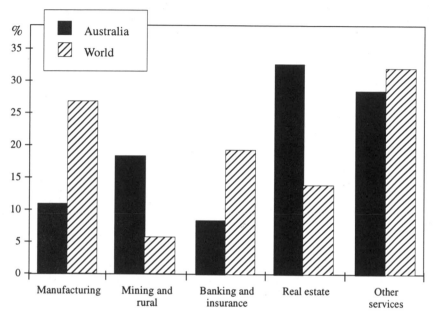

NOTE: Japanese fiscal year ends in March.
SOURCE: Ministry of Finance, Japan, *Monthly Finance Review*, June 1991, Tokyo.

Mining and Energy

Table 4.6 reveals that mining and energy companies still account for the
largest number of, and longest-established, Japanese firms operating in Australia. The huge resource trade between the two countries attracted investment to develop resource supplies for import by Japanese metal manufacturing and energy producers well before Japanese direct investment was significant globally. The scale of the resource trade, however, is not fully reflected in the stake of Japanese investors in the resource sector in Australia
for two main reasons.

In the 1960s, when this trade was opened up, severe capital constraints
in Japan and strict control policies prevented capital export from Japan on a
scale commensurate with the requirements of the growth of the industry and
resource trade (Crawford and Okita, 1976). Much of the foreign investment
that went into the mining and energy sector in this period was European and

American. Raw materials were delivered under long-term contracts from independent Australian and non-Japanese, foreign-owned suppliers to the Japanese steel mills and other users in Japan (Smith, 1980). Non-Japanese firms played the lead role in these developments not only because there were limited supplies of capital available from Japan but also because other foreign and Australian firms had the management and technological skills to get these huge projects into production. Japanese trading companies and (later) users took some equity in resource projects, but usually minority participation targeted monitoring conditions and developments in the industry more than securing control or an active role in management of the industry or trade. Japanese interest in minerals and energy developments did, however, provide important access to Japanese capital on preferred terms, in the form of loans from Japanese bank syndicates and official agencies (such as the Export-Import Bank of Japan), for financing these large-scale projects.

Japanese ownership of the Australian mining industry is last estimated to have been a mere 3.2 percent, compared with 21.7 percent U.S. ownership and 44.7 percent all other foreign ownership (Australia-Japan Foundation, 1991, p. 26). Ownership of coal output is somewhat larger at 12.5 percent, but small by comparison with European ownership, and the overwhelming proportion of the industry is in the hands of Australian companies (between 60 and 70 percent).

There was a new surge of Japanese direct investment in minerals and energy projects during the resources boom in the early 1980s. Between 1978–79 and 1981–82 the number of mining and energy proposals multiplied quickly and Japan became the second most important source of such investment proposals in this sector, after the United States. Again, in the late 1980s, investment in the minerals and energy sector rose steeply, with a large investment in the huge North West Shelf liquefied natural gas project dominating investment in this sector at this time.

Transport Equipment

Transport equipment, and later basic metals, led Japanese investment in Australian manufacturing. Japanese automakers began sales to Australia in the early 1960s and Australian Motor Industries (AMI) began assembly of Toyota vehicles in 1963. In 1966, Toyota entered the local contract plan for motor vehicle manufacture and, by 1991, Toyota's ownership of AMI rose to 50 percent.

It is significant that Australia represented the first major breakthrough into a Western market for Japanese motor car producers, around fifteen years before Japanese cars broke into the American and European markets. This pattern of Japanese entry into industrial-country markets was not atypical historically for other manufactured products. By 1972, Japanese vehicles already accounted for 18.6 percent of new registrations in Australia, with Toyota and Nissan supplying 74 percent of that share. By 1971, both Toyota and Nissan were complying with the 85 percent local-content arrangement. In 1972, the first Toyota engine was produced at the old Altona plant near Melbourne and in 1981 volume production of body panels began. Investments by both Toyota and Nissan were initially aimed at selling exports rather than manufacturing in Australia but both producers were drawn into local production as their stake in the local market and local policies developed. After the mid-1980s, following the yen appreciation, there was increased manufacturing of components and products in Australia, and Mitsubishi, which had earlier taken over Chrysler's ailing operations in Australia, began exporting cylinder heads and vehicles to the Japanese parent and Mitsubishi affiliates elsewhere in the Western Pacific.

In 1988, the impetus of a new motor vehicle plan, incorporating an export facilitation scheme and steady reduction of tariffs toward the year 2000, saw Toyota form a joint venture with General Motors, United Australian Automotive Industries (UAMI). The new company began integrated production of a range of models for both owners. Toyota Motors Australia is 70 percent owned by Toyota and 30 percent owned by UAMI, which is a 50/50 joint venture of Toyota and General Motors. At present, Toyota Australia operates three plants and is in the process of undertaking a large new investment, Australia's first new car production facility in over twenty-five years on a greenfields site at Altona. The first cars from this plant will be produced in 1994 and capacity will eventually reach 100,000 units a year. The value of this new investment is around $US 320 million.

Although Nissan has left the Australian market, Mitsubishi is undertaking improvements worth $US 163 million at its two South Australian sites. Mitsubishi's investment strategy focused on production of a local vehicle (also exported to the home market) and investment in plant and equipment for the manufacture of parts and components for export to the parent company and subsidiaries elsewhere in the region.

Agriculture and Foodstuffs

Direct investment in food processing and related agricultural activities grew rapidly in the late 1980s and early 1990s. Foodstuffs were the most important component of manufacturing investment in 1991. Most of the investment in this sector was induced by the abolition of quotas on imports of beef in April 1991 (McKenzie, 1990; Morrison, 1992). Tariffs on Japanese imports were also reduced, from 70 to 60 percent in the first year after the abolition of import quotas. Japanese investment in Australian agriculture and meat processing over this period has sought to exploit home country marketing and distribution advantages and provide quality assurances through ownership of upstream production facilities (Morrison, 1992).

Tourism and Real Estate

The share of real estate and tourism in Japanese FDI, as estimated from Japanese data, has been 35 to 53 percent of the flow of all direct investment from Japan over the past half decade. Despite the magnitude of Japanese real-estate-related investment, Japanese projects are on average smaller than North American and European projects (Committee for Economic Development and Keizai Doyukai, 1990, p. 81). Japanese property investments in Australia have also primarily involved development of new resort areas or business facilities, rather than the acquisition of established projects through takeover.

Table 4.7 shows the growing importance of Oceania (primarily Australia) as a destination for Japanese real estate investments from 1985 to 1991. Australia accounts for 12.5 percent of all Japanese property investment overseas in the postwar period, mostly undertaken in the past five years. Australia's share in recent years has frequently been higher than this, as shown in table 4.7.

Table 4.8 sets out the structure of Japanese property investment in all major Australian states and territories as of June 1992. A central feature of these data is the concentration of investment in office and tourism resort/hotel developments in New South Wales (NSW) and Queensland (QLD).

The large-scale growth of Japanese property development in Australia has been associated with rapid growth of tourism exports to Japan. In 1991, over half a million Japanese visitors came to Australia. Japan is now Australia's largest market for tourism; Australia is the destination for around 5 percent of Japanese travelers abroad. This association appears to underline

TABLE 4.7
JAPANESE DIRECT INVESTMENT IN REAL ESTATE BY REGION, 1985–1991
($US million and % share each year)

Region	1985	1986	1987	1988	1989	1990	1991	Cumulative 1950/51– 1990/91
North America	1,221	2,075	4,375	5,652	8,855	5,912	5,498	36,045
	92.9	81.9	80.6	65.4	62.6	53.2	61.8	65.8
Asia	15	308	442	384	1,121	640	357	3,348
	1.2	12.2	8.1	4.4	7.9	5.8	4.0	6.1
Europe	11	57	124	1,119	2,283	2,928	1,609	8,206
	0.9	2.2	2.3	12.9	16.1	26.4	18.1	15.0
Oceania	59	79	450	1,330	1,828	1,616	1,417	6,849
	4.9	3.1	8.3	15.4	12.9	14.5	15.9	12.5
Other	1	14	37	156	56	11	19	299
	0.1	0.6	0.7	1.8	0.4	0.1	0.2	0.5
Total	1,207	2,533	5,428	8,641	14,143	11,107	8,899	54,747

SOURCE: Ministry of Finance, Japan, *Monthly Finance Review*, 1985–1991, Information Systems Department, Institute of Fiscal and Monetary Policy, Tokyo.

TABLE 4.8

JAPANESE INVESTMENT IN AUSTRALIAN PROPERTY: LEVEL AS OF JUNE 1992

($US million)

Sector	New South Wales	Victoria	Queensland	South Australia	West Australia	Australia Commonwealth Territory
Office	2,896	1,728	328	23	371	50
Retail	250	273	585	0	0	78
Industrial	51	0	0	0	0	0
Residential	62	0	136	0	39	0
Tourism and leisure	1,504	111	1,935	156	319	61
Miscellaneous	29	0	171	0	0	0
Total	4,788	2,112	3,155	179	730	188

NOTES: Figures represent purchase price or likely development costs at time of construction (not current market value).
All sales represent actual value of investment into Australian property and may not necessarily represent current holdings.
All sales over $US 10 million.
0 indicates that investments in that sector over the threshold value are unknown.
All recorded sales until June 1992.
The information should be regarded only as a general guide and no responsibility is accepted for its accuracy.

SOURCE: Jones Lang Wooton Research and Consultancy, 1992, Sydney.

the traditional link between Japanese direct investment in Australia and trade complementarity with Japan. However, Forsyth and Dwyer (1990) suggest that the link between Japanese investment in Australian property and the increased flows of Japanese tourists may have been weak.

Much Japanese investment in property abroad has the character of portfolio investment, as Japanese holders of wealth adjusted their portfolios in response to low yields in Japan and the prospect of capital gains from property investment overseas during the property boom of the late 1980s (Farrell, 1992). Such investment did not involve active participation in, or control of, corporate activity in Australia. Yet, there was also a significant and active Japanese corporate interest in property development directly related to the growth of tourism.

The collapse of Australian property prices with the sharp monetary contraction after 1990 left many of the more entrepreneurial and prominent Japanese investors in Australian property severely exposed, and there has been a ragged retreat from this sector by these investors, covered largely by Japanese bankers.

Export Performance of Japanese Firms

The link between Japanese FDI and sales and purchases by Australian-based Japanese subsidiaries abroad is a question of considerable and more general interest. Do Japanese firms promote exports and direct a significant proportion of their sales abroad to Japan? How does the export performance of Japanese firms compare with that of U.S. firms in Australia?

A great deal of evidence can be assembled from MITI and the U.S. Commerce Department survey data to address these questions, but it has been surprisingly little used in the literature and discussion to date. MITI surveys cover data in Oceania as a whole, but these data can reasonably be taken to represent largely the performance of Japanese firms operating in Australia. Department of Commerce data treat Australia separately.

Selling into the Australian market, not selling abroad, was historically a strong rationalization for *manufacturing* investment from both Japan and America. The small size of the Australian market and the strategic purpose of investing in local operations (behind protective trade barriers) militated in the past against exporting from foreign-owned manufacturing firms in Australia. Brash (1966, p. 220) reports that exports of ninety-three American companies he surveyed in 1962 were a minuscule 2.3 percent of total sales.

Investors in mining and energy projects, as well as agriculture and tourism, on the other hand, might be expected to export a sizable proportion of their output.

An outstanding feature of Japanese corporate activity in Australia is its very strong export orientation. The ratio of exports to total sales has always been very high, and although it has fallen over the past twenty years, it still remains high. The export sales ratio was over 70 percent in the early 1970s, with most investment in trading companies and export-oriented resource projects. Yet, despite diversification of investment into manufacturing and other services, the export sales ratio was still a high 57.2 percent in 1980 and 44.4 percent in 1990. Australia stands out among Japanese foreign investment destinations as having among the highest average export sales ratios, including ratios of export sales to Japan, and the lowest ratios of purchases of imports from Japan to total purchases.

Figures 4.4 and 4.5 present data on export sales to Japan as a ratio of total sales and import purchases from Japan as a ratio of the total purchases of Japanese affiliates in Australia or Oceania and a range of other countries for the early 1970s and 1990. Exports to the home country and purchases from the home country are unusually low for Japanese firms in Australia. In the early 1970s, Japanese mining affiliates are reported to have exported around 80 percent of their sales while manufacturing affiliates exported around 12 percent (Hamada and Nishimura, 1975). Toyota and Nissan sold all their products to the domestic market at that time. Clearly, export-oriented resource producers and traders dominated Japanese business in Australia during that period.

There is an important element of double-counting in these Japanese data because of the role of trading companies. This factor tends to overstate both the export sales and the import purchase ratios when all sectors are included in these measures. Hence it is more instructive to examine direct exports and sales in each sector of investment activity.

Export sales for manufacturing were only 19.4 percent of total sales in 1980 and 10.9 percent in 1990. Motor vehicles, which are a sizable element in Japanese manufacturing investment in Australia, have a substantial depressing effect on the ratio. There were negligible sales of motor vehicles abroad in 1980 and the ratio of exports to total sales was only 1.6 percent in 1990. The export facilitation program and rationalization of capacity in this industry are likely to encourage higher exports in the coming decade. Exports of chemicals were nonexistent in 1980, but accounted for 85.4 percent of sales in 1990. The export sales ratio for agricultural goods was 90.9 percent in 1990 and the ratio for mining was 81.5 percent. A large proportion of the output of affiliates in basic metals manufacture is also sold abroad.

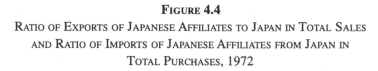

FIGURE 4.4

RATIO OF EXPORTS OF JAPANESE AFFILIATES TO JAPAN IN TOTAL SALES
AND RATIO OF IMPORTS OF JAPANESE AFFILIATES FROM JAPAN IN
TOTAL PURCHASES, 1972

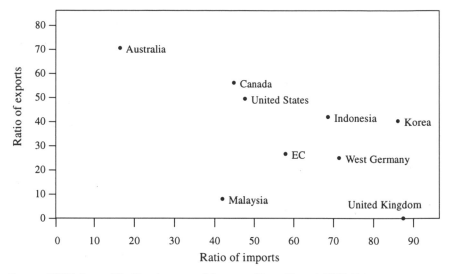

SOURCE: MITI, Japan, *The Development of Japanese Firms Abroad,* 1972, Tokyo.

Figures 4.6 and 4.7 present data on export sales to Japan as a ratio of total sales and import purchases from Japan as a ratio of total purchases for Japanese affiliates engaged in manufacturing in Oceania and other countries for 1980 and 1990. It is interesting to note that Oceania (and Australia) also appears to have a relatively high export sales ratio compared with other Japanese manufacturing bases. It is also noticeable that import purchases from Japan have declined considerably as a proportion of total purchases over the decade in Australia, while they have risen for North America and remained unchanged for Asia as a whole.

There is a marked contrast between the export performance of Japanese and American affiliates in Australia across all sectors. While the ratio of export to total sales for Japanese firms did not fall below 44.4 percent in the 1980s, the ratio of export sales to total sales for U.S. firms was only 13.3 percent in 1982, 11.4 percent in 1986, and 14.2 percent in 1989. Japanese firms are much more export-oriented than are U.S. firms operating in Australia, even if account is taken of the double-counting effect of the sales of Japanese trading companies abroad.

Comparison of the ratio of export sales to total sales of Japanese and

FIGURE **4.5**

RATIO OF EXPORTS OF JAPANESE AFFILIATES TO JAPAN IN TOTAL SALES
AND RATIO OF IMPORTS OF JAPANESE AFFILIATES FROM JAPAN IN
TOTAL PURCHASES, 1990

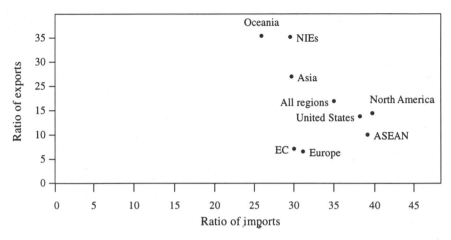

SOURCE: MITI, Japan, *Overseas Activites of Japanese Firms,* 1990, Tokyo.

U.S. firms in manufacturing activity is also interesting. In 1982, U.S. manufacturing affiliates exported 9.4 percent of their total sales; in 1986 the ratio was 13.5 percent; and in 1989 it was 10.9 percent. These data suggest that U.S. manufacturers in Australia, although much longer established than Japanese manufacturers, export a marginally lower proportion of total sales than do their Japanese counterparts. The export performance of U.S. and Japanese manufacturing firms in Australia at the beginning of the 1990s, and in the late 1980s, was not very different, however.

An interesting feature of the export performance of Japanese affiliates is the trend in sales to the home market in Japan. In 1980, 13.8 percent of sales of manufactures from Japanese affiliates went to Japan from Australia, comprising 71.1 percent of exports. By 1990, although this share of a much larger volume of sales had fallen to 9.5 percent, the proportion of exports going to Japan had risen to 87.2 percent. The tentative conclusion is that established Japanese manufacturing investment in Australia is not yet leading to the broader integration of Australian manufacturing into the regional economy. The share of Japan in the sales of all subsidiaries in 1990 was 34.3 percent; for chemicals it was 60.2 percent; for textiles, 76.9 percent; and for food products, 26.1 percent. Export sales of automobiles, parts, and components to Japan were negligible in the early 1980s but were 1.3 percent of the sales

FIGURE 4.6

RATIO OF EXPORTS OF JAPANESE AFFILIATES IN MANUFACTURING TO JAPAN IN TOTAL
SALES AND RATIO OF IMPORTS OF JAPANESE AFFILIATES IN MANUFACTURING FROM
JAPAN IN TOTAL PURCHASES, 1980

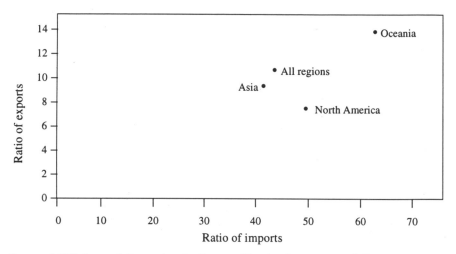

SOURCE: MITI, Japan, *A Comprehensive Survey of Foreign Investment and Overseas
Activities,* 1980, Tokyo.

of the companies surveyed in 1990, and comprised 81 percent of all exports.
About 4.0 percent of the total sales of all U.S. subsidiaries in Australia were
exported to the United States in 1989, or about 36.7 percent of the export
sales of these firms.

Purchasing Behavior of Japanese Firms

Japanese-owned subsidiaries are widely perceived to concentrate their purchases of equipment, components, and materials in Japan, in stark contrast
to subsidiaries from other countries. Corporate group (*keiretsu*) ties are pre-
sumed to bias purchases toward affiliates based in Japan and exclude local
and other foreign firms from supplying Japanese subsidiaries. The evidence
above throws some light on this issue, but it needs further exploration. It is
important to know whether Japanese corporations are very different from
other foreign firms in their impact on the local economy. The Australian case
also has more general significance. The purchasing behavior of Japanese

FIGURE 4.7

RATIO OF EXPORTS OF JAPANESE AFFILIATES IN MANUFACTURING TO JAPAN IN TOTAL
SALES AND RATIO OF IMPORTS OF JAPANESE AFFILIATES IN MANUFACTURING FROM
JAPAN IN TOTAL PURCHASES, 1990

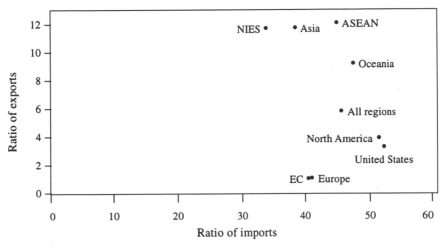

SOURCE: MITI, Japan, *Overseas Activites of Japanese Firms,* 1990, Tokyo.

firms in Australia has been cited prominently to substantiate the claim that
Japanese corporate practices are exclusionary, limiting access by foreign
suppliers to Japanese companies at home and abroad (Lawrence, 1991, p.
21). It is important to know whether the purchasing behavior of Japanese
firms in Australia provides any real support for these sweeping conclusions.

The principal evidence in this matter is presented in a survey by Kreinin
(1989) of sixty-two companies in Australia, of which twenty were Japanese,
twenty-two were American, and twenty were European. On the basis of responses to his questioning, he suggests that Japanese subsidiaries in Australia are highly controlled by the respective parent company, procure their
equipment mainly in Japan, and use and operate mainly Japanese machinery
(Kreinin, 1989, p. 540). Kreinin's conclusion is very strong and his interpretation of his findings unequivocally links this behavior to peculiar Japanese
corporate practice. His questionnaire appears open-ended, however, and there
is no summary statistical reporting of his findings whereby it is easy to assess his impression of the evidence, and he makes no comparison between
his findings and those of others, including the regular surveys by the responsible Japanese and U.S. agencies.

Kreinin reports that in fifteen out of the twenty Japanese companies surveyed either all or over 80 percent of the equipment was of Japanese origin (p. 535). Only five firms used international competitive bids for purchasing standardized equipment, compared with twenty-one of the twenty-two U.S.-owned subsidiaries, for machinery or materials not available in Australia. He did note that a few Japanese firms intended to move to open tendering but this observation did not qualify the interpretation of his findings.

There is a valuable reference point to Kreinin's work in the classic study of U.S. investment in Australia by Brash (1966). Brash undertook a careful survey of the sales and purchasing of U.S. investors in Australia in 1962. Interestingly, Kreinin appears unaware of Brash's earlier study or its relevance to his own.

Brash's work revealed that U.S. subsidiaries he surveyed were unlikely to purchase equipment or components from Australian suppliers, *even if they were cheaper* than equipment and materials sourced from affiliated or parent companies (pp. 203–11). Most of the imports of U.S.-owned companies were purchased from or through U.S.-affiliated firms, with wholly owned firms having a higher dependence on imports than joint ventures. The biggest factor affecting Australian content was reported to be Australian tariff policy. Significantly, Brash's data (p. 205) suggest that the more recently established U.S. subsidiaries imported a much higher proportion of their equipment and materials requirements than older established firms. Measured as a proportion of total sales (rather than purchases, for which data was not readily available), the import ratio for all firms was 18.7 percent, but for firms established in the previous five years it was 29.5 percent.

On the basis of both the impressionistic and the more comprehensive statistical evidence that Brash provides on U.S. subsidiary purchasing behavior in Australia, it would seem difficult to conclude that Japanese firms differ significantly in this respect from their U.S. counterparts. There is, in fact, much published quantitative evidence that can be used to analyze the purchasing behavior of Japanese and, to a lesser extent, U.S. subsidiaries in Australia.

The most complete data for Japan cover only purchases by subsidiaries of intermediate goods, not of plant and equipment. Table 4.9 summarizes these data for all sectors, manufacturing, and transport equipment. Imports comprised 35.5 percent of all purchases of materials by Japanese affiliates in Oceania in 1990s, of which 28.9 percent were from Japan. This ratio of imports from Japan has fallen from 36.7 percent in 1980. The ratio of purchases from Japan to total materials purchases for manufacturing enterprises was considerably higher, at 48.2 percent, but has fallen from 60.9 percent in 1980.

The ratio for transport equipment fell from 97.7 percent in 1980 to 50.5 percent in 1990. These trends are very pronounced and occurred in a period when Australian trade barriers were generally falling.

The data do not allow separation of intermediate goods purchases from purchases of capital equipment by U.S. subsidiaries operating in Australia. Furthermore, they only provide information on import purchases from the United States, not total import purchases. It is probable that a much larger proportion (almost all) of U.S. subsidiary purchases from the United States is capital equipment and that intermediate goods originating in the United States are relatively unimportant, given the character of U.S. comparative advantage and the vintage of U.S. investment in Australia. It is also probable that imports from affiliates outside the United States are more important for U.S. firms (such as in the case of IBM, Ford, or General Motors).

Imports of capital equipment and materials from the United States were indeed a much lower proportion of total purchases of these goods by U.S. subsidiaries in Australia than were purchases of intermediate goods from Japan for Japanese subsidiaries. The proportion was 7.8 percent in 1982 and 10.5 percent in 1988 (U.S. Department of Commerce, 1982, 1989).

TABLE 4.9

RATIO OF IMPORT PURCHASES OF INTERMEDIATE GOODS
BY JAPANESE AFFILIATES IN OCEANIA, 1980–1990

	1980	1987	1988	1989	1990
All sectors					
Import ratio	46.2	61.8	46.6	39.6	35.5
From Japan	36.7	51.8	43.3	35.6	28.9
From other countries	9.5	10.0	3.2	4.0	6.6
All manufacturing					
Import ratio	80.5	61.0	61.8	67.4	55.5
From Japan	60.9	52.9	59.6	65.6	48.2
From other countries	19.6	8.2	2.2	1.8	7.4
Transport equipment					
Import ratio	97.7	60.4	53.9	73.4	57.0
From Japan	97.7	49.9	53.3	72.7	50.5
From other countries	0.0	10.5	0.6	0.7	6.5

SOURCE: MITI, Japan, *Overseas Activities of Japanese Firms,* 1987/88, 1990, Tokyo; MITI, Japan, *A Comprehensive Survey of Foreign Investment and Overseas Activities,* 1980, 1989, Tokyo.

There are some separate data on Japanese subsidiaries' purchases of plant and equipment and these data are more likely to be more directly comparable with the U.S. data on U.S. subsidiary purchasing behavior. These data are also more directly relevant to the questions raised by Kreinin's study than are the data on purchase of intermediate goods.

Table 4.10 shows how much plant and equipment Japanese subsidiaries in all sectors and in manufacturing purchased locally, from Japanese suppliers and from third-country suppliers in 1989. The striking fact is that Japanese firms purchase a very large proportion of their plant and equipment in Australia locally. These data do not reveal whether these purchases are principally from other Japanese firms operating in Australia, but this is unlikely given the present structure of Japanese investment in Australia and the large presence of other firms in the machinery sector. Imports are only 12.5 percent of equipment purchases for all sectors, roughly half of which is drawn from Japan and half from other countries. Imports are 9.1 percent of plant and equipment purchases for manufacturing subsidiaries, 97.8 percent of which come from Japan. These data imply that Kreinin's results may have been distorted by sample bias. The very large proportion of equipment supplied by local firms (excluded from Kreinin's consideration) suggests little ground for interpretation of his findings in terms of exclusionary purchasing behavior by Japanese subsidiaries in Australia.

It is clear that Japanese subsidiaries imported a higher proportion of intermediate goods and equipment from the home country than did their American counterparts in the 1980s. It is also clear that there was a significant change in this pattern through the decade. Imports from Japan were consistently and significantly declining as a proportion of intermediate goods purchases over these years. Whatever drives this pattern of purchases, it is not a permanent feature of Japanese corporate behavior.

TABLE 4.10

RATIO OF IMPORT PURCHASES TO TOTAL PURCHASES OF PLANT AND EQUIPMENT
BY JAPANESE AFFILIATES IN OCEANIA, 1989

	Local Purchase	Import from Japan	Import from third countries
All sectors	87.5	6.2	6.3
All manufacturing	90.9	8.9	0.2

SOURCE: MITI, Japan, *A Comprehensive Survey of Foreign Investment and Overseas Activities,* 1989, Tokyo.

Kreinin's findings can be explained rather on grounds that have little do with discriminatory or exclusionary practices by Japanese firms or *keiretsu* (Saxonhouse, 1991). Most Japanese manufacturing operations in Australia are of recent origin. The bulk of these investments in the past were designed to produce substitutes for products that were previously imported to Australia from Japan. Japan continues to have a strong comparative advantage in what Japanese affiliates in these sectors are producing in Australia. By contrast, most of the U.S. and European firms with which Kreinin makes comparison are decades old, producing goods in which the home country has lost much of its comparative advantage. It is hardly surprising that the sourcing pattern of Japanese manufacturing firms in Australia is as it is. This has historically been typical also of the sourcing patterns of U.S. manufacturing firms in Australia. The evidence assembled here reinforces Saxonhouse's observation (Saxonhouse, 1991) that Kreinin's Australian study is entirely consistent with the histories of multinational corporations more generally (Wilkins, 1974). It does not suggest distinctive Japanese trade practices. This issue is endemic in the experience of multinational corporations and host countries as is attested by the prevalence of local-content requirements in the national regulation of FDI throughout the world.

Employment, Ownership, and Control

How important is Japanese investment in Australian employment and in ownership and control of Australian industry?

The most complete survey of employment in Japanese affiliates reveals that Japanese firms employ 109,268 persons in all sectors of the Australian economy. Employment in Japanese firms is heavily concentrated in manufacturing, and transport equipment is the sector with the largest employment within manufacturing. Almost 61 percent of the employees of Japanese subsidiaries in Australia are engaged in manufacturing.

Employment in U.S. subsidiaries in Australia totals 391,900, of whom 30 percent were engaged in manufacturing in 1989. Total employment in U.S. firms has also been growing steadily (up from 269,300 in 1977) but the proportion engaged in manufacturing has fallen dramatically (from 62 percent in 1977).

Australians employed in Japanese subsidiaries comprise a tiny proportion of total employment, only 0.6 percent, and although the proportion of those employed in U.S. subsidiaries is larger, it is still only 5 percent of the total workforce. Employment in U.S. subsidiaries is more important in manufacturing, where it was 9.4 percent of the manufacturing workforce in 1988, compared with 2.3 percent for Japanese subsidiaries (PECC, 1992).

About 3.8 percent of employees in all Japanese subsidiaries (4,033 persons) are Japanese nationals. Most of these are in senior management. There is no readily available data on the employment of U.S. nationals in U.S. subsidiaries, but the ratio is probably under 1 percent.

Data on foreign ownership and control of Australian industry are limited, although a number of surveys in the mid-1980s provide some picture of the stake foreign enterprises hold in the Australian economy. Table 4.11 shows that Japan was not a significant owner of Australian industry in this period. It is unlikely that Japanese ownership and control of mining or manufacturing has risen greatly since these data were compiled, but ownership in agriculture and tourism have grown, the latter significantly. What table 4.11 shows most clearly is how much more important U.S. and other foreign ownership of Australian industry has been.

Contrary to popular belief, Japanese FDI involves high levels of enterprise ownership. A very large proportion (77 percent) of Japanese affiliations in Australia are wholly owned. Joint ventures are more common in agriculture, foodstuffs, textiles, lumber and pulp, and other manufacturing than in other sectors . There are no recent data for ownership structure in U.S. affiliates but only 54 percent of the firms included in Brash's survey in 1962 were wholly owned. Japanese firms also appear to have a higher level of management control, with 49.8 percent of directors dispatched from headquarters in Japan. These figures suggest that the degree of home-country control is high in Japanese subsidiaries, but the extent to which management personnel dispatched from Japan play an active or merely a monitoring role varies from sector to sector is worthy of further study. There are no recent or comparable data for U.S. subsidiaries operating in Australia but Brash's early work suggests that head office management is directly involved mainly in the very early phases of establishment for U.S. firms.

Policy Perspectives

The growth of Japanese FDI in Australia over the past decade has occurred at a time of considerable reform and liberalization of the Australian economy. There has been no comparable development since the big wave of American investment in the 1950s and 1960s.

TABLE 4.11
FOREIGN OWNERSHIP OR CONTROL BY SECTOR
(% share)

ABS Catalog No.	Industry	Year	Foreign	Japan	United States	United Kingdom
5322.0	Manufacturing	1982–83	32.9	1.4	12.2	12.7
5333.0	Private new fixed capital expenditure[a]	1982–83	29.9	1.6	15.6	10.5
5309.0	General insurance[a]	1983–84	28.5	na	2.0	13.3
5311.0	Life insurance	1983–84	33.4	na	1.2	15.5
5335.0	Transport	1983–84	5.1	na	1.0	2.9
5336.0	Agricultural land	1983–84	5.9	0.1	1.8	3.4
5336.0	Agricultural production	1983–84	1.8	na	0.5	0.7
5317.0	Mining	1984–85	44.7	3.2	21.7	13.3
5323.0	Mineral exploration (excl. oil)[a]	1984–85	35.9	1.4	14.6	13.2
5343.0	Private construction	1984–85	9.6	na	1.4	3.6
5341.0	Imports[a]	1984–85	53.2	10.6	18.9	12.5
5348.0	Exports[a]	1985–86	35.6	6.5	13.9	7.9
5334.0	Financial corporations	1986	38.1	3.4	12.5	11.4
5347.0	Banks	1986	21.0	na	5.3	−7.5
5330.0	Research and development	1986–87	31.5	1.7	12.5	8.9

NOTES: a Data are for control. All other industries' data are for ownership.
na Not available.

SOURCE: Australia-Japan Foundation, *Japanese Investment in Australia*, 1991, p. 26.

Australia has always had, as an active objective of national policy, a generally welcoming attitude toward foreign investment, with capital inflow seen as an important complement to policies encouraging strong population growth through migration, industrial growth, and national development. This attitude has been qualified by concerns in the community about foreign ownership levels and control of key sectors of the Australian economy.

In the past there were specific controls on investment in mining and energy, among other sectors. Restraints on foreign investment in the media and telecommunications remain The Foreign Investment Review Board monitors large-scale investments and takeovers. Nonetheless, Australia is very open to FDI and has a foreign investment presence as high as, or higher than, most OECD economies. The national regulation of foreign investment in the past was qualified by active promotion of foreign investment and prodevelopment interests, both at the state and national level.

The significant change in policy environment affecting foreign investment in the past decade was the impact of deregulation and liberalization of the foreign exchange and financial markets and the implementation of trade reforms on incentives to invest in Australia.

In the early postwar period, foreign investment in Australia was motivated as much by the desire of foreign manufacturers to get behind protective trade barriers as it was by the desire to take advantage of the natural and commercial advantages of investment in Australia. In the 1980s this changed dramatically. Unlike Japanese investment in North America and Europe, Japanese investment in Australia in the 1980s was not motivated by a defensive interest in protected markets.

Japanese and other foreign investors in Australia now face a radically different policy environment, especially in manufacturing activity. Trade barriers have come down and the prospect is for negligible tariff protection by the end of the decade.

The retreat of Nissan, the expansion of Toyota, and the rationalization of Japanese and U.S. capacity in the motor vehicle industry is one aspect of this change. The focus on tourism investment is another. Yet another is the growth of Japanese investment interest in high-technology industry and Japanese corporate interest in capitalizing on research and development capacity in Australian organizations.

These developments are likely to have a profound effect on the structure and character of Japanese investment in Australia in the 1990s, although it is not yet clear how Japanese investors will develop their role in the next phase of Australia's economic internationalization.

Appendix

Statistical Sources

Australia-Japan Economic Institute (AJEI), *Japanese Business Activity in Australia,* 1981–1992, AJEI, Sydney

Australian Bureau of Statistics, *Foreign Investment: Australia,* 1980/81–1990/91, Australian Government Publishing Service, Canberra

J. P. Morgan, *World Financial Markets,* various issues, J. P. Morgan, New York

Jones Lang Wooton Research and Consultancy, 1992, Sydney

Ministry of Finance, Japan, *Monthly Finance Review,* monthly issues, Information Systems Department, Institute of Fiscal and Monetary Policy, Ministry of Finance, Tokyo, Japan

Ministry of International Trade and Industry (MITI), Japan, *The Development of Japanese Firms Abroad,* 1972, MITI, Tokyo

Ministry of International Trade and Industry (MITI), Japan, *Wagakuni Kigyo no Kaigai Jigyo Katsudo* [Overseas Activities of Japanese Firms], 1979–1992, MITI, Tokyo (in Japanese)

Ministry of International Trade and Industry (MITI), Japan, *Kaigai Jigyō Katsudō Kihon Chōsa: Kaigai Toshi Tōkei Sōran* [A Comprehensive Survey of Foreign Investment and Overseas Activities], 1980, 1983, 1986, 1989, MITI, Tokyo (in Japanese)

U.S. Department of Commerce, *Survey of Current Business,* monthly issues, U.S. Department of Commerce, Washington

U.S. Department of Commerce, *U.S. Direct Investment Abroad: 1982 Benchmark Survey Data,* Department of Commerce, Bureau of Economic Analysis, Washington

U.S. Department of Commerce, *U.S. Direct Investment Abroad: Operations of U.S. Parent Companies and Their Foreign Affiliates, Revised Estimates,* 1983–1988, U.S. Department of Commerce, Bureau of Economic Analysis, Washington

U.S. Department of Commerce, *U.S. Direct Investment Abroad: 1989 Bench-mark Survey, Preliminary Results,* U.S. Department of Commerce, Bureau of Economic Analysis. Washington

Sources of Data

The data in this paper on direct investment come from four sources—the Australian Bureau of Statistics (ABS), the Australian Foreign Investment Review Board (FIRB), the Japanese Ministry of Finance, and the U.S. Department of Commerce.

ABS data record a direct investment when a foreign individual or enterprise has an equity interest of at least 10 percent. However, for foreign investment statistics for periods prior to 1985/86, the equity threshold used to determine a direct investment relationship is 25 percent.

The U.S. Department of Commerce and the Japanese Ministry of Finance also define a direct investment as one in which an overseas investor holds at least 10 percent of the ordinary shares or voting stock. However, the Japanese Ministry of Finance data are based on *notifications* of investment that may or may not proceed. The Japanese Ministry of Finance data also exclude retained earnings and the cumulative figures do not value previous investment flows at market prices.

The main shortcoming of the ABS data is that property investment is not separately identified and not all foreign investment transactions in real estate are included in the statistics. Japanese data appear, therefore, to provide a more complete record of real estate investment. The ABS data should be treated with caution with respect to the sector or industry breakdown because investment is allocated in the sector in which the enterprise is mainly involved although this may be very different from the industry in which the funds are ultimately used.

The FIRB publishes data on foreign investment proposals, and should not be taken to indicate the amount actually invested in any year.

The data on the activities of subsidiaries in Australia are largely based on surveys conducted at regular intervals by the Japanese Ministry of International Trade and Industry, the U.S. Department of Commerce, and the Australia-Japan Economic Institute. The data from MITI, however, refer to Oceania in most cases, without a separate identification of Australia, whereas the survey data from the AJEI refer specifically to activities carried out in Australia. Both the U.S. and Japanese data define a majority-owned affiliate as one that has ownership of 50 percent or more. Much of the U.S. Department of Commerce data refers to majority-owned affiliates, although a U.S. parent is a U.S. person or organization that owns or controls, directly or indirectly, 10 percent or more.

Another difference between the Japanese and U.S. data is that in relation to purchase patterns, MITI separates out intermediate and capital goods. In sales patterns, the export ratio of subsidiaries in trading forms an important part of Japanese subsidiaries' activities. As a result, a more accurate picture of Japanese foreign corporate activities can be gained from looking at the sectoral or industry breakdowns rather than focusing on export ratios or sales of Japanese affiliates as a whole.

Where data are presented in Australian dollars, they have been converted to U.S. dollars through a fiscal year average exchange rate provided by the ABS. All the ABS data and the data from Jones Lang Wooton have been converted to U.S. dollars. The exchange rates are as follows:

Year	Rate	Year	Rate	Year	Rate
1980–81	1.1588	1984–85	0.7728	1988–89	0.7553
1981–82	1.1024	1985–86	0.6956	1989–90	0.7642
1982–83	0.9360	1986–87	0.6956	1990–91	0.7799
1983–84	0.9032	1987–88	0.6580	1991–92	0.7788

References and Bibliography

Australia-Japan Foundation (1991), *Japanese Investment in Australia*, report prepared by Access Economics, Canberra.

APEC Ad Hoc Economic Group Meeting (1992), *Vision for the Economy of the Asia-Pacific Region in the Year 2000 and Tasks Ahead,* August 10–11, Tokyo.

Australia-Japan Economic Institute (1981), *Japanese Business Activity in Australia, 1981: A Survey of Japanese Investment,* AJEI, Sydney.

———— (1983), *Japanese Business Activity in Australia, 1983: A Survey of Japanese Investment,* AJEI, Sydney.

———— (1992a), *A Directory of Japanese Business Activity in Australia, 1992,* AJEI, Sydney.

————— (1992b), *Australia-Japan Business Outlook Conference: Conference Proceedings,* AJEI, Sydney, March.

—————, *AJEI Newsletter,* June 1990, December 1991, January 1992, February 1992, March 1992, June 1992, AJEI, Sydney.

Brash, Donald (1966), *American Investment in Australian Industry,* Australian National University Press, Canberra.

Bureau of Tourism Research and David H. Jacobs (1992), *Japanese Tourism in Australia, Market Segmentation: A Key to New Opportunities,* Bureau of Tourism Research, Canberra.

Committee for Economic Development of Australia (CEDA) and Keizai Dōyūkai (1990), *Encouraging Direct Investment Between Australia and Japan,* CEDA, Sydney, July.

Crawford, Sir John, and Saburo Okita (1976), *Australia, Japan and Western Pacific Economic Relations: A Report to the Governments of Australia and Japan,* Australian Government Publishing Service, Canberra.

Davis, Kevin (1990), "Japanese investment in the Australian financial sector," paper presented to the Australia-Japan Research Centre (A-JRC) workshop on Japanese Investment Abroad, A-JRC, Australian National University, Canberra, July 23.

Drysdale, Peter (1972), ed., *Direct Foreign Investment in Asia and the Pacific,* Australian National University Press, Canberra.

Edgington, David (1990), *Japanese Business Down Under: Patterns of Japanese Investment in Australia,* Routledge, London.

————— (1991), "Japanese manufacturing investment in Australia: Corporations, governments and bargaining," *Pacific Affairs,* Vol. 64, No. 1, Spring.

Farrell, Roger (1992), "Japanese direct investment in overseas property in the 1980s: Overview and assessment," paper presented to the Australia-Japan Research Centre (A-JRC) workshop on Japanese Direct Investment, A-JRC, Australian National University, Canberra, December 10.

Forsyth, P., and L. Dwyer (1990), "Japanese investment in Australian tourism," paper presented to the Australia-Japan Research Centre (A-JRC) workshop on Japanese Investment Abroad, A-JRC, Australian National University, Canberra, July 23.

Froot, Kenneth (1992), "Japanese foreign direct investment," presentation to the Japan Economic Seminar, Harvard University, Cambridge, February 15.

Graham, Edward, and Paul Krugman (1991), *Foreign Direct Investment in the United States* (2d ed.), Institute for International Economics, Washington.

Hamada, Koichi (1972), "Japanese investment abroad," in Peter Drysdale, ed., *Direct Foreign Investment in Asia and the Pacific,* Australian National University Press, Canberra.

————— and Sadao Nishimura (1975), "Japanese direct investment in Australia," in Kiyoshi Kojima, ed., *Harmonisation of Japanese and Australian Economic*

Policies: Japanese-Australian Project, Report No. 3, Japan Economic Research Center, Tokyo, Center Paper No. 27, June 1975.

Hutchinson, Diane, and Stephen Nicholas (1990), "Japanese involvement in Australian manufacturing in the 1980s: A comparative perspective," paper presented to the Australia-Japan Research Centre (A-JRC) Workshop on Japanese Investment Abroad, A-JRC, Australian National University, Canberra, July 23.

Japan Committee for Pacific Economic Outlook (1992), "Changing patterns of foreign direct investment in the Pacific region," Pacific Economic Cooperation Conference, Background Papers for Final Report, Vol. 1, March.

Japan External Trade Association (1991), *1991 JETRO White Paper on Foreign Direct Investment: Direct Investment Promoting Restructuring of Economies Worldwide* (Summary), JETRO, Tokyo, March.

Kojima, Kiyoshi (1986), "Japanese-style direct foreign investment," *Japanese Economic Studies,* Vol. 14, No. 3, Spring, pp. 52–82.

_____ (1990), *Japanese Direct Investment Abroad,* International Christian University, Mitaka, Tokyo.

Kreinin, Mordechai E. (1989), "How closed is the Japanese market? Additional evidence," *The World Economy,* Vol. 11, No. 4, pp. 529–42.

Lawrence, Robert (1991), "How open is Japan?" in Paul Krugman, ed., *Trade with Japan: Has the Door Opened Wider?* University of Chicago Press, Chicago.

McKenzie, Colin (1990), "Japanese investment abroad and the regulatory environment," paper presented to the Australia-Japan Research Centre workshop on Japanese Investment Abroad, A-JRC, Australian National University, Canberra, July 23.

McKern, R. B. (1976), *Multinational Enterprise and Natural Resources,* McGraw-Hill Book Company, Sydney.

Ministry of International Trade and Industry (MITI) (1991), *Wagakuni kigyō mo kaigai jigyō katsudō* [Overseas Activities of Japanese Firms], MITI, Tokyo (in Japanese).

Misawa, Keiko (1991), "Latest trends of Japanese business activities abroad and measures to facilitate direct investment abroad," Australia-Japan Research Centre (A-JRC) seminar, A-JRC, Australian National University, Canberra, November 4.

Morrison, Julian (1992), "FDI and other contractual arrangements in the Australian beef industry: The Japanese response to domestic market liberalisation," Australia-Japan Research Centre (A-JRC) public seminar, A-JRC, Australian National University, Canberra, April 6.

Ozawa, T. (1979), *Multinationalism, Japanese Style: The Political Economy of Outward Dependency,* Princeton University Press, Princeton, N.J.

PECC (Pacific Economic Cooperation Conference) (1992), "Changing patterns of foreign direct investment in the Pacific region," Background Papers for Final

Report, Vol. 1, Orientation Papers.

Saxonhouse, G. R. (1991), "Comment" on Robert Z. Lawrence, "How open is Japan?" in Paul Krugman, ed., *Trade with Japan: Has the Door Opened Wider?* National Bureau of Economic Research, University of Chicago Press, Chicago.

Sheard, Paul (1992), *International Adjustment and the Japanese Firm,* Allen and Unwin, Sydney, in association with the Australia-Japan Research Centre, Australian National University, Canberra.

Smith, Ben (1980), "Long-term contract and financing arrangements for mineral developments," *Research Paper* No. 72, Australia-Japan Research Centre, Australian National University, Canberra.

Tejima, Shigeki (1992), "Japanese foreign direct investment in the 1980's and its prospect for the early 1990's, with the results of a 1991 survey on Japanese FDI," Research Note No. 15, Research Institute of Overseas Investment, Export-Import Bank of Japan, Tokyo.

Treasury Department of Australia (1992), "Foreign direct investment: Australia's investment links with PECC," paper presented to the Pacific Economic Outlook Meeting, Osaka, Japan, March 25–26.

U.S. Department of Commerce (1982), *U.S. Direct Investment Abroad: 1982 Benchmark Survey Data,* Department of Commerce, Bureau of Economic Analysis, Washington.

U.S. Department of Commerce (1989), *U.S. Direct Investment Abroad: 1989 Benchmark Survey Data,* Department of Commerce, Bureau of Economic Analysis, Washington.

Wheelwright, E. L., and Judith Miskelly (1967), *Anatomy of Australian Manufacturing Industry,* The Law Book Company, Sydney.

Wilkins, Mira (1974), *The Maturing of Multinational Enterprise: American Business Abroad from 1914 to 1970,* Harvard University Press, Cambridge, Mass.

CHAPTER 5

Japanese Direct Investment in Thailand

• •

MINGSARN SANTIKARN KAOSA-ARD

Toward the end of the 1980s, Thailand emerged as one of the world's fastest-growing economies. The Thai economy exhibited double-digit real GDP growth rates between 1988 and 1990. Consequently, Thailand becomes another success story among the market-oriented economies of the East. To what extent did foreign direct investment (FDI) contribute to Thailand's development process? Was accelerated growth in Thailand stimulated by massive FDI flow into Thailand during the late 1980s?

The popular belief is that the United States has been the largest investor in Thailand. In recent years, however, Japanese investments have attracted attention because of the concentration of Japan's investment in the consumer-product industries. How has the pattern of Japanese investment compared with that of other foreign investors? How have scholars evaluated the contribution of foreign investments to Thailand's economic development?

After briefly discussing the performance of the Thai economy, this chapter examines the global trend of foreign investment, describes the pattern of FDI in Thailand and, finally, explores the behavior of foreign investors and their Thai partners according to their negotiation experience.

The information about foreign investors and their Thai partners has only surfaced recently and is preliminary. Few local firms having joint investments with transnational corporations (TNCs) have willingly supplied information. Local firms with multi-country experience also were extremely large and among the top 1 percent of the country. When a large firm has multi-source connections, an executive with language skills will be assigned to deal with foreign investors. From these individuals we can learn how foreign investors and their Thai counterparts have interacted.

The Thai Economy: An Overview

Thailand experienced rapid gross domestic product (GDP) growth rates of over 6.8 percent between 1970 and 1980. During the global recession in 1985–1986 the growth rates of Thailand slowed down (table 5.1) but quickly picked up again in 1987 as the GDP growth rate almost doubled that of 1986. The accelerated growth period starting from 1987 was unexpectedly checked by the Gulf War in 1990. Since then, political disturbances arising from the coup d'état in 1991 and a military showdown in May 1992 have rocked the economy. The 1993 GDP growth rate was around 7 percent.

The manufacturing sector in particular showed a remarkable performance. Between 1950 and 1952, the share of agriculture to GDP averaged 46.5 percent, almost four times larger than that of the manufacturing sector (12.3 percent). In 1985 the share of manufacturing exports (49.5 percent) exceeded the share of agricultural exports (37.9 percent) for the first time, and by 1991 exports of manufactured products constituted more than 75 percent of the total exports of Thailand. The performance of the manufacturing sector suggested that Thailand might join the ranks of the newly industrialized economies (NIE) in the 1990s.

Global Trend of Foreign Direct Investment

As the world economy emerged from recession in the mid-1980s, global FDI outflow increased from $US88 billion to $US225 billion, or an average growth rate of 24 percent per annum, which far exceeded the growth rate of merchandise exports of 13 percent (TCMD, 1992). Over the same period, Japan emerged as the world's largest investor (table 5.2). Its share in the global FDI outflow increased from 10 percent for the period 1980–1985 to 20 percent between 1986 and 1990, surpassing the United Kingdom (17 percent) and the United States (14 percent). Much of the slowdown of FDI

TABLE 5.1

INDICATORS OF THE THAI ECONOMY

	1983	1984	1985	1986	1987	1988	1989	1990	1991ᴾ	1992ᵉ
A. Production and investment*										
Real GDP growth	7.3	7.3	3.5	4.9	9.5	13.2	12.0	10.0	7.5	7.5
agriculture and mining (%)	3.8	5.6	6.2	0.3	-0.2	10.2	6.6	-1.8	2.8	3.8
industry (%)	8.9	8.9	0.7	7.7	11.9	16.2	15.5	14.8	10.3	9.4
trade and services (%)	7.9	6.3	4.9	4.6	11.6	11.8	10.9	9.8	6.1	9.6
GDP at current prices ($ billion)	39.57	41.16	37.33	41.68	48.74	59.64	43.46	80.24	94.08	104.4
Domestic investment to GDP ratio (%)	25.9	24.9	24.0	21.8	23.9	28.8	31.5	36.8	37.9	38.3
National saving to GDP ratio (%)	21.2	20.6	19.4	20.9	23.7	28.6	30.2	30.4	31.4	31.7
B. Population										
level (million persons)	49.5	50.6	51.8	53.0	53.9	55.0	55.9	56.3	57.0	57.6
growth (%)	1.4	2.2	2.4	2.3	1.7	2.0	1.7	0.7	1.2	1.2
GDP per capita (US$)	799	802	710	776	893	1,076	1,231	1,410	1,628	1,812
Labor force (million persons)	25.9	26.4	27.1	28.0	28.6	29.5	30.3	31.1	31.9	32.7
C. External sector										
Exports										
value (US$ billion)	6.3	7.3	7.1	8.8	11.6	15.8	19.9	22.8	28.3	32.5
growth (%)	-7.7	16.4	-3.8	24.8	31.6	36.2	25.7	14.9	23.9	14.5
Imports										
value (US$ billion)	10.2	10.3	9.3	9.4	13.3	19.7	25.2	32.6	37.8	40.7
growth (%)	21.2	0.6	-9.0	0.2	42.0	48.7	27.7	29.1	16.1	7.2
Trade balance (US$ billion)	-3.9	-2.9	-2.3	-0.5	-1.7	-4.0	-5.4	-10.0	-9.7	-8.2
Current account balance (US$ billion)	-2.9	-2.1	-1.5	0.2	-0.4	-1.6	-2.5	-7.3	-7.6	-6.7
(as percent of GDP) (%)	-7.3	-5.1	-4.1	0.6	-0.7	-2.7	-3.6	-9.1	-8.1	-6.4
Net capital inflow (US$ billion)	1.5	2.5	1.9	0.4	0.8	2.9	5.9	8.1	11.5	8.0
Overall balance of payments (US$ billion)	0.8	0.4	0.5	1.3	0.7	1.6	4.3	2.2	4.4	1.2
Official reserves (US$ billion)	2.56	2.69	3.00	3.78	5.21	7.11	10.51	14.27	18.42	21.2
(in months of imports)	3.0	3.2	3.9	4.9	4.7	4.3	5.0	5.3	5.8	6.5
D. Exchange rate										
Baht/dollar exchange rate (average)	23.00	23.64	27.16	26.27	25.71	25.27	25.68	25.56	25.49	25.34

NOTES: ᵉEstimated

ᴾProvisional.

SOURCE: Office of the Board of Investment, *Key Investment Indicators of Thailand* (Bangkok: Office of the Board of Investment, 1992), p. 3.

outflow after 1990 was because Japanese FDI declined from $US48 billion in 1990 to $US31 billion in 1991 (table 5.2).

Apart from North America, Japanese TNCs have tended to concentrate their investment in the Pacific Rim countries. Following the international currency realignment in late 1985, Thailand became a new production base in Southeast Asia, along with Malaysia and Indonesia. Although Japanese investment inflows to ASEAN countries increased substantially, the ASEAN share in the total Japanese outflow has in fact diminished. This evidence seems to suggest that Japan's direct investment is motivated more by demand than by supply factors.

Pattern of Foreign Direct Investment in Thailand

Until the Thai economy took off in 1987, Thailand was considered as one of those countries with relatively low levels of foreign investment. Prior to the mid-1960s, the annual net inflow of FDI was very small, contributing less than $US25 million. This is partly because during that period foreign firms were more often found in trade-related activities that required less capital investment. Although FDI flow started to gain momentum in the early 1970s, the oil shock in 1973 and the political uncertainties in Indochina following the fall of Saigon in 1975 kept foreign investment inflow relatively stable between 1974 and 1976. Foreign direct investment inflow only began to increase steadily in the early 1980s but was dampened for two years between 1985 and 1986 as a result of the global recession (table 5.3). In spite of the surge of FDI, the Republic of Korea and Thailand still had the lowest level of investments among the NICs and ASEAN countries (ESCAP/UNCTC, 1986).

From 1988, the net FDI inflow to Thailand increased by leaps and bounds, tripling between 1987 and 1988, and almost doubling between 1988 and 1989. The net investment flow in 1990, which stood at 62 billion baht, exceeded the total cumulative flow between 1975 and 1987.

When compared with gross domestic investment (GDI), foreign investment accounted for considerably less than 5 percent of GDI during 1970–1987 (table 5.3). This ratio dropped to less than 1 percent during 1978–1979 but regained its normal trend in 1980. Toward the end of the 1980s, the contribution of net FDI flow to GDI rose to 8 percent. When gross private business investment is considered, the FDI contribution reached 10 percent in 1989 but dropped to 5.9 percent in 1991.

Various internal factors caused this quantum jump in FDI. Since the early

TABLE 5.2
FOREIGN DIRECT INVESTMENT FROM FIVE COUNTRIES, 1986–1990

Country	Outflows (billions of dollars)						Share in total (percentage)		Growth rate (percentage)	
	1986	1987	1988	1989	1990	1991ᵃ	1980–85	1986–90	1980–85	1986–90
France	5	9	15	19	35	21	6	10	–6	59
Federal Republic of Germany	10	9	11	14	23	23	8	8	4	22
Japanᵇ	15	20	34	44	48	31	10	20	22	35
United Kingdom	18	31	37	36	21	18	20	17	–1	6
United Statesᶜ	14	28	14	29	29	29	26	14	–16	20
Total	61	97	112	142	156	122	69	72	–5	26

NOTES: [a]Preliminary estimates.
[b]Data for Japan do not include reinvested earnings.
[c]Excluding outflows to the finance (except banking), insurance, and real estate sectors of the Netherlands Antilles. Also excludes currency translation adjustments.

SOURCE: *Thailand Economic Information Kit* (Bangkok: Bank of Thailand, 1992), Table 3, p. 16. (Henceforth, "Bank of Thailand.")

TABLE 5.3
THAILAND'S FDI AND GROSS DOMESTIC INVESTMENT, 1970–1991
(\$US million)

Years	FDI Inflows	Gross Domestic Investment	FDI to Gross Domestic Investment	FDI to Gross Private Business Investment	Gross Private Business Investment	Japanese FDI
1970	42.8	1,814.0	2.4	1,181.1	3.6	15.49
1971	38.8	1,785.4	2.2	1,225.1	3.2	12.67
1972	68.6	1,772.7	3.9	1,308.5	5.2	16.38
1973	78.7	2,939.1	2.7	1,888.5	4.2	34.69
1974	191.8	3,718.3	5.2	2,731.4	7.0	37.48
1975	87.3	4,056.7	2.2	2,683.8	3.3	21.18
1976	80.7	4,155.4	1.9	2,792.4	2.9	21.21
1977	108.2	5,424.0	2.0	3,743.5	2.9	40.19
1978	49.7	6,759.9	0.7	4,222.8	1.2	33.83
1979	55.2	7,446.1	0.7	4,918.4	1.1	12.04
1980	189.4	8,498.3	2.2	5,229.7	3.9	44.09
1981	294.0	9,153.2	3.2	5,502.2	5.3	64.48
1982	188.3	8,242.5	2.3	5,469.3	3.4	45.10
1983	357.6	10,264.8	3.5	6,296.0	5.7	105.73
1984	408.0	10,258.3	4.0	6,622.1	6.2	109.48
1985	163.7	8,991.9	1.8	5,468.6	3.0	56.54
1986	263.0	9,084.2	2.9	5,903.6	4.5	116.06
1987	351.8	11,660.4	3.0	8,513.0	4.1	127.14
1988	1,106.6	17,196.1	6.4	13,043.7	8.5	578.06
1989	1,779.5	21,795.4	8.2	17,830.6	10.0	730.88
1990	2,445.9	35,044.4	7.0	29,043.5	8.4	1,088.44
1991	2,016.0	41,955.0	4.8	34,035.8	5.9	611.75

SOURCE: Compiled from data in *Bank of Thailand* and statistical file of the National Economic and Social Development Board.

1980s, the Thai economy gradually shifted away from agriculture to manufacturing. Unlike many other developing countries in Asia, in the 1970s the land/man ratio in Thailand continued to rise and agriculture dominated the economy. Since foreign ownership of land was never allowed, foreign investment in agriculture remained low. The closing of the land frontier in the 1980s, however, forced rural labor to seek jobs outside agriculture. As the country's factor endowment changed, manufacturing industries could draw on a large pool of cheap, trainable labor. After 1980 the labor market supplied the manufacturing sector with low-cost labor. Benefiting from the cheap labor, the expanding manufacturing sector also benefited from government fiscal and monetary policies that controlled inflation and from new policies designed to attract foreign investment into Thailand.

External factors also played a role. The appreciation of the Japanese and Chinese (ROC) currencies in the mid–1980s greatly encouraged their FDI to seek low-wage countries to develop new sources of production.

The pattern of net inflow of FDI classified by industry can be found in table 5.4. Prior to the 1970s, FDI mainly flowed to the tertiary sector, such as trading. A sectoral shift from the primary to the tertiary sector then took place. The share of FDI in secondary industries was relatively stable at 33 percent between 1970 and 1984. After 1985, investment inflow became increasingly concentrated in manufacturing at the expense of the primary sector. In 1988 the share of inflow of the manufacturing sector peaked at 58 percent, and investment in the primary sector declined to about 3 percent of total inflow in 1990.

Meanwhile, investments from the NIEs increased markedly in the latter half of the 1980s, and finally their cumulative inflow exceeded that of the United States between 1980 and 1990 (table 5.5). Among the Asian NIEs, Hong Kong was the largest investor, followed by the ROC; Singapore's investment flow was unstable, and the Republic of Korea's investment was negligible. The share of investors from Europe and other advanced countries declined.

Japan and the United States rotated as the largest source of investment inflow between 1970 and 1985 (Santikarn Kaosa-ard, 1990). The United States held the largest share of FDI inflow in the early 1970s just when there occurred a campaign against Japanese investment. U.S. activities, however, concentrated in nonmanufacturing and nontrading areas, which made the U.S. activities less visible to the public. Then in the latter half of the 1970s, Japan became the largest investor as the U.S. share fell. The United States regained its position of top investor in the first half of the 1980s, but Japanese inflow sharply increased to exceed U.S. investment in 1986 and the following year. The U.S. FDI inflow continued to decline after 1987 despite Thailand's rapid economic growth, while Japan's investment remained high and eventually Japan emerged as Thailand's largest investor.

The pattern of sectoral distribution of Japanese and U.S. FDI inflow markedly changed in the late 1980s. In the latter half of the 1970s, the manufacturing sector received the largest share of investment from both Japan (41.8 percent) and the United States (35.4 percent) (table 5.6). After

TABLE 5.4
NET INFLOWS OF FOREIGN INVESTMENT BY INDUSTRY, 1970–1990 (%)

	1970–1979	1980–1984	1985	1986	1987	1988	1989	1990	Cumulative FDI Inflows 1970–1990
Primary	12.0	23.5	13.3	6.4	5.3	2.8	2.6	3.0	7.3
Secondary	33.2	32.3	30.6	30.7	52.5	57.8	47.8	46.5	44.4
Food	3.5	1.0	8.9	4.2	4.8	3.8	4.3	3.1	3.4
Textiles	12.6	2.6	1.3	1.2	11.0	4.0	1.5	2.8	3.7
Metal and nonmetallic	1.5	4.4	-2.8	-0.3	4.0	7.6	6.0	4.5	4.7
Electrical appliances	7.1	9.8	6.3	8.9	12.6	22.6	19.4	17.3	15.8
Machinery and transport equipment	2.0	3.0	0.7	-0.2	1.8	2.3	2.4	3.9	2.8
Chemicals	4.0	3.5	11.0	7.0	9.6	3.8	6.2	6.9	5.7
Petroleum products	1.3	6.3	0.0	0.1	-0.2	2.8	-2.6	1.4	1.3
Construction materials	-0.4	0.1	0.9	0.1	0.1	0.1	0.2	0.0	0.1
Tertiary	54.8	44.2	56.1	62.9	42.2	39.4	49.6	50.5	48.3
Total	100.0	100.0	100.0	100.0	100.0	100.0	100.0	100.0	100.0

NOTES: Including equity and loans from parent or related companies, including capital funds of foreign commerical banks.
SOURCE: Bank of Thailand.

manufacturing, U.S. FDI went into mining (25.6 percent), and the second largest inflow from Japanese firms went into trading activities (25.3 percent). United States investment was more resource-oriented than was Japanese investment.

Toward the end of the 1980s, Japan's FDI in manufacturing industries sharply increased; it had averaged 58 percent of its total inflow during 1986 and rose to 87 percent in 1991, whereas similar U.S. investment in 1991 stood at 40 percent (table 5.6).

These annual data underestimate the part of foreign capital that may be accumulated by plowing back profits and might underestimate the growth of foreign enterprises that relied on capital raised in local capital markets. The stock data originating since 1915 suggest that Japan had been the largest investor in Thailand throughout the period 1915 to 1984, followed by the United States, the United Kingdom, Hong Kong, and Malaysia (Pongpisanu-pichit 1985). Both stock and flow data confirm that Japan has been the largest source of FDI for Thailand.

Foreign Investment in the Promoted Sector

Since 1960, the Thai government has provided special financial incentives to foreign and local enterprises to stimulate investment in a broad range of industries considered vital for national development. The Board of Investment (BOI) manages these incentives. The incentive scheme initially comprises income tax holidays; reduction of or exemption from import duties on capital goods, raw materials, and intermediates; double deduction of utility costs from taxable income, and the like. These incentives attracted Japanese investors more than any other foreign investors. Exemption from import duties has been considered the most important privilege. In 1991, in an attempt to simplify, systematize, and reduce distortive effects of the tariff protection, duties on imported capital goods were reduced to 5 percent. This action greatly reduced the role of the BOI in attracting foreign enterprises to locate in Thailand.

According to the BOI guideline of 1983, tax privileges varied with the level of foreign ownership. For example, eligible projects for investment privileges in agriculture, mineral exploration and mining, and services must have at least 60 percent Thai capital. For export enterprises, foreign ownership is allowed in the same proportion as exported output. For example, a fully foreign-owned firm must export all of its output to be eligible for pro-

TABLE 5.5

DISTRIBUTION OF OTHER COUNTRIES' FDI IN THAILAND, 1981–1991 (%)

Country	1981–1985	1986–1990	1991
United States	32.19	11.41	11.52
Japan	27.17	44.38	30.34
NIE	12.87	30.36	41.03
South Korea	0.07	0.71	0.58
Taiwan	0.78	10.63	5.36
Singapore	3.59	7.34	12.59
Hong Kong	8.44	11.68	22.51
ASEAN	0.66	0.37	0.04
Malaysia	0.66	0.37	0.04
EC	15.04	7.21	7.41
Germany	2.37	2.10	1.64
United Kingdom	5.11	1.83	0.50
France	0.88	1.12	2.43
Belgium	0.40	0.46	1.39
Netherlands	6.28	1.70	1.45
Others	−0.80	−24.08	−31.36
Total	100.00	100.00	100.00

SOURCE: Bank of Thailand.

motion privileges. In 1992, this condition was relaxed to 80 percent exported output for foreign subsidiaries. For large public utilities and the transport system, the state allows full foreign ownership.

The trend of foreign investment in Thailand's promoted sector is similar to the general trend shown by net capital inflow. Foreign direct investment in the promoted sector between 1987 and 1991 far exceeded investment two decades earlier, i.e., 2.5 times measured in terms of the number of projects, 2.6 times measured in terms of capital investment, and 2.2 times measured in terms of employment (Sibunruang and Brimble, 1992; tables 4.1, 4.2, 4.3). Foreign investments in the form of joint ventures totaled 599 projects before 1987, but from 1987 to 1991 the number of and investment in joint-venture projects tripled. The number of foreign subsidiaries showed a sharply increasing trend, from 82 projects from 1960 to 1987 to 623 projects from 1987 to 1991, due to special equity conditions for export-oriented projects, as mentioned earlier. In terms of employment, the share of employment of foreign subsidiaries and joint ventures in total employment generated by investment promotion increased from 53.6 percent for the period 1960–1987 to 65.1 for

TABLE 5.6

NET INFLOW OF DIRECT INVESTMENT FROM JAPAN
AND THE UNITED STATES (%)

	1976–1980		1986–1990		1991	
	Japan	U.S.	Japan	U.S.	Japan	U.S.
Financial institutions	3.65	−13.38	3.6	5.3	0.6	3.4
Trade	25.25	20.60	10.6	23.6	7.1	21.9
Construction	20.24	9.49	11.7	2.4	6.0	2.9
Mining and quarrying	0.19	25.57	0.0	7.8	0.0	10.4
Oil exploration	0.18	23.88	0.0	7.3	0.0	10.4
Other	0.01	1.69	0.0	0.5	0.0	0.1
Agriculture	0.49	0.31	1.7	1.4	3.1	0.4
Industry	41.87	35.40	58.0	44.9	86.6	39.6
Food	0.82	3.41	2.4	5.4	5.6	6.3
Textiles	19.75	1.77	1.3	2.7	4.1	0.2
Metal-based	1.27	0.47	8.5	1.6	8.1	7.7
Electrical appliances	3.30	25.77	27.7	13.4	40.5	11.8
Machinery and transport	6.31	4.97	6.0	0.9	8.5	0.9
Chemicals	7.59	0.14	4.6	10.6	13.7	0.9
Petroleum products	0.53	1.69	1.5	0.0	3.2	0.0
Construction materials	−0.08	−5.43	0.0	0.2	0.0	0.5
Other	2.00	2.67	6.0	10.1	9.2	11.4
Services	9.30	22.00	2.8	9.6	1.6	10.2
Transport and travel	7.50	12.22	1.0	3.0	1.2	1.6
Other services	0.40	0.25	1.8	6.6	0.4	8.6
Hotels and restaurants	0.10	0.25	0.0	0.0	0.0	0.0
Other	1.30	0.28	0.0	0.0	0.0	0.0
Investment	0.00	0.00	0.0	0.0	0.0	0.0
Real estate	0.00	0.00	10.6	4.9	5.3	5.8
Housing and real estate	0.00	0.00	5.0	3.2	7.6	4.7
Hotels and restaurants	0.00	0.00	5.7	0.0	12.9	0.0
Other	0.00	0.00	0.0	0.0	0.0	0.0
Other	0.00	0.00	1.0	0.1	0.3	5.5
Total	100.00	100.00	100.00	100.00	100.00	100.00

SOURCE: Bank of Thailand.

1987–1990.

    The purpose of attracting foreign investment projects in the promoted sector was to stimulate Thai exports. Before 1987 export joint-venture projects and export foreign subsidiaries accounted for 13 and 3 percent of all promoted projects, respectively. By 1991, the ratios increased to 42.3 and 17 percent, respectively; i.e., 59 percent of all export projects are foreign affiliates. The revaluation of the yen increased Thailand's export competitiveness, encouraged Japanese firms to set up production bases in Thailand, and also allowed those firms to increase their contribution to the volume of goods exported.

Traditionally, Japan was known to be the largest investor in the promoted sector. Between the inception of BOI and 1987, the registered capital of Japanese-promoted projects was three times larger than the second-biggest investor, the United States (table 5.7). The share of Japanese registered capital of the approved projects was 40 percent for the investment between 1960 and 1987. The share of Japanese investment peaked at 53 percent in 1988 and declined to around 23 percent in 1991. The U.S. share, which was the second highest in the period prior to 1987, declined rapidly thereafter and was superseded by the ROC share after 1988.

Japanese investment, therefore, has influenced the overall foreign-investment pattern in the promoted sector. Prior to 1987, a larger proportion of Japanese investments entered joint ventures rather than fully foreign-owned subsidiaries. Since the latter half of the 1980s, however, Japanese TNCs made two major changes in their investments. First, they placed less emphasis on import-substitution production such as automobile assembly, paints, and consumer chemical products. After the currency realignment in late 1985, Japanese investment projects in Thailand concentrated on producing for export rather than import-substitution; examples include microwave ovens, toys, floppy-disk drives, computer keyboards, ski-related products, metallic dies, and the like. Second, Japanese investors increasingly preferred wholly Japanese-owned enterprises over joint ventures. In an export enterprise, a local partner is unnecessary for local distribution. Before 1987, 71 percent of Japanese projects in the promoted sector were joint ventures. After 1987 the share of Japanese joint ventures in total projects fell to 68 percent.

Contribution of FDI

Thailand always welcomed foreign investment. A brief anti-Japanese investment campaign in 1974 was the only incident to oppose FDI, and that campaign was brief and ineffective. Contemporary popular attitudes toward foreign investment as reflected in the mass media are very positive. In fact, all political factions have wanted to maintain a favorable investment atmosphere to appease dissatisfied interest groups. They believe foreign invest-

TABLE 5.7

PROPORTION OF REGISTERED FOREIGN CAPITAL IN THAILAND,
1960/86–1991 (%)

Nationality of ownership	1960/86	1987	1988	1989	1990	1991
Thai	7.2	68.9	47.0	63.3	63.8	76.8
Foreign	27.8	31.1	53.0	39.7	36.2	24.2
	100.0	100.0	100.0	100.0	100.0	100.0
Japan	25.7	39.6	57.2	38.1	27.0	35.1
Taiwan	9.5	8.2	12.5	15.1	10.2	13.2
United States	16.9	12.7	5.8	3.9	6.4	14.1
United Kingdom	6.6	5.9	5.2	3.9	1.7	7.6
Republic of Korea	na	na	1.7	2.6	3.0	1.2
Singapore	4.4	3.2	1.5	4.0	4.5	2.0
Australia	2.9	2.2	0.8	0.8	0.4	0.5
Malaysia	2.3	1.8	0.7	0.3	0.7	2.5
Germany	1.6	1.3	0.6	1.2	2.5	0.2
India	1.6	1.1	0.3	2.4	3.4	0.2
Netherlands	2.8	2.0	0.1	0.8	3.1	4.5
Others	25.7	22.0	11.0	20.5	10.9	12.2
	100.0	100.0	100.0	100.0	100.0	100.0

SOURCE: Office of the Board of Investment.

ment will enhance growth, exports, and technology transfer. Let us examine these separately.

Growth

To date, only one study has tried to cite FDI as a factor to explain growth. It used a simple Solow model to demonstrate that net foreign capital inflow between 1973 and 1990 accounted for an important share of the Thai economy's growth. However, the FDI variable had a negative sign and was statistically insignificant (Sibunruang and Kijbunchu, 1992). Two reasons might explain this result. Until recently the ratio of FDI to gross domestic investment was relatively low (table 5.5). Moreover, the authors used a nonlagged model for their estimate.

One causal hypothesis states that Thailand's high growth in the 1980s was export-led. Foreign direct investment might have contributed to Thailand's recent remarkable growth performance, but the most recent estimate of manufactured exports' contribution to Thailand's economic growth (Brummit and Flatters, 1992) shows that in the past decade the trade in manufactures accounted for only one-quarter of income growth. Between 1984 and 1987, 40 to 60 percent of income growth could be explained by export activities, especially of manufactured goods. Between 1987 and 1990, the manufactured export drive began to lose steam, precisely when Thailand exhibited double-digit growth. During this accelerated growth period, the export sector contributed only 23.6 percent to income growth. The economy's rapid growth performance perhaps could be explained by the growth of the services sector. Before 1987, FDI was relatively small in Thailand, but because FDI increased after 1987, just when the push from manufactured exports subsided, the hypothesis that growth was export-led should be rejected.

Export Increase

The conceptual framework for predicting different export behavior of TNCs from different countries hinges on the motives for direct investment. Kojima (1973) has advanced the proposition that Japanese FDI increased as Japan's comparative advantage changed and became trade-promoting. United States investment, on the other hand, seems to have been motivated by monopolistic advantage and was less trade-enhancing except in the case of natural-resource-based industries.

From the data of firms promoted by the BOI, the average propensity to export by foreign firms, except Japanese, exceeded that of local firms throughout 1970s (Sibunruang, 1994). Foreign investors from industrializing countries showed high, rising export propensities, increasing from 3.7 to 27.1 and 51.8 percent in 1971, 1975, and 1979, respectively. The same trend was also observed for U.S. firms (7.1, 18.1, and 41.7 percent, respectively). The Japanese joint ventures, on the contrary, showed a fluctuating performance (2.9, 18.4, and 17.6 percent for 1971, 1975, and 1979, respectively). Another study for 1974–1975, of seventy Japanese and nineteen U.S. firms, also confirmed that Japanese affiliates exported less than U.S. affiliates. Both types of investors had very high propensities to import, but the Japanese-related firms tended to import more. Subsequent studies by Kanchanaphankha (1978) of sixty-nine samples also confirmed the earlier studies. Another study of 134 samples (Chinwanno and Tambunlertchai, 1982) suggested that exports of Japanese companies were small, averaging around 2 percent annually between 1974 and 1979. Only the textile industry showed a higher export ratio of about 20 percent of sales.

A later study by Sibunruang and Brimble (1987) indicated that in 1984, the local firms outperformed the foreign firms. An examination of 388 technology contracts deposited at the Bank of Thailand (Santikarn, 1984) revealed that 26 percent of Japanese contracts stipulated some forms of export restrictions but only 19 percent of contracts concluded with U.S. suppliers had such arrangements. These findings suggest that, until the mid–1980s, Japanese investments in Thailand were oriented toward penetrating local markets and expanding market share rather than promoting exports as the Kojima hypothesis argued.

After 1985, the Japanese TNCs in Thailand shifted their strategy from a local-market orientation to developing an export base, and the export performance of Japanese affiliates substantially improved (Sibunruang and Brimble, 1992). In a survey of 771 promoted manufacturing firms, which accounted for almost one-third of Thailand's manufacturing exports in 1990, the export propensities of Japanese joint ventures increased to 60 percent and for Japanese subsidiaries they increased to 89.5 percent, surpassing the propensities of North American firms (84.7 percent) but lower than the export propensities of European (89.4 percent) and other Asian export ventures (table 5.8). Firms with FDI from NIEs tended to have the highest export propensities. On the whole, the average export propensities of all Japanese projects were close to the sample average. As Japanese exporting joint ventures and subsidiaries tended to be larger enterprises, however, the share of export of Japanese joint ventures constituted a high of 55 percent of the total exports of all joint ventures and about 34.5 percent of all exports for foreign subsidiaries.

Sibunruang and Brimble (1992) calculated the total export contribution of the 771 sample firms to Thailand's total export earnings at 24 percent. Those authors argued that because the sample constituted about 40 percent of total promoted manufacturing enterprises, the total export contribution of all foreign affiliates could be between 30 and 40 percent of total export earnings. Considering that the above result was estimated from enterprises already exporting in 1990, this sample might not have included export projects

TABLE 5.8

MANUFACTURED EXPORTS AND EXPORT PROPENSITIES
BY NATIONALITY GROUP AND OWNERSHIP (%)

	Thai-owned Total	Joint ventures Total	Subsidiaries Total	Total companies Total
Thai-owned				
Export share in total	100.0	0.0	0.0	23.5
Export propensity	62.6	n.d.	n.d.	62.6
North America				
Export share in total	0.0	3.6	52.4	23.0
Export propensity	n.d.	71.8	84.7	76.6
Japan				
Export share in total	0.0	65.0	34.5	33.5
Export propensity	n.d.	59.6	89.5	66.5
Europe and other DCs				
Export share in total	0.0	14.1	3.0	6.2
Export propensity	n.d.	52.2	89.4	61.6
NICs				
Export share in total	0.0	17.0	7.5	9.1
Export propensity	n.d.	76.6	97.0	83.3
ASEAN				
Export share in total	0.0	2.7	1.7	1.6
Export propensity	n.d.	45.0	100.0	51.5
Other LDCs				
Export share in total	0.0	7.3	0.8	2.9
Export propensity	n.d.	54.3	100.0	59.2
Unknown				
Export share in total	0.0	0.5	0.2	0.2
Export propensity	n.d.	33.6	100.0	50.2
Total exports				
Export share in total	100.0	100.0	100.0	100.0
Export propensity	62.6	68.6	91.3	66.5

NOTES: Export propensities are export sales divided by total sales.
      n.d. = no data available.
SOURCE: Sibunruang and Brimble (1992), Table 4.7.

approved from 1989 onward. These findings suggest that FDI projects will play an increasing role in enhancing Thailand's future export activities.

Technology Transfer

No rigorous research has been done to compare technology transfer in Thailand for TNCs of different nationalities. The reasons are twofold. First, there is no satisfactory theoretical explanation of why nationality ought to explain the effectiveness of transmitting technology. What reason is there to believe that Japanese TNCs would be more or less generous in transferring their technologies than other nations' firms? Suppose one argues that Japan as an emulator of technology of Western countries might have adapted the technology to its own needs depending on relative factor endowment. There would be great benefit from any second-stage transfer of this same technology if it could be effectively absorbed by less developed countries (LDCs). Because Japanese industries have rapidly advanced, the technology gap between Japan and such LDCs is not likely to be narrower than that between those LDCs and other developed countries. Second, Japanese, American TNCs, and TNCs from the NIEs tend to have slightly different patterns of investment. They do not often produce the same product or operate in the same industry. Thus, most studies on technology transfer cover only one foreign nationality of investors. Third, case studies on technology transfer tend to refer to local management as a key to technological mastery (Santikarn, 1987; Surakanvit and Chiowatana, 1988). Only when a foreign firm interacts with aggressive and eager local partners and management can local enterprise absorb technology and use it effectively.

The most comprehensive study on comparative technology transfer of 388 technology contracts revealed three interesting features (Santikarn, 1984). First, Japanese technology suppliers tended to charge less than American or European suppliers, but they also charged a fee for every item of know-how, including basic specifications or standards. Second, Japanese technology suppliers (42 percent Japanese contracts) tended to be more generous with the training to be undertaken at suppliers' plant compared with the U.S. TNCs (26 percent) and United Kingdom (27 percent) and European countries (24 percent).

Further evidence from interviews of 251 employees from 100 enterprises in 26 industries confirmed that Japanese firms tended to put more emphasis on training than did other TNCs and had a more effective in-house training system (Poapongsakorn et al., 1992). As the Japanese in-house training system stresses teamwork and evaluation revolving around a particular task, the skills developed were company- or system-specific. Given that Japanese TNCs invest greater effort to train workers, it is logical that even in Thailand they would adopt a lifetime employment policy. When, however, the data from interviews were subject to regression analysis with other controlling variables such as size of firm, market orientation, and so forth, the contribution of Japanese TNCs in training of Thai workers was found to be statistically insignificant and unrelated.

Technology transfer at the management level is normally measured by the number of foreign to local managers. A questionnaire survey of 100 enterprises revealed that the ratio of Thai to Japanese executives of exporting firms rose from 31 to 42 percent between 1986 and 1990 (Tiralap and Chiowatana, no date). For importing firms, the ratio rose more sharply, from 33 to 67 percent over the same period, because local managers are more familiar with local markets. The same study indicated that Japanese TNCs tended to place more emphasis on training of production workers and technicians. The study also cited a number of well-known Japanese manufacturers that allowed Thai executives to reach no higher than the number-two position in Japanese affiliates.

A preliminary study by this writer on the hiring policies of TNCs suggests a different pattern of career path for local managers who join Japanese and Western TNCs (Santikarn Kaosa-ard, 1991). In a typical Western TNC there are two sets of staff, local and foreign. The former may enter the latter's career path if there are merits. Once elevated into the international rank, the Thai staff may even be posted overseas. In the Japanese case, the two sets of staff, local and Japanese, are distinctly separated.

Western TNCs attempt to encourage their staff to adopt their corporations' cultures, but the local staff of Japanese TNCs must adapt to Japanese general business culture. Although Japanese TNCs appear internationalized in their operation, this does not appear to be the case in their internal business culture, especially when communicating with headquarters. As a result, it is much more difficult for local managers to ascend to the highest rank in a Japanese firm. To confirm this finding, we identified the proportion of Japanese managing directors in Japanese-affiliated firms and compared it with similar measures for other foreign firms. Out of 84 Japanese affiliates appearing in the Million Baht Business Directory (1991), only 15 firms (or 18 percent) had a Thai managing director compared with 52 out of 159 other foreign firms (33 percent) with Thai managing directors. This evidence seems to confirm the complaint that Japanese firms do not use Thai talent. Ironically, neither Japanese nor other TNCs have won praise from their host countries. In the developing economies where local staff members have become successful in joining the international rank, many accuse the TNCs of promoting a brain drain. The Japanese TNCs, on the other hand, seem reluctant to use local talent in their business.

Negotiating with Foreign Partners

Two local executives were interviewed regarding different characteristics of foreign partners. One executive was involved in manufacturing and construction activities; the other engaged mainly in trading operations. Both operated more than one-billion-baht businesses and had numerous contracts with foreign partners. We compared Japanese negotiators with U.S., French, Italian, and Taiwanese partners and learned the following.

Expected Rate of Return

It is widely believed within Thai business and academic circles that Japanese firms tend to accept lower rates of return in order to maximize market share. Both interviewed executives confirmed that Japanese partners tended to accept lower rates of return than their Western partners. The expected rate of return of U.S. partners in a trading enterprise was said to be more than ten times larger than that of Japanese partners. However, the distribution of gain between partners expected by both U.S. and Japanese partners was thought to be equally fair.

Authority and Speed of Decision-Making

American negotiators appear to have more authority in decision-making. Japanese partners consult their Tokyo head office all through the negotiation, but Thai partners felt that this was to buy time. In general, a business deal is more rapidly concluded with Americans than with Japanese. Both executives mentioned that communication with Japanese partners is more difficult because of the language barrier.

Consistency and Commitment

For Japanese partners, once a deal is closed, a lifelong commitment can be expected. Japanese partners tend to honor their local partners more than the (imperial) European partners and were willing to discuss matters at length with local partners to avoid undue misunderstanding.

Other investors often changed their minds after the deal was concluded. When interviewed, one executive said,

> In my experience, American traders changed their mind on a quarterly basis. So did the French and the Taiwanese. The Taiwanese agreed on one thing but did exactly the opposite.

Both executives concluded that, although it is difficult to strike a good deal with a Japanese, once a deal is made, the partnership is more stable. Japanese partners were also very willing to back up their local partners, even in bad times. However, lower margins from working with Japanese partners must be expected.

Information

All partners were well prepared and informed before negotiations. The difference was in the source of information. Japanese partners relied on information from in-house department and trading companies whereas Western firms relied on consultant firms.

Emphasis on Quality

Partners of all nationalities were quality-conscious and observed very high quality standards, but Japanese partners were slightly more strict. Japanese partners put more emphasis on training local workers, but U.S. firms stressed R & D activities.

Home Country Support

All foreign partners have secured financial backup from their national banks, but the French partners also received support from their government in the form of tied loans and risk guarantee (COFACE, Commission Frangaise pour l'Assurance Commerce Extérieur). The Japanese conglomerates tended to compete as a system of enterprises-cum-government much more than did the other TNCs.

On the whole, the two executives believed that to form a joint venture with other foreign partners to compete with a Japanese joint venture is very difficult. In such a case, one must be ready to offer lower prices and be very efficient. This information helps to explain the statistical results given above.

Concluding Remarks

Although Japanese enterprises have a long, stable history of FDI in Thailand, until 1987 their FDI contribution was still small as a share of total FDI, and their production went to the domestic market. In fact, before the mid–1980s Japanese affiliates contributed less to promoting Thai exports than did the affiliates of TNCs from other nations. In addition, as Thailand only recently entered the first stage of industrialization, the industrial technologies required were still simple. Since 1987, however, the pattern of Japanese investment has substantially changed, greatly increased, and become more specialized in manufacturing. Therefore, Japanese investors can be expected to play an increasing role in export promotion and technology transfer in the future.

United States investments, on the other hand, have been more unstable; some investors have even abandoned local markets in some industries. United States investors have shown more interest in investing only after noting Thailand's recent spectacular growth performance.

A new investment phenomenon has been the rapidly increasing role of the NIEs, especially the ROC and Hong Kong, with more and more of their labor-intensive industries moving into Thailand.

In the future, the inflow of Japanese investment is more likely to be influenced by infrastructural bottlenecks, the shortage of skilled manpower, and the fluctuating value of the yen.

References

Blythe, Stephen E., "Japanese Management System: A Comparison with U.S. Management Systems and Their Application to U.S. Industry," University of Arkansas, Ph.D. thesis, 1979.

Brummitt, William E., and Frank Flatters, "Exports, Structural Change and Thailand's Rapid Growth." Background Report for the 1992 TDRI Year-end Conference, Ambassador City Jomtien Chonburi, December 12–13, 1992.

Chinwanno, Chulacheeb, and Somsak Tambunlertchai, "Japanese Investment in Thailand and Its Prospect in the 1980's," Asian Dialogue Oiso Conference, May 22–23, Tokyo, 1982.

ESCAP/UNCTC Joint Unit on TNCs, *Costs and Conditions of Technology Transfer Through Transnational Corporations.* Publication Series B, No. 3, Bangkok, 1985.

————, *Transnational Corporations and External Financial Flows of Developing Economies in Asia and the Pacific,* Publication Series B, No. 10, Bangkok, 1986.

Kanchanapankha, Phoranee, "Joint Ventures in Thailand: Case Studies of Japanese-Thai Joint Ventures." Master's thesis, Faculty of Economics, Thammasat University, Thailand, 1978.

Kojima, Kiyoshi, "A Macroeconomic Approach to Foreign Direct Investment," *Hitotsubashi Journal of Economics,* Vol. 16, pp. 1–12, 1973.

Phongpaichit, Pasuk, "The New Waves of Japanese Direct Investment in Thailand," paper prepared for the conference on "External Capital and the Role of Japan" organized by Chulalongkorn University and Japan Foundation, Pattaya, March 27–28, 1988.

Poapongsakorn, Nipon, et al., "On the Job Training in the Manufacturing and Services Industries," report prepared for National Social and Economic Development Board, 1992.

Pongpisanupichit, Jirasak, "Direct Foreign Investment and Thai Investment Promotion Policy," Public Policy Study Project, Social Sciences Association of Thailand, September, 1985.

Santikarn, Mingsarn, "Trade in Technology: ASEAN and Australia." Australia Economic Papers, No. 8, ASEAN Australia Joint Research Project, Canberra, 1984.

————, "Technology Acquisition Under Alternative Arrangements with Transnational Corporations: Selected Industrial Case Studies in Thailand," in *Technology Transfer Under Alternative Arrangements with Transnational Corporations,* ESCAP/UNCTC Publication Services B, No. 11, 1987.

Santikarn Kaosa-ard, Mingsarn, "Japanese Investment in Thailand: Looking Back and Into the Future," in Seiji Naya and Akira Takayamd, eds., *Economic Development in East and Southeast Asia: Essays in Honor of Professor Shinichi Ichinmura*, IEAS, Singapore, 1990, pp. 185–201.

———, "A Preliminary Study of TNCs' Hiring and Localization Policies in Thailand," *TDRI Quarterly Review*, December, pp. 11–18, 1991.

———, "TNC Involvement in the Thai Auto Industry," *TDRI Quarterly Review*, March, 1993.

Sibunruang, Atchaka, "Foreign Investment and Manufactured Exports in Thailand," Ph.D. thesis, Graduate School of Social Study, University of Sussex, 1994.

———, and Peter Brimble. "Foreign Investment and Export Orientation: A Thai Perspective," in Naya S. Vichitvadakan and U. Kerdpibule, eds., *Direct Foreign Investment and Export Promotion: Policies and Experiences in Asia*. Southeast Asian Central Banks Research and Training Centre and the East West Resource Systems Institute, 1987.

———, "The Employment Effects of Manufacturing Multinational Enterprises in Thailand," paper prepared for the International Labour Organization on behalf of the Human Resources Institute, Thammasat University (draft report), 1988.

———, "Export-Oriented Industrial Collaboration: A Case Study of Thailand," study prepared for UNCTC, Bangkok, 1992.

Sibunruang, Sathien, and Thongdee Kijbunchu, "Investment, Exports and the Growth of the Thai Economy," *Thammasat Economic Journal*, Vol. 10, No. 4, December, 1992, pp. 43–56.

Surakanvit, Banyat, and Prayoon Chiowatana, "Technology Transfer: View from Technology Recipient and a Case Study of Thailand's Electronics Industries," paper prepared for symposium, "Toward Restructuring of the International Division of Labour in the Asian Pacific Region: Economic Relations of Japan, China, NICs and ASEAN in the Year 2000," November 2–3, Pattaya, 1978.

Tambunlertchai, Somsak, "Japanese and American Investments in Thailand's Manufacturing Industries: An Assessment of Their Relative Economic Contribution to the Host Country," Institute of Developing Economy, Tokyo, 1977.

Tejima, Shigeki, "Japanese MNCs' Overseas Business Operations in the Asia Pacific Region," paper prepared for Kyushu University International Symposium 1992, Fukuoka, Japan, July 27–28, 1992.

Tiralap, Anupap and Prayoon Chiowatana, "Study on the Role of Japanese Investment in the Thai Manufacturing Sector," paper prepared for ASEAN Center for Investment, Trade and Tourism Promotion, no date.

TCMD (Transnational Corporations and Management Division). "World Investment Report 1992: Transnational Corporations as Engines of Growth," United Nations, New York, ST/CTC/130, 1992.

UNCTC. "World Development Report 1991. The Triad in foreign direct investment." United Nations, New York, ST/CTC/118, 1991.

Chapter 6

Japanese Direct Investment in the Republic of China

• • • • • • • •

CHI SCHIVE

Compared with other investors in the Republic of China (ROC), Japanese investors prefer joint ventures and small to medium firms and emphasize longer-term commitments. Long-term relationships between Japan and the ROC have fluctuated, however. For instance, certain regulations on foreign direct investment (FDI) were applied to Japanese investors. The ROC only imposed a large-scale trade embargo against Japan, yet Japan has been the ROC's largest deficit-trade partner, with deficits increasing since the mid-1960s. In the late 1980s, Japan finally replaced the United States as the most important source of FDI in the ROC. The amount of Japanese capital was very significant: By the end of 1980s, Japan actually contributed the largest FDI share in the ROC. The ROC welcomed Japanese investment, and its impact on the ROC economy, particularly the manufacturing sector, has been significant. The ROC's rapid economic growth and rapid structural changes also have important links with Japan's FDI.

To show these links, we first compare Japanese FDI in Korea and in the ROC. This account is followed by a review of the key characteristics of Japanese FDI made by Japanese general trading companies (*sogo shosha*) and by the Japanese government and major Japanese banks. The discussion then focuses on how ROC industrial development benefited from the exports and technology transfer generated by Japanese capital investment. Finally, some ideas about Japanese FDI are closely examined, followed by a brief summary.

Japanese FDI into Taiwan and Korea

After the Sino-Japanese War ended in 1895, the Ching empire ceded Taiwan to Japan, and in 1910 Korea became a colony of Japan (until 1945). Japanese capital, both direct and portfolio, significantly helped to develop Taiwan's agriculture and industry. Taiwan became Japan's major suplier of essential food products because of the speed and efficiency with which the Japanese reformed the land system, built a modern irrigation system, and established agricultural research institutes. As a result, Japanese sugar imports from Taiwan increased markedly, from 8.7 percent of all sugar imports in 1903 to 81 percent in 1935. Rice exports to Japan also increased greatly. Food processing industries, such as pineapple-canning also took off. Japan moved toward economic self-sufficiency in the 1930s, however, and began to invest in heavy industries such as cement, chemicals, pulp and paper, fertilizer, petroleum refining, and metallurgy (Chang, 1980).

Table 6.1 shows Japanese capital investment in Taiwan and Korea during the colonial period. Japanese corporate enterprise investment took the lion's share, between 80 and 90 percent of the total capital inflow to Taiwan, but between 50 and 70 percent for Korea. Before 1924, Taiwan's indigenous entrepreneurs could not form joint stock companies unless Japanese businessmen participated. Even after 1924, the regulations and licensing procedures imposed by the colonial administration virtually excluded non-Japanese firms. It is not surprising that the Japanese colonial regime made certain that all large-scale industrial activity on the island remained in Japanese hands at the beginning of World War II. Japanese owned 76.4 percent of all paid-up capital in Taiwan as of 1929. Four-fifths of all Japanese capital was concentrated in the industrial sector, and 90.0 percent of the total paid-up capital in that same sector belonged to the Japanese.

Japanese capital investment was nonexistent in the ROC until the 1950s, and in Korea, only by the 1960s. The Nationalist government had confiscated most of the previous Japanese corporate investments in Taiwan and diverted them to public enterprises, which made up 80 percent of industry's total production in Taiwan in the early 1950s.

In the ROC, FDI remained low and fluctuated in the 1950s, partly

TABLE 6.1

JAPAN'S INVESTMENT IN TAIWAN AND KOREA DURING THE COLONIAL REGIMES

	Government Loans	Corporate Investment	Private Investment	Total	Exchange Rates
Taiwan					
1924	52.5	581.4	——	633.0	¥100 = $46.875
1939	39.8	282.0	——	321.8	¥100 = $23.437
1943	39.8	452.3	——	492.1	¥100 = $23.437
Korea					
1931	438.9	530.6	70.9	1,040.4	¥100 = $48.871
1938	370.4	618.6	41.7	1,030.3	¥100 = $28.496
1941	460.8	1,004.7	219.6	1,684.7	¥100 = $23.437

SOURCE: Ken'ichi Yasumuro (1982), "The Contribution of Sogo Shosha to the Multinationalization of Japanese Industrial Enterprises in Historical Perspective," in Akio Okochi and Tadakatsu Inoue, eds., *Overseas Business Activities*, University of Tokyo Press, cited from Ippei Yamazawa and Yuzo Yamamoto, *Foreign Trade and Balance of Payments—Estimates of Long-Term Economic Statistics of Japan Since 1968*, Tokyo, 1979, p. 56 (in Japanese).

because of a limited local market and the threat of political instability (Jacoby, 1966; Schive, 1990a), and partly because of little international private capital movement in that decade. Inflow of FDI into the ROC quickly increased in the 1960s, and that trend has continued ever since. A new Investment Law in 1960, the overhaul of the foreign exchange system, and peace across the Taiwan Straits helped to create a favorable environment for attracting FDI to the ROC (Schive, 1988). Table 6.2 clearly indicates this new trend.

Foreign investors in the ROC consisted of overseas Chinese and other foreigners, with the former contributing around 30 percent of the total approval FDI before 1970, but only 10 percent in the 1980s (table 6.2). Among foreigners, Americans provided the largest share before 1985, and Japanese took the lead after 1986. The share of European capital started from a low level of 6 percent before 1970, increased to 10 percent in the 1970s, and to 17 percent in the second half of 1980s. Capital from other sources showed an even higher rate of expansion than that from Europe. In short, a significant shift of investment position among foreign investors took place during the past four decades; Japanese, European, and other investors gradually replaced Americans and overseas Chinese as the major suppliers of FDI capital in the ROC.

The rapid increase of FDI into the ROC, along with a significant change in the composition of investment in the second half of the 1980s, reflected some key internal and external factors. First, the economy underwent great change during that period. The mounting trade surplus that culminated in the early 1980s strengthened the local currency sharply after 1986. Moreover, many reforms occurred: The average tariff rate fell from 30 percent in 1984 to below 10 percent in 1990; nontariff barriers to trade declined; regulations on foreign exchange remittance and investment eased. A good example is that any individual can now remit $5 million abroad per year, and FDI is now allowed in retailing and insurance. In 1988, some industries formerly unavailable for FDI could receive foreign capital, which helped expand FDI even more. In the foreign-exchange market, after the NT dollar significantly appreciated over a four-year period, only the Japanese yen surpassed the NT dollar in being revalued. The surge of Japanese FDI into the ROC in the second half of 1980s was in large part due to the great strength of the Japanese yen in those years.

Capital from Europe and other sources may not always reflect reality. First, many well-known multinational corporations investing in the ROC were not registered in the country where the companies originally formed. For instance, Ford Company formed a joint venture in Taiwan in the earlier 1970s through Canada Ford. The famous Singer investment in Taiwan was

TABLE 6.2
FOREIGN DIRECT INVESTMENT IN TAIWAN AND SOUTH KOREA BY SOURCE

Taiwan Source	1952–1970 Amount no.(%)	1952–1970 Case[a] no.(%)	1971–1980 Amount no.(%)	1971–1980 Case no.(%)	1981–1985 Amount no.(%)	1981–1985 Case no.(%)	1986–1991 Amount no.(%)	1986–1991 Case no.(%)	1952–1991 Amount no.(%)	1952–1991 Case no.(%)
Overseas Chinese	163 (29)	710 (54)	801 (37)	(774 (53)	210 (9)	272 (37)	999 (10)	506 (19)	2,173 (14)	2,253 (37)
Foreign	396 (71)	587 (46)	1,358 (63)	675 (47)	2,232 (91)	462 (63)	8,871 (90)	2,185 (81)	12,857 (86)	3,909 (63)
United States	242 (43)	156 (12)	534 (25)	173 (12)	940 (38)	176 (24)	2,163 (22)	367 (14)	3,879 (26)	872 (14)
Japan	89 (16)	386 (30)	369 (17)	370 (26)	673 (28)	144 (20)	3,078 (31)	1,057 (39)	4,209 (28)	1,957 (32)
Europe	36 (6)	16 (1)	225 (10)	46 (3)	272 (11)	53 (7)	1,699 (17)	347 (13)	2,232 (15)	462 (7)
Others	29 (5)	29 (2)	230 (11)	80 (6)	347 (14)	89 (12)	1,931 (20)	414 (15)	2,537 (17)	618 (10)
Total	559 (100)	1,288 (100)	2,159 (100)	1,449 (100)	2,442 (100)	734 (100)	9,870 (100)	2,691 (100)	15,030 (100)	6,612 (100)

South Korea Source	1962–1971 Amount (in $US million)	1962–1971 Percent	1972–1981 Amount	1972–1981 Percent	1982–1984 Amount	1982–1984 Percent	1985–1988[b] Amount	1985–1988[b] Percent	1962–1988 Amount	1962–1988 Percent
United States	$172	45	$371	23	$348	40	$745	23	$1,636	27
Japan	140	37	926	58	373	42	1,736	54	3,175	52
Europe	30	8	135	8	88	10	531	16	784	13
Others	38	10	168	11	71	8	217	7	494	8
Total	380	100	1,600	100	880	100	3,229	100	6,089	100

NOTES: [a]Number of contract investments finalized.
[b]Korea's data for 1988 based on January–September total.

SOURCES: Investment Commission, MOEA, Statistics on Overseas Chinese and Foreign Investment, Technical Cooperation, Outward Investment, Outward Technical Cooperation, various issues; Chi Schive (1990), The Foreign Factor: The Multinational Corporation's Contribution to the Economic Modernization of the Republic of China. Stanford: Hoover Institution Press. Lee and Ramstetter (1991).

partly financed by Singer Company in Switzerland.[1] Gulf's joint venture with the Chinese Petroleum Company, a public enterprise, came from Gulf Panama. American FDI in Taiwan has probably been underestimated by using U.S. government statistics. Another bias comes from a problem caused by the financial liberalization mentioned above. When capital outflow became easier and increased in the late 1980s, foreign companies still enjoyed a certain degree of tax benefit; many local companies, including large ones, made outward investment first in some tax-haven countries or territories belonging to the British or Dutch. That same capital was remitted back to the ROC as FDI. A rough estimation of this particular FDI in 1989 and 1990 accounted for about 20 percent of the total FDI approved. As a result, the approved FDI figure in the late 1980s exaggerated the actual FDI capital inflow.

Foreign direct investment in Korea reveals a similar pattern but with a minor difference. When FDI in Korea began in the 1960s, the United States was the largest investor. After Japanese outward investment experienced a boom in the 1970s, Japan became the largest FDI capital supplier. It is worthwhile to point out that Korean statistics on FDI never distinguish overseas Koreans, mainly from Japan, from foreigners. Thus, some Japanese FDI in Korea resembled "neighboring country" investment, such as the overseas Chinese investment into the ROC from Hong Kong, Southeast Asian countries, and Japan. Relatively speaking, Japan has played a greater investment role in Korea than in Taiwan.

Characteristics of Japanese Investment in Taiwan

All studies of Japanese FDI in the ROC and Korea consistently show that Japanese outward investment prefers joint venture ownership (Chou, 1988; Schive, 1990a; Lee, 1980; Koo, 1985; Kojima, 1985). This finding, shown in table 6.3, seems more applicable to Korea than to the ROC. By 1991, 48 percent of all Japanese firms in Korea were those with foreign ownership between 40 and 59 percent, compared with only 28 percent in the ROC. Minority-owned Japanese firms also accounted for more in Korea than those in the ROC, 25.6 percent and 14.4 percent, respectively. There were wholly owned Japanese firms in both countries, but more so in the ROC. It may be noted that one-fifth of those wholly owned Japanese companies in the ROC were located in three export processing zones, an indication that the minimum requirement of local contact reduced the incentive to have a local

TABLE 6.3

OWNERSHIP STRUCTURE OF JAPANESE ENTERPRISES
IN TAIWAN AND S. KOREA, 1991 (percent)

Ownership Share	Taiwan	South Korea
< 40%	14.4	25.6
40–59%	28.1	48.0
60–99%	29.1	15.7
100%	28.3	10.7

NOTE: If we exclude the Japane firms of EPZ, the percentage of wholly
owned in Taiwan decreases to 23.5%.
SOURCE: Toyo Keizai (1992).

partner. In addition, 40 percent of Japanese ventures in the electronics industry, noted for its very high export propensity, were wholly owned. In the late
1980s, when the ROC government allowed Japanese investment in trading
businesses, many investors quickly took advantage of the opportunity.[2]

The ownership structure of Japanese FDI has been influenced by the
attitude of local governments and the incentives to form joint ventures. The
Korean government made it clear in 1973 that foreign ownership was limited to 50 percent, although exceptions have existed. A similar situation prevailed in the ROC but with some differences. On the investor side, capital is
limited, and if the risk of investment is low and the technology options are
feasible, a minority-owned venture is preferred. Because of a long-existing
economic and social relationship between Japan and Korea, both sides tend
to prefer small-scale investments in joint ventures. When a Japanese general
trading company made foreign investments, the Japanese generally insisted
on having more than two participants in the same venture (more on this point
below).

Japanese FDI in the ROC and Korea has been associated with small
amounts of investment capital per project or case. The Japanese investor
tends to be a small firm, which usually does not invest abroad. However,
Japanese small and medium enterprises (SMEs) have been very active in
investing in East Asia. One survey showed that 72.7 percent of all outward
investment made by Japanese SMEs in manufacturing has been concentrated
in Asia, and 46.3 percent of that amount went to Taiwan, Korea, and Hong
Kong in 1987 (JETRO, 1991).

Japanese general trading companies, or *sogo shosha*, have participated
in making foreign investments. By 1991 the top ten *shosha* produced a total

of 2,570 foreign ventures, of which 76 were in Taiwan and 49 in Korea. Kojima and Ozawa's earlier study (1984a) showed that the top nine *shosha* had 682 investments in the manufacturing sector by 1980, of which 547 (80.2 percent) were in the developing world, and 364 (53.4 percent) were in Asia. Their study and that of Sazanami (1992) strongly suggest that *shosha* have promoted Japanese outward investment in the manufacturing, extractive, and services sectors.

As the *shosha* make their foreign investments, they build a well-organized international network. *Shosha* can then provide other companies with services in their foreign operations or coordinate activities so as to launch large-scale investment. The investor can be a small- or medium-sized business with the *shosha* as a minority participant. The *shosha* are also unlikely to play a major role in providing capital. The *shosha* do not go abroad alone except to make their initial set-up investment in the network. After a joint venture is formed, *shosha* seek partnership with a small firm or company.

This foreign investment pattern associated with *shosha* can be explained as follows. The *shosha*'s specific advantage is not associated with any manufacturing skill, but with the ability to reduce transaction costs, such as in gathering information. It is unnecessary to have a majority-owned venture develop these advantages. By having a small stake in a company abroad, a *shosha* can win the contract for shipping, procurement of equipment, materials, and making final products for that company. There are great incentives for partner(s) to allow a *shosha* to assume the marketing costs.

The *shosha*'s typical investment behavior in the ROC and Korea is similar, with only slight differences. In Korea, the *shosha* have made no majority-owned joint ventures. Among minority-owned ventures, their ownership was limited to no more than 30 percent. In the ROC, there were seventy-six joint ventures with *shosha* capital, of which only eight were majority-owned and only three wholly owned. The exceptional ones include an apparel factory, which involved no particular manufacturing skill but were an investing company and a trading company. As far as the partnership is concerned, two-thirds of the joint ventures had at least two partners, one local and one Japanese, in addition to *shosha* as the third participant. Among the rest, nine were with only Japanese partners and fourteen with only local collaborators. In Korea, 40 out of 49 ventures involved the cooperation of three parties—a *shosha*, a Japanese company, and a local partner. There was only one case without any local capital. Thus, the *shosha* went to the ROC and Korea as matchmakers for foreign and local investors.

If we compare *shosha* investment in Korea and the ROC, more investments related to trading companies were approved after 1985 in the ROC. In the tertiary sector, 24 out of 29 ventures were established after 1985. As a matter of fact, of all ventures in the service subsector, mainly retailing and chain food-service industries, three construction companies and a transportation firm could operate in the ROC since 1985, as compared with only four ventures existing before that year. This dramatic change in relation to *shosha*'s investment reflects the FDI policy switch in the ROC in general, and that toward Japanese investment after 1985 in particular. A scrutiny of two data sources of Japanese investment in the ROC indicates that several Japanese trading companies set up their ventures long before they were legally permitted. For instance, Marubeni set up its Taipei office in 1949, Mitsubishi in 1950, Sumitomo in 1953, Kanematsu in 1955, and Tomen in 1955.[3]

These arrangements involved a very limited transfer of capital and foreign exchange, merely the transfer of information. Similar arrangements existed elsewhere when the law or the administrative body did not favorably treat Japanese investment. In Korea, only 13 out of a total of 49 ventures related to *shosha* were set up after 1985. There was only one case in the trading industry. It seems that Korea's *zaibatsu* (the *chaebol*) have not allowed the *shosha* to expand their activities.

In the 1960s, the ROC's society was still poor, and businesspeople eagerly wanted to establish new industry. The government worried about the cutoff of U.S. aid in 1965. Therefore, the ROC government sought capital from the Japanese government and its banks (see table 6.4)

The first contract with the Japanese government, signed in 1965, amounted to a total of 54 billion yen, or $150 million equivalent loans to finance procurement of Japanese equipment and engineering consultancy over a five-year period. The Japan Eximbank and Japan Overseas Economic Cooperation Fund provided funds to public enterprises and the central government, which financed the construction of a large water reservoir, expanding Kaoshiung harbor, and building new power plants and communication facilities. The total amount, 43 billion yen or $140 million, financed nineteen projects. A second contract, signed with the Japan Eximbank in 1972, committed 7.17 billion yen or $23.5 million. When formal diplomatic ties between the ROC and Japan ended, that contract also terminated, but the government loans amounted to 49.9 billion yen, or $163 million, and were repaid by 1988.

The local economy benefited from these government loans. Developing infrastructure absorbed 34 percent of the capital, and the rest went to public enterprises, with the Taiwan Fertilizer Company and Taiwan Sugar Company being the largest recipients. Interest rates varied between 3.5 percent and 5.75 percent. These loans linked Japanese businesses more tightly to the

TABLE 6.4
JAPANESE GOVERNMENT LOANS TO TAIWAN ($US millions)

	Agreement Amount	Disbursement	Principal Repaid	Outstanding Balance
1965	150.0	0.0	0.0	0.0
1966	na	7.7	0.0	7.7
1967	110.7	36.9	0.0	36.9
1968	99.2	58.4	0.0	58.4
1969	109.3	75.1	4.7	70.4
1970	137.3	93.8	11.3	82.4
1971	145.6	119.3	23.3	96.0
1972	176.7	136.4	34.6	101.8
1973	176.7	136.6	57.9	82.0
1974	176.7	162.2	69.6	92.6
1975	176.7	163.6	81.7	81.9
1976	176.7	163.6	95.2	68.4
1977	176.7	163.6	106.8	56.8
1978	163.6	163.6	116.5	47.1
1979	163.6	163.6	125.7	37.9
1980	163.6	163.6	132.6	31.0
1981	163.6	163.6	137.6	25.9
1982	163.6	163.6	142.2	21.3
1983	163.6	163.6	145.8	16.7
1984	163.6	163.6	151.5	12.1
1985	163.6	163.6	155.9	7.7
1986	163.6	163.6	160.1	3.5
1987	163.6	163.6	163.3	0.3
1988	163.6	163.6	163.6	0.0

SOURCES: Council for Economic Planning and Development, *Taiwan Statistical Data Book,* 1968–1989. Directorate-General of Budgets, Accounts, and Statistics, Executive Yuan, *Statistical Abstract of the Republic of China,* 1965–1967.

local economy. The U.S. Eximbank was also motivated to provide a loan to Taiwan Power Company after the ROC and Japanese governments signed the first contract in 1965.

Turning to bank loans, the Dai-Ichi Kangyo Bank broke the ice by investing in the ROC in 1959. It was the sole Japanese bank in Taiwan until 1993, when the Bank of Japan upgraded its Taipei office into a branch, although there were already thirty-six foreign banks in the ROC by 1991.[4] Given the unique position of this Japanese bank in the ROC, its business rapidly expanded. The Dai-Ichi Kangyo Bank accounted for only 1.5 percent of total loans, 2.3 percent of deposits, and 4.9 percent of total income before taxes of all foreign banks in 1981, but all these figures jumped to 9.5 percent, 16.4 percent, and 29.9 percent, respectively, in 1991. That Japanese bank grew faster and made more profit than its foreign competitors in the 1980s. Moreover, the bank's income return was more than three times that of its loans, giving it an outstanding earning performance.

Foreign banks in the ROC profited from their loans foreign exchange settlements. Their original paid-up capital, retained earnings, and interbank loans provided them with working capital. The excellent income statement shown by the Dai-Ichi Kangyo Bank can be attributed to its unique FDI relationship, one not available to other foreign banks, even U.S. banks. Interview data indicate that 80 percent of the Dai-Ichi Kangyo Bank's customers were either Japanese companies in the ROC or firms doing business with Japan. The bank's long-term, stable relationship with customers helped reduce risk. Meanwhile, the largest foreign bank in Taiwan, Citibank, heavily relied on consumer loans, which came to 64 percent of all its loans in 1991. Finally, the Japanese bank's low cost of capital and large undistributed profits also represented its successful investments in the ROC (Tiao, 1993).

Performance of Japanese Investment in Taiwan

Sazanami (1992) pointed out that Japanese FDI in Asia had shifted to the service sector in the 1980s, and the same trend occurred in the ROC. Its service sector attracted only 3 percent of Japanese FDI before 1980, but 11.3 percent and 26.6 percent in the first and second half of 1980s, respectively (see table 6.5). In the late 1980s, Japanese capital targeted trading firms, and then Japanese investments in retailing, chain stores, and department stores boomed in the 1980s. During the second half of 1980s, Lee and Ramstetter (1991) argue that 47 percent of Japanese FDI in Korea went to the service sector.[5]

TABLE 6.5
JAPANESE PAID-UP CAPITAL AND FIRM BY INDUSTRY AND BY YEAR OF ESTABLISHMENT, TAIWAN AND S. KOREA

Year of Establishment	Pre 1971				1971–1980				1981–1985				1986–1991				Total			
	Amount	%	Case	%	Amount	%	Case	%	Amount	%	Case	%	Amount	%	Case	%	Amount	%	Case	%
TAIWAN																				
Primary Sector	0.0	0.0	0	0.0	0.0	0.0	0	0.0	0.0	0.0	0	0.0	0.7	0.1	1	0.3	0.7	0.0	1	0.1
Manufacturing	721.6	97.0	132	93.6	366.6	96.5	121	84.6	290.5	88.7	57	64.0	526.4	73.4	173	49.7	1,905.0	87.8	483	67.0
Food/beverage	14.7	2.0	4	2.8	1.0	0.3	2	1.4	0.5	0.2	2	2.2	17.0	2.4	11	3.2	33.2	1.5	19	2.6
Textiles/apparel	8.9	1.2	8	5.6	19.7	5.2	3	2.1	0.0	0.0	0	0.0	10.1	1.4	7	2.0	38.8	1.8	18	2.5
Wood/paper/ leather	2.5	0.4	3	2.1	19.5	5.1	3	2.1	0.4	0.1	1	1.1	6.2	0.8	4	1.1	28.6	1.3	11	1.5
Rubber/plastics	15.4	2.1	8	5.7	30.2	7.9	6	4.2	1.4	0.4	3	3.4	13.5	1.9	10	2.9	60.6	2.8	27	3.7
Chemicals	63.9	8.6	22	15.6	23.9	6.3	14	9.8	30.9	9.4	12	13.5	44.9	6.3	20	5.7	163.6	7.5	68	9.4
Nonmetallic products	5.2	0.7	3	2.1	1.8	0.5	4	2.8	1.9	0.6	1	1.1	29.6	4.1	13	3.7	38.4	1.8	21	2.9
Basic metals	21.7	2.9	19	13.5	21.4	5.6	20	14.0	37.5	11.4	16	18.0	78.8	11.0	33	9.5	159.3	7.3	88	12.2
Machinery	42.8	5.8	9	6.4	39.7	10.4	21	14.7	123.5	37.7	7	7.9	90.3	12.6	23	6.6	296.3	13.7	60	8.3
Electronic/ electrical	526.2	70.7	43	30.5	200.9	52.9	44	30.8	94.5	28.8	14	15.7	227.1	31.6	41	11.8	1,048.7	48.3	142	19.6
Other manufacturing	20.3	2.7	12	8.5	8.4	2.2	4	2.8	0.0	0.0	1	1.1	8.7	1.2	12	3.4	37.5	1.7	29	4.0
Services	22.5	3.0	9	6.4	13.5	3.5	22	15.4	37.1	11.3	32	35.9	191.1	26.6	174	50.0	264.3	12.2	237	32.9
Construction	0.0	0.0	0	0.0	1.5	0.4	3	2.1	8.6	2.6	2	2.2	11.6	1.6	13	3.7	21.7	1.0	18	2.5
Trade	5.2	0.7	5	3.5	8.4	2.2	15	10.5	5.6	1.7	14	15.7	120.6	16.8	103	29.6	139.9	6.4	137	19.0
Banking/ insurance	0.0	0.0	0	0.0	0.0	0.0	0	0.0	0.0	0.0	0	0.0	1.8	0.3	1	0.3	1.8	0.1	1	0.1
Transportation	0.0	0.0	0	0.0	0.0	0.0	0	0.0	0.6	0.2	3	3.4	0.6	0.1	6	1.7	1.2	0.1	9	1.2
Other services	17.3	2.3	4	2.8	3.6	0.9	4	2.7	22.3	6.8	13	14.6	56.5	7.9	51	14.6	99.7	4.6	72	10.0
Total	744.1	100.0	141	100.0	380.1	100.0	143	100.0	327.6	100.0	89	100.0	718.2	100.0	348	100.0	2,170.0	100.0	721	100.0

NOTES: 1. Due to rounding, figures may not sum to total.
2. Japanese firm is Japanese ownership above 10%.

SOURCE: Toyo Keizai (1992, Japanese Multinationals Facts and Figures, Tokyo).

Year of Establishment

S. KOREA

	Pre 1971				1971–1980				1981–1985				1986–1991				Total			
	Amount	%	Case	%	Amount	%	Case	%	Amount	%	Case	%	Amount	%	Case	%	Amount	%	Case	%
Primary Sector	0.0	0.0	0	0.0	0.1	0.0	1	0.6	0.0	0.0	0	0.0	0.0	0.0	0	0.0	0.1	0.0	1	0.3
Manufacturing	24.5	100.0	17	100.0	541.8	91.6	152	93.3	136.1	84.1	35	81.4	341.8	98.0	119	75.8	1044.2	92.6	323	85.0
Food/beverage	0.0	0.0	0	0.0	7.2	1.2	7	4.3	7.2	4.5	2	4.6	18.8	5.4	5	3.2	33.2	2.9	14	3.7
Textiles/apparel	0.5	2.7	2	11.8	166.9	28.2	14	7.6	4.9	3.0	1	2.3	1.7	0.5	2	1.3	173.9	15.4	19	5.0
Wood/paper/leather	0.0	0.0	0	0.0	0.0	0.0	1	0.6	0.0	0.0	1	2.3	1.5	0.4	2	1.3	1.5	0.1	3	0.7
Rubber/plastics	0.0	0.0	0	0.0	2.1	0.4	3	1.8	2.0	1.2	3	7.0	18.3	5.2	10	6.4	22.5	2.0	16	4.2
Chemicals	0.2	0.8	1	5.9	145.5	24.6	29	17.8	12.0	7.4	7	16.3	46.7	13.4	20	12.7	204.4	18.1	57	15.0
Nonmetallic products	6.9	28.2	0	0.0	12.1	2.0	7	4.3	7.2	4.4	1	2.3	3.3	0.9	5	3.2	22.6	2.0	13	3.4
Basic metals	4.2	17.1	4	23.5	21.7	3.7	26	15.9	1.7	1.1	2	4.7	36.5	10.5	19	21.1	34.1	5.7	51	13.4
Machinery	6.9	28.2	6	35.3	27.8	4.7	16	9.8	86.2	53.3	10	23.3	26.4	7.6	21	13.4	147.2	13.1	53	13.9
Electronic/electrical	12.8	52.2	3	17.6	155.1	26.2	42	25.8	8.8	5.4	6	13.9	181.5	52.0	29	18.5	358.3	31.8	80	21.1
Other manufacturing	0.1	0.4	1	5.9	3.1	0.5	7	4.3	6.1	3.8	2	4.6	7.0	2.0	6	3.8	16.3	1.4	16	4.2
Services	0.0	0.0	0	0.0	50.0	8.4	10	6.1	25.5	15.9	8	18.6	7.1	2.0	38	24.2	82.6	7.4	56	14.7
Construction	0.0	0.0	0	0.0	0.0	0.0	0	0.0	1.0	0.6	1	2.3	0.4	0.1	1	0.6	1.4	0.1	2	0.5
Trade	0.0	0.0	0	0.0	0.2	0.0	1	0.6	0.4	0.2	2	4.6	2.4	0.7	12	7.6	3.0	0.3	15	3.9
Banking/insurance	0.0	0.0	0	0.0	23.2	3.9	2	1.2	22.4	13.9	2	4.6	0.1	0.0	2	1.3	45.8	4.1	6	1.6
Transportation	0.0	0.0	0	0.0	0.0	0.0	0	0.0	0.0	0.0	0	0.0	0.1	0.0	1	0.6	0.1	0.0	1	0.3
Other services	0.0	0.0	0	0.0	26.6	4.5	7	4.3	1.7	1.2	3	7.0	4.1	1.2	22	14.0	32.3	2.9	32	8.4
Total	24.5	100.0	17	100.0	591.8	100.0	163	100.0	161.6	100.0	43	100.0	348.9	100.0	157	100.0	1,126.8	100.0	380	100.0

NOTES: 1. Due to rounding, figures may not sum to total.
2. Japanese firm is Japanese ownership above 10%.

SOURCE: Toyo Keizai (1992, Japanese Multinationals Facts and Figures, Tokyo).

Japanese electrical and electronics manufacturers also wanted to invest in the ROC. Before 1970, up to 70.7 percent of Japanese FDI in the ROC went to that particular industry, 52.9 percent in the 1970s, and the percentage fell to around 30 percent in the 1980s. The machinery industry took the lion's share of 37.7 percent of Japanese total FDI between 1981 and 1985 when Toyota took over a joint venture from General Motors assembling heavy trucks, and Nissan expanded its Taiwan operation. Metal products and chemicals were the next two major industries receiving Japanese direct investment capital. Japanese FDI in the trade and other service industries ranked as the second or third most important industries in the 1980s. American FDI behaved the same as Japanese in the 1980s and even in the 1970s.

In Korea the investment pattern in the manufacturing sector resembles that in the ROC with minor differences (see table 6.5). Japanese FDI also concentrated in the electrical and electronics industry; Japanese textile producers preferred the Korean market to the ROC market, and so did Japanese chemicals producers.

If we define foreign firms as local companies with any amount of foreign capital, they played an important role in promoting ROC exports—more so in the 1970s than in the 1980s. Foreign firms, excluding companies with overseas Chinese capital, exported a total amount of $1.8 billion commodities in 1976 and $5.4 billion in 1986, so that 22.3 percent and 14.2 percent of Taiwan's total export in those years came from FDI. Some well-known companies in the ROC had a small percentage of capital owned by foreigners, such as the Tatung Company and Taiwan Cement Company. Taking care not to overestimate foreign firms' exports as representing all FDI, we observe that the weighted foreign-firm exports as a share of Taiwan exports decreased to 16.0 percent in 1976 and 10.3 percent in 1986, or roughly 30 percent lower than the unweighted figures. In spite of foreign firms' exports' increasing 1.95 times between 1976 and 1986, the ROC's total exports expanded 3.86 times, making foreign firms' contribution to exports less important in the 1980s.[6]

Japanese companies occupied the largest share of foreign-firm exports: 54.8 percent in 1976 and 52.8 percent in 1986. The shares pertaining to U.S. companies were 34.1 percent and 21.3 percent in both relevant years. Japanese firms' share of the country total reveals a significant drop between 1976 and 1986; U.S. ones had an even more significant degree of decline, an indication that native exporting firms, mostly small- and-medium-sized enterprises (SMEs), have grown rapidly in that market. As a matter of fact, SMEs in the manufacturing sector exported 57.2 percent of their total products in 1976, but 71.1 percent in 1985, to contribute 70 percent of the ROC's total export in the mid-1980s.[7]

As foreign firms' share of total exports gradually declined, many manufacturing industries came to depend on foreign firms for their long-term exports. In 1976, foreign firms controlled 80.7 percent of the ROC's total exports of electrical and electronic products, of which half were attributable to Japanese companies and about one-fourth to U.S. companies. Ten years later, foreign-firm shares in total exports of the same industry declined to 42.0 percent, of which still around half belonged to Japanese companies and only 7.4 percent to U.S. ones. The electrical and electronic industry has been export-oriented since the 1960s, and its growth has been linked to FDI from the very beginning.

Foreign firms accounted for more than two-digit export shares in 1976 in the textiles, rubber and plastics, chemicals, nonmetallic products, basic metals, and machinery industries. Japanese firms also outperformed U.S. ones in all these industries. Ten years later, foreign-firm export shares declined in all industries except for machinery, because of the surge of Japanese investment in that industry. Nevertheless, Japanese firms did record a decline in their exports for the textile, apparel, wood, bamboo and rattan, and chemical industries, of which the first three were labor-intensive and became declining industries. Many traditional electronic products such as home appliances also fit this category. Therefore, even before the ROC began making significant structural adjustments in the second half of 1980s, largely caused by a sharp appreciation of local currency (Schive, 1993), FDI already had quickly responded to the changing economic environment.

One reason that foreign firms have had a relatively large impact on exports is because they tended to export a large proportion of their output (table 6.6). When direct and indirect exports are combined, they accounted for over 62.3 percent of all sales by foreign firms in 1976 and 49.2 percent in 1986. In the strategic and targeted electrical and electronic industries, this ratio was over 70 percent in both years. In most other sectors, the share of total exports to foreign firms' sales tended to fall over time, with the exception of the apparel and nonmetallic industries. In addition to the electrical and electronic industries, exports still accounted for over 40 percent of all sales in the textiles, apparel, wood, bamboo and rattan, leather products, rubber and plastics, and basic metals industries in 1986.

Therefore, foreign firms have generally been very export-oriented and have used the ROC as an export base in their worldwide networks. One reason for this pro-export market orientation in the past was their ability to exploit the ROC's abundant labor. Indeed, as confirmed by Riedel (1975), low wages provided a strong incentive for labor-intensive and export-oriented FDI throughout the 1970s. However, not all FDI has been

TABLE 6.6
EXPORTS AND MARKET ORIENTATION OF FOREIGN FIRMS IN TAIWAN, 1976 AND 1986

Industry	Total		Overseas Chinese		Non-Overseas Chinese		Japan		United States	
	1976	1986	1976	1986	1976	1986	1976	1986	1976	1986
Unweighted total foreign-firm exports[a] ($US million)										
All industries	2,334	6,166	513	790	1,821	5,376	998	2,839	620	1,145
Manufacturing[b]	2,214	5,817	474	713	1,730	5,213	962	2,705	573	1,050
Food, beverages	43	39	23	2	21	38	19	25	0	11
Textiles	344	304	125	25	219	281	163	50	56	220
Apparel	156	207	85	101	71	107	39	10	22	26
Wood, bamboo, rattan	37	37	19	25	18	12	13	10	0	0
Paper, paper products	4	32	1	23	2	9	1	1	2	8
Leather, leather products	29	27	13	11	16	16	7	6	2	9
Rubber, plastics	106	256	25	115	82	167	62	71	16	0
Chemical, petrol. products	261	326	145	218	117	191	45	35	34	49
Nonmetalic products	23	119	9	23	15	96	7	22	0	33
Basic metals, products	58	200	8	9	51	191	39	152	11	8
Nonelec. mach., trans. eq.	96	587	5	24	91	562	57	494	23	62
Electric, electronic mach.	1,057	3,680	28	138	1,029	3,543	510	1,828	406	625

Unweighted total foreign-firm exports as a share of Taiwan exports[a] (percent)

Industry	Total 1976	Total 1986	Overseas Chinese 1976	Overseas Chinese 1986	Non-Overseas Chinese 1976	Non-Overseas Chinese 1986	Japan 1976	Japan 1986	United States 1976	United States 1986
All industries	28.6	16.3	6.3	2.1	22.3	14.2	12.2	7.5	7.6	3.0
Manufacturing[b]	31.3	18.8	6.9	2.3	24.5	16.8	13.6	8.7	8.1	3.4
Food, beverages	6.4	2.1	3.7	0.1	3.0	2.1	2.8	1.3	0.0	0.6
Textiles	37.8	12.2	13.8	1.0	24.0	11.2	17.9	2.0	6.1	8.8
Apparel	11.7	4.7	6.3	2.3	5.3	2.4	2.9	0.2	1.7	0.6
Wood, bamboo, rattan	6.7	2.2	3.5	1.5	3.2	0.7	2.4	0.6	0.0	0.0
Paper, paper products	6.7	13.6	2.2	9.9	4.5	3.7	1.3	0.4	3.2	3.3
Leather, leather products	11.1	2.2	5.1	0.9	6.0	1.3	2.7	0.5	0.8	0.8
Rubber, plastics	17.5	6.9	4.0	3.1	13.4	4.5	10.3	1.9	2.7	0.0
Chemical, petro. products	93.9	30.8	52.0	20.6	41.9	18.0	16.3	3.3	12.3	4.6
Nonmetallic products	23.6	15.9	8.9	3.0	14.7	12.9	7.3	2.9	0.04.3	
Basic metals, products	15.4	6.9	2.0	0.3	13.4	6.6	10.3	5.2	3.0	0.3
Nonelec. mach., trans. eq.	14.8	26.5	0.7	1.1	14.1	25.4	8.9	22.3	3.5	2.8
Electric, electronic mach.	82.9	43.6	2.2	1.6	80.7	42.0	40.0	21.7	31.9	7.4

NOTES: na = Not available.
[a] Total exports include direct and indirect exports. Indirect exports are sales of intermediate goods, parts, and materials to other firms which are subsequently exported by the purchaser.
[b] Data refer to the sum of the individual industries listed below, i.e., it excludes miscellaneous manufacturing.
[c] Foreign-firm ownership shares wee used to approximate the purely foreign contribution to foreign-firm export.
[d] Figures are not weighted by ownership shares.

SOURCE: Schive and Tu (1991). Original data from Central Bank of China, *Financial Statistics, Taiwan District, Republic of China,* various years; Liu et al. (1983, 111); Ministry of Economic Affairs, Investment Commission, *An Analysis of Operations and Economic Effects of Foreign Enterprises in Taiwan,* various years; Wu (1987, 189); Wu et al. (1980, 124).

TABLE 6.6 (CONTINUED)

Industry	Total 1976	Total 1986	Overseas Chinese 1976	Overseas Chinese 1986	Non-Overseas Chinese 1976	Non-Overseas Chinese 1986	Japan 1976	Japan 1986	United States 1976	United States 1986
Weighted total foreign-firm exports as a share of Taiwan exports[a,c] (percent)										
All industries	18.8	11.4	2.8	1.1	16.0	10.3	8.0	4.9	6.0	2.2
Manufacturing[b]	20.5	13.5	2.9	1.1	17.6	12.4	8.8	5.8	6.4	2.5
Food, beverages	2.3	1.2	0.6	0.1	1.7	1.1	1.5	0.7	0.0	0.3
Textiles	12.5	3.2	5.6	0.5	6.9	2.6	6.3	1.0	0.6	1.7
Apparel	8.0	3.1	5.2	2.0	2.7	1.0	1.7	0.4	0.3	0.3
Wood, bamboo, rattan	5.0	1.8	3.2	1.2	1.8	0.6	1.3	0.6	0.0	0.0
Paper, paper products	2.6	4.9	0.2	2.4	2.6	2.5	1.0	0.3	1.6	2.2
Leather, leather products	6.4	1.2	2.8	0.2	3.5	1.0	1.2	0.2	0.8	0.7
Rubber, plastics	11.0	3.1	2.9	1.4	8.2	1.7	7.0	1.1	0.6	0.0
Chemical, petrol. products	21.8	21.6	3.1	3.6	18.7	18.0	3.4	2.0	7.2	2.9
Nonmetalic products	5.7	3.2	0.7	0.0	5.0	3.2	3.2	0.6	0.0	0.8
Basic metals, products	10.8	4.3	1.7	0.3	9.2	4.0	6.6	2.9	2.5	0.2
Nonelec. mach., trans. eq.	22.4	18.5	0.7	0.7	10.7	17.8	8.0	15.5	1.1	2.1
Electric, electronic mach.	72.0	35.5	1.3	1.2	70.7	34.3	30.7	14.6	31.4	7.3

Total exports as a share of foreign-firm sales[a,d] (percent)

Industry	Total 1976	Total 1986	Overseas Chinese 1976	Overseas Chinese 1986	Non-Overseas Chinese 1976	Non-Overseas Chinese 1986	Japan 1979	United States 1976	United States 1986
All industries	61.4	46.4	58.6	33.4	62.3	49.2	na	na	na
Manufacturing[b]	62.3	47.8	61.1	34.1	62.6	51.7	57.5	68.0	na
Food, beverages	26.0	10.5	40.8	1.0	18.5	17.4	47.2	3.5	na
Textiles	85.3	43.4	85.1	33.8	85.4	44.8	81.1	88.2	na
Apparel	96.9	49.7	98.4	93.6	95.2	44.5	97.4	99.8	na
Wood, bamboo, rattan	90.3	94.8	88.9	95.5	91.8	93.6	100.0	na	na
Paper, paper products	12.1	15.6	6.4	20.7	17.6	9.4	21.8	17.5	na
Leather, leather products	100.0	60.1	100.0	96.3	100.0	54.3	99.0	100.0	na
Rubber, plastics	89.5	50.9	97.4	72.0	87.3	48.5	90.4	60.5	na
Chemical, petro. products	50.3	16.3	79.4	24.5	34.6	17.1	39.3	22.4	35.5
Nonmetallic products	8.0	21.1	4.8	10.3	13.6	28.0	62.4	100.0	na
Basic metals, products	58.2	39.9	75.2	23.8	56.3	41.3	44.5	82.1	43.9
Nonelec. mach., trans. eq.	849.0	32.7	79.1	22.2	48.1	33.4	69.6	37.6	73.3
Electric, electronic mach.	70.6	72.3	66.4	76.1	70.7	72.1	51.1	98.4	94.0

NOTES: na = Not available.
[a] Total exports include direct and indirect exports. Indirect exports are sales of intermediate goods, parts, and materials to other firms which are subsequently exported by the purchaser.
[b] Data refer to the sum of the individual industries listed below, i.e., it excludes miscellaneous manufacturing.
[c] Foreign-firm ownership shares wee used to approximate the purely foreign contribution to foreign-firm export.
[d] Figures are not weighted by ownership shares.

SOURCE: Schive and Tu (1991). Original data from Central Bank of China, Financial Statistics, Taiwan District, Republic of China, various years; Liu et al. (1983, 111); Ministry of Economic Affairs, Investment Commission, An Analysis of Operations and Economic Effects of Foreign Enterprises in Taiwan, various years; Wu (1987, 189); Wu et al. (1980, 124).

export-oriented, and the ROC's expanding local market was crucial for attracting FDI, a point long emphasized in industrial organization research (Hymer, 1960).

Looking at the market orientation of foreign firms in another way, we observe that figure 6.1 shows three curves based on census data of 1978, 1982, and 1986, depicting the export ratio in total sales and the year when the foreign firm was established. All three curves reveal the same patterns of change: Companies set up before 1962 exported the least in all three survey years; those established in 1970 or in 1974 reported the highest export propensity, but latecomers paid more attention to the local market. Thus, export-oriented FDI came to Taiwan mainly from 1966 to the year of the first oil crisis, 1972. Since then, the late arrivals exported less in total sales when compared with their predecessors as well as over time. In the late 1980s, when trade liberalization accelerated and FDI shifted to the tertiary sector, the export ratio for foreign firms can be expected to decline further.

In short, the export behavior of FDI in general and of Japanese firms can be summarized as follows: (1) Foreign firms have been very export-oriented and have made significant contributions to Taiwanese exports, but more so during the period of the late 1960s and the 1970s; (2) foreign firms' contributions have been concentrated in a few industries, especially the electrical

FIGURE 6.1
THE EXPORT RATIO OF FOREIGN FIRMS

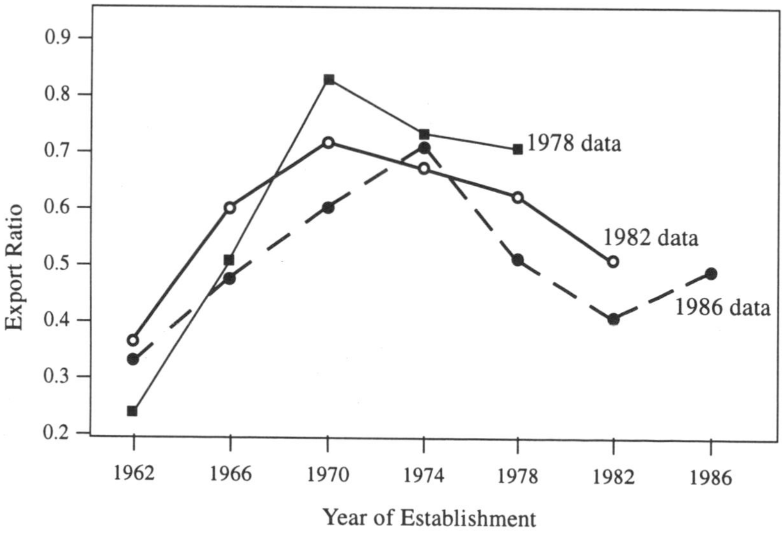

Year of Establishment

SOURCE: Wu, Schive, and Tsai (1990).

and electronic industries; (3) the relative volume of foreign-firm export activity declined over time, but more so for U.S. companies than for Japanese ones; (4) foreign investors never ignored the Taiwanese local market, including its strong derived demand for local intermediates created by booming exports during all three decades observed. (More on this point later.)

Theory so far suggests that FDI is an efficient channel of international technology distribution. Empirical studies of foreign firms' behavior in the ROC (Schive, 1990a) reveal that the participation of foreign capital did encourage their use of foreign technology. As to the specific technologies imported through FDI, foreign firms played an important role in introducing new products and technologies in the auto and auto parts, electrical and electronic products, and plastic and plastic products industries, but they were less active in the machinery and textile industries, in which processing instead of product improvement was more important.

The close link between hardware-technology transfer and FDI seems applicable to that of software technology, mainly in management and marketing skills. The empirical results in the ROC in the earlier 1970s show that 74.8 percent of exporting foreign firms relied to some extent on their foreign parent companies or partners for marketing their exports. Detailed data in the electrical and electronic industries indicate that foreign subsidiaries can be set up on a larger scale from the outset when they do not face export-marketing difficulties. Finally, foreign investors are able to obtain the most favorable contract terms for the technology provided to the recipients if they are the investors' subsidiaries. The ROC's experience shows that the majority-owned foreign firms in the electrical and electronic industries signed slightly longer-term and somewhat more expensive contracts for their parent companies' technologies than did national or even minority-owned foreign firms. All these findings generally apply to foreign firms without distinguishing the sources of investors.

Relatively smaller in size, larger in amount of investment, and having closer economic and noneconomic ties to the local business community, the Japanese FDI pattern of industrial distribution increasingly became one form of technical cooperation. By 1979 there were a total of 1,318 valid technical cooperation projects, of which 70 percent were from Japan, 19 percent from the United States, and 9 percent from Europe. By 1991, the number of formal technical transfer contracts increased to 3,608, or 1.74 times, those from Japan decreased to 60 percent, shares for the United States and Europe increased 5 and 4 percentage points, respectively. Thus, Japan dominated the ROC's technology market for a long time, yet its relative importance has been declining, a positive sign that the ROC is becoming more independent of foreign technology.

At the industrial level, four leading industries—electrical and electronic, machinery, basic metal, and chemicals—accounted for three-quarters of all technology-transfer contracts during the period observed. Proportionately, the ROC has sought more technology from the United States and Europe in the electrical and electronic industries over time. In comparison with Japan, technology inflows from these two particular sources were concentrated more in the chemical industry.

In 1975, the ROC granted 30 percent of the total technical cooperation cases to foreign firms, of which 73 percent represented intracompany transfer. Given the declining position of FDI in the 1980s, the contribution to technology transfer from FDI might decline in the relative sense. Nevertheless, FDI has effectively promoted technology transfer to the ROC through formal or informal channels in spite of overcharging for royalties and fees. One hears that Japanese firms became more sensitive than U.S. firms in guarding their technical know-how.[8] This behavior probably produced a larger technology gap between the licenser and the licensee in the case of Japanese technology than for U.S. firms. Moreover, the renewal of existing collaboration cases was high, although complaints prevailed.[9]

The Kojima Hypothesis and Other Issues

The well-known Kojima hypothesis argues that the industrial pattern of Japanese FDI in a developing country fits the host country's comparative advantages, or potential comparative advantages, better than that of the U.S. one. Why? Japanese investors moved those industries abroad that had lost their international competitiveness. Because of the existing or potential differences of comparative advantage between the source and host countries, such an investment is most likely to promote trade with Japanese capital and technology. In comparison, the U.S. FDI in the developing world involves the industries in the United States that still enjoy comparative advantage. Therefore, U.S. FDI does not fit the host developing country's comparative advantage, and less trade will be created (Kojima, 1973, 1977; Kojima and Ozawa, 1984b; Kojima, 1985). An important implication from this hypothesis is that Japanese FDI tends to facilitate trade, whereas U.S. FDI does not.

Quite a few studies have been carried on in the ROC and Korea to test this hypothesis. Ranis and Schive (1985) found that the investment pattern among industries did not differ much between U.S. and Japanese capital in the 1970s. United States companies in Taiwan reported 65 percent of export ratio in total sales, including indirect export; Japanese ones, 53 percent; and European firms, 96 percent in 1975. In a similar study, Chou (1988) showed that the industrial rankings of U.S. and Japanese investment in Taiwan did not differ significantly. Moreover, the export ratios of U.S. and Japanese firms were 61 percent and 60 percent in 1983, respectively. Liu, Schive, and Tsai (1990) have measured the foreign-firm export ratios in 1976, 1981, and 1985: for U.S. firms, they were 73.4 percent, 56.4 percent, and 51.0 percent, respectively; those for Japanese firms were 63.8 percent, 57.2 percent, and 50.7 percent. To take into account the capital-ownership problem, Ranis and Schive (1985) calculated export per unit of paid-up capital for the United States and Japan. They were $2.44 for the United States and $1.98 for Japan in 1975. No evidence, so far, supports the Kojima hypothesis.[10]

Kojima's own study (1985) also refuted his hypothesis. He calculated the index of revealed comparative investment advantage for the United States and Japan in the ROC, which he defined as the ratio of U.S. FDI share in the given industry over the Japanese share in the same industry. The results showed that U.S. FDI led the Japanese in the paper and products, nonmetallic products, chemical, service, and food and beverage industries in the ROC by 1982, while the opposite held in the electrical and electronic, textile, apparel, and leather products industries. Furthermore, the export propensity of U.S. firms was slightly higher than that of Japanese ones. Kojima attributed these findings to the close relationship between the United States and the ROC.

Lee (1980) analyzed the export behavior of U.S. and Japanese firms in Korea during the period 1962–1974. He found that only 10 percent of the former were in the industries exporting half of the production, whereas 61 percent of Japanese investments were in export-oriented industries. A later study (Lee, 1983) showed that Japanese companies exported 49 percent in their total sales compared to only 21 percent for U.S. companies between 1974 and 1978. United States FDI concentrating in the chemical, technology, and capital-intensive industries was responsible for the bias toward the local market. The Kojima hypothesis receives more support in Korea than in the ROC.

Foreign firms are well known for their close ties with the home economy, but they are only loosely connected to the local market (Kindleberger, 1968). Abundant evidence supports this assertation, but the issues centering around this topic do not have easy answers. Export-oriented FDI should not be blamed for not supplying the local markct if the demand is not there. Even the heavy reliance on imported machinery and materials is acceptable on the ground of covering costs. The typical export-processing-zone operation for FDI is to create jobs and promote exports, and has less to do with increasing linkages between sectors in the economy. Moreover, Meier (1970) claims that "every new development (investment) is initially an enclave and it takes time for all innovation to work through and be absorbed." Foreign firms cannot be faulted for not purchasing local materials if the supply is not there. In short, the linkage effect from FDI is not expected to work immediately, and it may not be in line with the comparative advantage of the host country economy (Schive, 1990b).

Empirical data in the ROC for the 1970s and 1980s show that FDI located in export-processing zones (EPZs) or foreign companies, compared to those controlled by overseas Chinese, has a tendency to import more, and hence form enclaves. However, this group of alien foreign firms improved its procurement policies over time, and those located in EPZs did so in particular. In the short run, the enclave phenomenon associated with FDI becomes less significant over the long run, as the ROC experience shows (Schive, 1990a, 1990c).

Foreign firms with longer experience in dealing with local suppliers, or simply arriving earlier, are expected to buy more locally. Figure 6.2 confirms this development. Both older U.S. and Japanese companies in the ROC have bought more locally. However, most European and Japanese latecomers seem to buy more. This seemingly contradictory phenomenon may be the other side of the linkage argument. If a foreign company chooses the ROC as the offshore base for its strong supply capability in the local market, the local procurement will be high from the very beginning of the investment. In other words, the forward linkage possibilities influence the newly arrived FDI.

In addition to the time factor, the foreign-ownership structure, export propensity, status as a producer of either final or intermediate goods, status as overseas Chinese or foreigners, and the scale of operation all influence foreign firms' local purchasing behavior. Table 6.7 covers four industries and provides further information about the behavioral differences between U.S. and Japanese firms. The best-fitting results indicate that U.S. firms did show a tendency to buy more than others, mainly Japanese in the basic metal and machinery industries. In the chemical industry Japanese firms were buying less than others. These crude findings provide only limited information on the possible behavioral differences in local purchasing between Japanese and others, but findings on other explanatory variables were more solid.

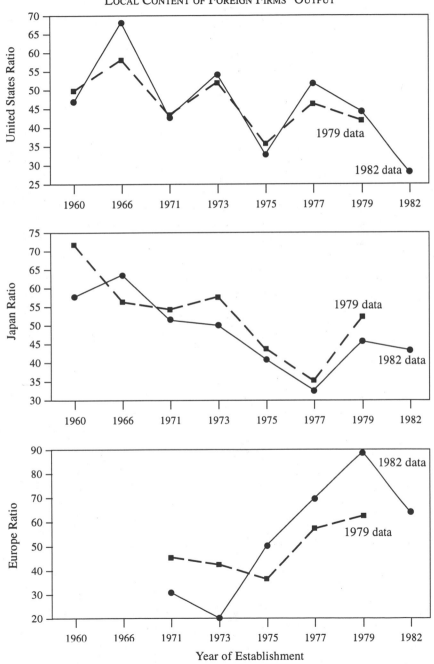

FIGURE 6.2
LOCAL CONTENT OF FOREIGN FIRMS' OUTPUT

SOURCE: Schive (1986, 73).

TABLE 6.7
MULTIPLE REGRESSIONS ON FOREIGN FIRM'S LOCAL CONTENTS, 1979 AND 1982

	No. of Firms (1)	Foreign Ownership	Export Ratios (2)	Overseas or Non-Overseas Chinese (3)	Total Sales as Firm Sale	United States (4)	Japan (5)	Year of Estab. (6)	EPZ (7)	Time (8)	R^2
Electronics											
(A) 183			-0.132 (-1.98)**	-9.01 (-1.25)	0.0209 (1.34)						0.303
(B) 189		-0.150 (-2.34)**	-0.935 (-1.42)			6.42 (1.35)		-4.40 (-1.02)			0.0481
(C) 2 X 142		-0.101 (-2.00)**	-0.125 (-2.30)					-3.75 (-1.17)		4.49 (1.42)	0.0594
Machinery											
(A) 60		-0.239 (-1.87)*			-0.471 (-1.62)*		-14.23 (-1.54)	-12.88 (-1.50)	-26.77 (-2.29)*		0.2469
(B) 68		-0.254 (-2.57)**	-0.176 (-2.24)				9.58		-26.19 (-3.09)		0.2585
(C) 2 X 46		-0.234 (-2.55)			-0.019 (-1.70)*	15.50 (1.80)*	1.36		-18.77 (-2.29)**		0.3016
Basic metal products											
(A) 101		-0.242 (-1.57)		39.23 (2.82)**	-0.447 (-2.07)**	18.57 (1.83)*					0.667
(B) 94					-0.449 (-2.15)**	17.50 (1.83)*			-7.704 (-0.73)		
(C) 2 X 72					-0.502 (-2.98)**	23.34 (3.25)**					
Chemicals											
(A) 96		-0.256 (-2.03)**	-0.232 (-2.27)**	-15.79 (-1.47)	0.112 (2.74)**			9.24 (1.61)*			0.2512
(B) 99		-0.365 (-4.46)**							-34.99 (1.77)*		0.1633
(C) 2 X 76		-0.340 (-5.17)**	-0.226 (-2.95)**			-11.44 (-2.64)**					0.2061

NOTES:
1. (A) and (B): data of 1979 and 1982, respectively; (C): data of both years.
2. (2) Export rations = exports/total sales.
   (3) Non-overseas Chinese investment as dummy variable 1, overseas Chinese 0.
   (4) U.S. firms as dummy 1.
   (5) Japanese firms as dummy 1.
   (6) Year of establishment as dummy variable; before 19710, after 1972 = 1.
   (7) EPZ as dummy variable; EPZ = 1, others = 0.
   (8) Time as dummy variable; 1982 = 1, 1979 = 0.
3. *: as 5% significance level, **: as 1% significance level.

Source: Schive (1986, p. 70).

Summary

Japanese FDI in the ROC goes back to the colonial period. At that time, most large and incorporated companies were either controlled or owned by the Japanese. Japanese FDI returned to the ROC slowly after the war but grew so fast in the late 1980s that it again became the dominant source of foreign capital investment.

Japanese firms in the ROC are smaller in size compared to U.S. and European ones, but their number is larger than those of the non-Japanese. This pattern owes much to the complex ties between Japan and Taiwan, Japanese investment through trading companies, and investments via the Japanese government and banks.

Japanese firms also contributed significantly to the ROC's trade, exports in particular, although Japan has enjoyed a trade surplus with the ROC since the mid–1960s. In comparing Japanese and U.S. enterprises' contributions to trade, both become less important in export promotion, but more so for U.S. companies.

Japanese FDI also imported both hardware and software technology to the ROC. Although complaints are often heard about Japanese companies having a conservative attitude toward introducing foreign technology, Japanese technology cost less than other foreign technology.

The well-known Kojima hypothesis does not apply to the ROC, unlike Korea. United States FDI performed as well as Japanese direct investment in promoting ROC exports. As far as local purchasing behavior is concerned, Japanese firms tended to buy less in Taiwan compared with their U.S. counterparts. Over time, however, all FDI increasingly was associated with greater purchases from Chinese firms.

The ROC has greatly benefited by attracting FDI while guiding market trends. Moreover, no serious dysfunctions associated with the concentration of FDI in certain economic sectors have occurred. As a matter of fact, trade liberalization in the 1980s did not reduce FDI. The latest wave of FDI into the ROC tended to be more local market-oriented and concentrated in the service sector or the capital- and knowledge-intensive industries. Of course, older foreign companies had to adjust to cope with this new environment of higher wages, tougher environmental-standards protection, higher quality requirements, and more competition from imports.

The investment opportunity for foreign capital in the ROC remains favorable. In addition to the enlarged local market for consumer goods—helped by a strong New Taiwan dollar—the ROC government is committed to expanding investment in infrastructure. Local financing can easily be obtained because of the world's largest foreign exchange reserves. An advanced industrial sector with a well-trained labor force is another big plus in attracting new FDI. Finally, the ROC now plays the same role as Japan once did by exporting capital, technology and equipment, and intermediate goods to other Asian countries (Schive, 1993). Its investors go to the People's Republic of China (PRC) and enjoy great advantages compared with "foreigners." The ROC is in an excellent position to cooperate with foreign capital from other sources to penetrate the PRC market.

Notes

1. Statistics of FDI in Taiwan include intercompany loans over two years.
2. Thirty-five percent of Japanese investment in the trading sector in Taiwan was wholly owned.
3. These two data sources are *Tōyō Keizai* (1992) and *Statistics on Overseas Chinese and Foreign Investment, Technical Cooperation, Outward Investment and Outward Technical Cooperation,* Ministry of Economic Affairs (various issues). It may be pointed out that no permission was granted for Japanese investment in the trading business until 1987. Over a short period of four years, a total of 350 Japanese investment projects were approved in the trading industry, accounting for 53 percent of the total amount of FDI in that industry.
4. A variety of sources revealed that pressure from the People's Republic of China was responsible for the rigid Japanese policy governing the bank operation in Taiwan until recently. In Korea there were fourteen Japanese banks by 1989 (Sazanami, 1992).
5. Inconsistencies in FDI data are common because: (1) Different definitions of FDI exist. For instance, the approved FDI data in Taiwan include all capital registered under foreigners without distinguishing between direct and portfolio investment. Data shown in *Tōyō Keizai* refer to capital owned by Japanese with ownership above 10 percent. (2) Industrial classification of the same investment may differ because of host country's regulations or preferential treatment among industries. A good example is the ROC's FDI policy toward Japanese investment in the trading business. (3) Withdrawn investments may be included or excluded. Survey data of existing firms usually exclude such cases, but not the approval data. Of course, FDI approved but not arriving at the same time also create a discrepancy. A comparison of the approved FDI data with those from balance of payments in the case of the ROC reveals a 50 percent discrepancy (Schive, 1990a). It is unclear which factor(s) contributed to the data inconsistency for Japanese FDI in Korea.

6. There is another bias in foreign-firm export data. From export data, products of
material sold to the downstream processors and ending up in exports were also
reported as exports. The so-called "indirect" exports should not be treated as
exports, to avoid double-counting.
7. The official definition of SME varied over time. Usually the paid-up capital and
the employment level were applied. In the 1979 definition a manufacturing firm
hiring 300 or fewer employees, with paid-up capital $NT20 million and below,
and total value of assets less than $NT60 million was classified as an SME.
8. In a case study of Taiwan Singer (Schive, 1990a), interviews of local sewing-
machine-parts suppliers did reveal some negative views about Japanese sewing-
machine companies in providing technical assistance to their local subcontractors.
9. Referring to the technical cooperation data, each contract lasted 7 years for U.S.
technology, 6.9 years for European, and 4.9 years for Japanese in the machinery
industry in 1980. The same figures in the electrical and electronic industry from
these three sources varied from 8.2 years, 9.2 years, and 4.8 years in 1979
(Schive, 1980, 1981). As for royalty fees, 66.7 percent of U.S. licensers charged
4 percent of sales or more in the electrical and electronic industry in 1979, but
only 2.7 percent of Japanese licensers did so. In comparison, most Japanese
technology providers, 82.1 percent of the total, charged a fee between 2 and 4
percent, but the same range covered only 16.7 percent of U.S. technology in
1979. A regression analysis of the machinery industry indicated that the U.S. and
European technology cost 1.26 percentage more in terms of royalty fee than the
Japanese one in 1980 (Schive, 1981). It may be concluded, thus, that Japanese
technology cost less and lasted a shorter time compared to that from other
sources in Taiwan. The same source of data in the machinery industry revealed
that 26.5 percent of all technology licensees were not satisified with the results,
yet 60 percent of all technology receivers continued the contract when it expired.
10. For similar studies at the industrial level, see Wu (1980), Liu (1983), and
Ramstetter (1992).

References

Central Bank of China, *The Annual Report of Financial Institution Activities,*
various issues. Taipei.

Chang, Chung-Han (1980), *Industrialization in Taiwan Before 1945.* Taipei:
United Press (in Chinese).

Chou, Tein-Chen (1988), "American and Japanese Direct Foreign Investment in
Taiwan: A Comparative Study," *Hitotsubashi Journal of Economics,* 29:2,
165–79.

Council for Economic Planning and Development, *Taiwan Statistical Data Book,*
various issues. Taipei.

Hymer, S. H. (1960), *The International Operations of National Firms: A Study of*

Direct Foreign Investment. Ph.D. diss., Massachusetts Institute of Technology.

Jacoby, Neil H. (1966), *U.S. Aid to Taiwan.* New York: Praeger.

JETRO (1991), *Sekai to Nihon no kaigai chokusetsu toshi* [FDI of the World and Japan]. Tokyo.

Kindleberger, C. P. (1968), *American Business Abroad: Six Lectures on Direct Investment.* New Haven, Conn.: Yale University Press.

Kojima, Kiyoshi (1973), "A Macroeconomic Approach to Foreign Direct Investment," *Hitotsubashi Journal of Economics,* 14:1, 1–21.

—— (1977), "Transfer of Technology to Developing Countries: Japanese Type Versus American Type," *Hitotsubashi Journal of Economics,* 17:2, 1–14.

—— (1985), "Japanese and American Direct Investment in Asia: A Comparative Analysis," *Hitotsubashi Journal of Economics,* 26:1, 1–35.

Kojima, Kiyoshi, and Terutomo Ozawa (1984a), *Japan's General Trading Companies: Mechants of Economic Development.* Paris: OECD.

Kojima, Kiyoshi, and Terutomo Ozawa (1984b), "Micro- and Macro-Economic Models of Direct Foreign Investment: Toward a Synthesis," *Hitotsubashi Journal of Economics,* 25:1, 1–20.

Koo, Bohn Young (1985), "The Role of Direct Foreign Investment in Korea's Recent Economic Growth," in Walter Galenson, ed., *Foreign Trade and Investment.* Madison: University of Wisconsin Press, 176-216.

Lee, Chung H. (1980), "United States and Japanese Direct Investment in Korea: A Comparative Study," *Hitotsubashi Journal of Economics,* 20:2, 26–41.

—— (1983), "International Production of the United States and Japan in Korean Manufacturing Industries: A Comparative Study," *Weltwirtschlafliches Archiv,* 119:4, 744–53.

Lee, Chung H. and Eric D. Ramstetter, (1991), "Direct Investment and Structural Change in Korean Manufacturing," in Eric D. Ramstetter, ed., *Direct Foreign Investment in Asia's Developing Economies and Structural Change in the Asia-Pacific Region.* Boulder: Westview Press, 105-141.

Liu, Jin-Tan, Chi Schive, and Wei-der Tsai (1990), "The Export Behavior of Multinational Firms in Taiwan," *Taiwan Economic Review,* 18:4, 427–48 (in Chinese).

Liu, T. Y., and C. C. Chien, with P. W. Chang, J. H. Chiu, and C. J. Chuang (1983), *The Effects of Japanese Investment on the National Economy.* Taipei: Taiwan Institute of Economic Research (in Chinese).

Meier, G. M., ed. (1970), *Leading Issues in Economic Development Studies: International Poverty.* 2d ed. Oxford: Oxford University Press.

Ministry of Economic Affairs, Investment Commission (MOEA), *Statistics on Approved Overseas Chinese and Foreign Investment, Technical Cooperations, Outward Investment, and Outward Technical Cooperation,* various issues. Taipei.

Ramstetter, Eric D. (1992), "The Macroeconomic Effects of Inward Direct Investment in Taiwan: A Multifirm Econometric Analysis," in Mitsuru Toida and Daisuke Hiratsuka, eds., *Projections for Asian Industrializing Region* (1). Tokyo: Institute of Developing Economies, 53-154.

Ranis, Gustav, and Chi Schive (1985), "Direct Foreign Investment in Taiwan's Development," in Water Galenson, ed., *Foreign Trade and Investment.* Madison: University of Wisconsin Press, 85-137.

Riedel, S. (1975), "The Nature and Determinnants of Export-Oriented Direct Foreign Investment in a Developing Country: A Case Study of Taiwan," *Weltwirtschlaflich Archiv*, 111:3, 505-525.

Sazanami, Yoko (1992), "Japanese Service Foreign Direct Investment to the Asia Pacific," paper presented at "Economic Regionalism: Macroeconomic Core and Microeconomic Optimization," sponsored by the American Committee on Asian Economic Studies and the Chulalongkorn University, December 16-18, 1992, Bangkok.

Schive, Chi (1980), *The Report of Technical Cooperation Effect in Taiwan's Electrical and Electronic Industry.* Taipei: Ministry of Economic Affairs Investment Commission (in Chinese).

——— (1981), "A Study of Foreign Firms' Local Purchasing Behavior: Its Relationship to the Development in Taiwan," in Proceedings, Industrial Trade and Taiwan's Economic Development in Taiwan. Taipei: Academia Sinica (in Chinese).

——— (1986), *The Effects of Overseas Chinese and Foreign Investment on the National Economy.* Taipei: Ministry of Economic Affairs Investment Commission (in Chinese).

——— (1988), "Policy Reform in Taiwan's Economic Development, 1950–1965. Working Paper.

——— (1990a), *The Foreign Factor: The Multinational Corporations' Contribution to the Economic Modernization of the Republic of China.* Stanford: Hoover Institution Press.

——— (1990b), "Linkages: Do Foreign Firms Buy Locally?" *Asian Economic Journal*, 4:1, 1–15.

——— (1990c), "Direct Foreign Investment and Linkage Effects: The Experience of Taiwan," *Canadian Journal of Development Studies*, 11:2, 325–42.

——— (1993), "How Did Taiwan Solve Its Dutch Disease Problem?" *Journal of Asian Economies* (forthcoming).

——— and Jenn-Hwa Tu (1991), "Foreign Firm and Structural Change in Taiwan," in Eric D. Ramstetter, ed., *Direct Foreign Investment in Asia's Developing Economic and Structural Change in the Asia-Pacific Region.* Boulder: Westview Press, 142–71.

Tiao, Man Peng (1993), "The Dai-Ichi Kangyo Bank: Super Performance of Adhesiveness." *Common Wealth,* March 1993. Taipei (in Chinese).

Tōyō Keizai (1992), *Kaigai shinshutsu kigyō sōran* [Japanese Multinationals: Facts and Figures]. Tokyo.

Wu, Rong I. (1987), "U.S. Direct Investment in Taiwan: An Economic Appraisal," in *Asia-Pacific Economies: Promises and Challenges, Research in International Business and Management,* Vol. 6, Part B: 185-98.

Wu, Rong I., L.C.H. Wong, T. C. Chou, and C. K. Li (1980), *The Effects of United States Investment on the National Economy.* Taipei: Institute of American Culture, Academia Sinica (in Chinese).

Contributors

PETER DRYSDALE. Professor in the Economics Division, Research School of Pacific Studies at the Australian National Unviersity (ANU) and Executive Director of the Australia-Japan Research Centre (A-JRC), which is responsible for an Australia-wide research program on economic relations with Japan and the Asia-Pacific region, based at the ANU and involving research cooperation with economists in Japan and other countries. Professor Drysdale is one of Australia's foremost authorities on Australia's international trade and economic diplomacy. He has written extensively on Asia-Pacific economic cooperation and is the author of *International Economic Pluralism: Economic Policy in Asia and the Pacific* (translated into Japanese and Chinese), on economic policy in Asia and the Pacific and international trade diplomacy. That work was awarded the Asia-Pacific Prize in Japan. He has been a consultant to the Australian government and international organizations. He is a member of *Time* magazine's Asia-Pacific Board of Economists and a member of the Order of Australia, awarded for services to Australia's relations with Japan and Asia-Pacific.

LEON HOLLERMAN. Professor of economics in the Peter F. Drucker Graduate Management Center, Claremont Graduate School. Professor Hollerman has been a visiting professor in Japan at Tokyo University and Hitotsubashi University. His books include *Japan's Economic Strategy in Brazil* (1988); *Japan, Disincorporated: The Economic Liberalization Process* (1988); and *Japan's Dependence on the World Economy* (1967).

RAMON H. MYERS. Senior fellow and curator-scholar of the East Asian Collection of the Hoover Institution, Stanford University.

TERUTOMO OZAWA. Professor of economics at Colorado State University. Professor Ozawa's research interests include the role of foreign direct investment in structural upgrading, the operations of Japanese multinationals, and the era of flexible manufacturing in modern capitalism. He is an author of numerous publications, including *Multinationalism, Japanese Style: The Political Economy of Outward Dependency* (1979), *Recycling Japan's Surpluses for Developing Countries* (1989), and *In Search of Flexibility: The Japanese Manufacturing Paradigm and Developing Countries* (forthcoming).

CLARK E. REYNOLDS. Graduated *summa cum laude* from Claremont Men's College, did graduate work at the Massachusetts Institute of Technology and the Harvard Divinity School, and received his Ph.D. in economics from the University of California at Berkeley. After teaching for five years at Yale University, Professor Reynolds joined the faculty of Stanford University in 1967. His research interests include international trade, finance, labor economics, the political economy of development, and regional integration. His publications include *The Mexican Economy: Twentieth Century Structure and Growth* (1970), coedited volumes including *The Dynamic of North American Trade and Investment: Canada, Mexico, and the United States* (1990) and *U.S.-Mexico Relations: Labor Market Interdependence* (1992), and *Open Regionalism in the Andes* (1994), which he coauthored with Francisco Thoumi and Reinhart Wettmann. His current interests include research on the labor market impact of alternative integration strategies, including the Caribbean Basin's accession to the North American Free Trade Agreement.

MINGSARN SANTIKARN KAOSA-ARD. Director of the Natural Resources and Environment Program and former head of the Department of Economics, Faculty of Social Sciences, Chiang Mai University.

CHI SCHIVE. Professor of economics, Department of Economics, National Taiwan University; vice chairman, Council for Economic Planning and Development, Executive Yuan, Republic of China.

KAR-YIU WONG. Associate professor of economics at the University of Washington. Professor Wong's special areas are the theory of international trade and foreign direct investment and the economic relationship between the United States and Japan. He is the author of *International Trade in Goods and Factor Mobility* (1995).

KOZO YAMAMURA. Job and Gertrud Tamaki Professor of Japanese Studies, Henry M. Jackson School of International Studies, University of Washington. Professor Yamamura specializes in Japanese economic history and economic policy and has published extensively. Most recently he coedited and contributed to *Land Issues in Japan: A Policy Failure?* (1992) and *The Legacies and Lessons of Macroeconomic Policy of the United States and Japan in the 1980s* (1995). He is currently preparing a book on the motivations and effects of the increasing economic presence of Japan in Asia.

Index